SECRETS AND PUZZLES
SILENCE AND THE UNSAID IN CONTEMPORARY ITALIAN WRITING

THE EUROPEAN HUMANITIES RESEARCH CENTRE

UNIVERSITY OF OXFORD

Director
Professor Martin McLaughlin, Magdalen College

The European Humanities Research Centre of the University of Oxford organizes a range of academic activities, including conferences and workshops, and publishes scholarly works under its own imprint, LEGENDA. Within Oxford, the EHRC bridges, at the research level, the main humanities faculties: Modern Languages, English, Modern History, Classics and Philosophy, Music and Theology. The Centre stimulates interdisciplinary research collaboration throughout these subject areas and provides an Oxford base for advanced researchers in the humanities.

The Centre's publishing programme focuses on making available the results of advanced research in medieval and modern languages and related interdisciplinary areas. An Editorial Board, whose members are drawn from across the British university system, covers the principal European languages. Titles currently include works on Arabic, Catalan, Chinese, English, French, German, Italian, Portuguese, Russian, Spanish and Yiddish literature, and linguistics. In addition, the EHRC co-publishes with the Society for French Studies, the Modern Humanities Research Association and the British Comparative Literature Association. The Centre also publishes a Special Lecture Series under the LEGENDA imprint, and a journal, *Oxford German Studies*.

Enquiries about the Centre's academic and publishing programme
should be addressed to:
Kareni Bannister, Senior Publications Officer
European Humanities Research Centre
University of Oxford
76 Woodstock Road, Oxford OX2 1HP
enquiries@ehrc.ox.ac.uk
www.ehrc.ox.ac.uk

LEGENDA

EUROPEAN HUMANITIES RESEARCH CENTRE
University of Oxford
MODERN HUMANITIES RESEARCH ASSOCIATION

Secrets and Puzzles

Silence and the Unsaid in Contemporary Italian Writing

NICOLETTA SIMBOROWSKI

LEGENDA

European Humanities Research Centre, University of Oxford
Modern Humanities Research Association
2003

Published by the
European Humanities Research Centre
of the University of Oxford
47 Wellington Square
Oxford OX1 2JF
in conjunction with the Modern Humanities Research Association

LEGENDA is the publications imprint of the
European Humanities Research Centre

ISBN 1 900755 74 2

First published 2003

British Library Cataloguing in Publication Data
A CIP catalogue record for this book is available from the British Library

LEGENDA series designed by Cox Design Partnership, Witney, Oxon
Printed in Great Britain by
Information Press
Eynsham
Oxford OX8 1JJ

Copy-Editor: Dr Jeffrey Dean

CONTENTS

FOR MY MOTHER AND FATHER

ACKNOWLEDGEMENTS

I should like to express thanks to the Modern Humanities Research Association, co-publisher of this book, for its generous support.

I am grateful to all the colleagues in Oxford who at various times have offered advice and commented on the ideas in this book, in particular Martin McLaughlin and Peter Hainsworth. During my work on this project, early drafts of chapters have appeared in journals, and I am grateful to their editors and publishers for permission to make use of the following material here: 'From *La famiglia* to the *Taccuino* and *La casa in collina*: Pavese and the Need to Confess', *The Modern Language Review* 92 (1997), 70–85; 'Music and Memory in Natalia Ginzburg's *Lessico famigliare*', ibid., 94 (1999), 680–90; '"Il ritegno": Writing and Restraint in Primo Levi', *Romance Studies* 19 (2001), 41–57. The Taylor Institution Library and the Bodleian Library, both in Oxford, and their staffs have been invaluable. I thank Kareni Bannister at the European Humanities Research Centre for her help and attention to detail right from the beginning.

Most of all, I am indebted to my beloved husband Daniel Gill for his unfailing encouragement and support whilst this book was being written.

ABBREVIATIONS

For full references see Bibliography

BB   Warner, *From the Beast to the Blonde*
CC   Pavese, *La casa in collina*
CO   Sanvitale, *Camera ottica*
IWW   Wood, *Italian Women's Writing, 1860–1994*
LEF   Pavese, *La luna e i falò*
LF   Ginzburg, *Lessico famigliare*
MF   Sanvitale, *Madre e figlia*
MV   Pavese, *Il mestiere di vivere*
SP   Pizzardo, *Senza pensarci due volte*
SW   Wright, 'Intervista a Francesca Sanvitale, Roma 17 luglio 1995'
VP   Sanvitale, *Verso Paola*

PREFACE

This book came into being as a result of the perception that, despite comparative freedom of expression for writers in the latter part of the twentieth century in Italy, all writers nevertheless choose to 'censor' their own work in some way and often to a far greater extent than one might have expected. The sense of something left 'unsaid' is particularly strong in some authors, though the fact of selectivity is a central aspect of all good writing, and, it could be argued, defines art of all kinds. When researching this book I was struck by how often theoretical debate about the nature of literature and what can be derived from it led to considerations of the unsaid. Stefan Collini's comment, in his introduction to a stimulating debate on the nature of reading and interpretation, *Interpretation and Overinterpretation*, is at the heart of my book, when he talks of being 'willing to let the text determine the range of questions we put to it: there can always be interesting questions about what it does not say, and the range of what it may come to us to find interesting here cannot be limited in advance'.[1]

In order to examine the notion of the unsaid, I had to make some selections myself. Analysis of any text reveals that elements have been elided or suppressed: narrative is the organization and expression of a tiny proportion of the available material, whether fictional or 'fact'. The awareness of this overlap has been central to a great deal of recent work on autobiography and its relationship to fiction. I was therefore concerned with something both more elusive yet ultimately more definable: aspects of the text that were omitted within the structure of what had ostensibly been selected. In other words, authors had provided us with a picture that was to be read as an artistic whole, yet within that apparently integrated whole, gaps and elisions occurred. It emerged that there existed what could be termed a 'poetics of omission', the writer's subtlety and characteristic tone depending on what was left unsaid as much as on what was said. In the end, the works that form the basis of this book selected themselves: in all cases, my study is the investigative consequence of an initial intuitive response, specifically, puzzlement regarding some aspect of a text. The interesting result has been that aspects of a work that might have been dismissed as 'flaws' (and sometimes were described as such in some criticism) have revealed significant new layers of meaning.

All the writers I discuss are mainstream, canonical authors, well respected and thoroughly researched. Nevertheless, these were writers in some of whose works, I felt, the immediate surface reading of the text left too many unanswered questions, whatever the position of the reader, whether reading for casual pleasure or for the purposes of study. Ideally, both pleasure and study go hand in hand, but all would admit that the 'uses' of reading are as various as readers themselves, and all the writers I discuss have been put to 'use' in University courses.

Faced with texts by skilled writers, which nevertheless in some cases seemed to demonstrate flaws in plot, consistency or style, I decided to consider the possibility of reading these 'flaws' from a different angle. What if they were not flaws at all? And might it be that writers of such undoubted talent did not write loosely, and the 'flaws' were the surface evidence of a gap in the text, consciously or unconsciously created, a small hole in the weave of the fabric of the text, as important and meaningful as the compact and integrated text around it?

Twentieth-century literary theory, alert to the paradoxes of language and how it functions independently of its generators, was immensely helpful in focusing my thoughts, as was all the work on the theory of silence that has gained momentum in the latter part of the twentieth century, but I was aware of the dangers of falling foul of the interpretation-versus-use debate, or of forcing an interpretative and restrictive grid over literature. The intention of the author became an issue, along with the *intentio operis* and *intentio lectoris*. I found the field of autobiography was sharply relevant, where debate and theory about the coincidence of authorial voice and the text, problems of expression and issues of truth and memory were all fruitful and thought-provoking stimuli. Feminist criticism, work on the fantastic, and psychoanalytical approaches all proved essential and enlightening and turned my early curiosity about individual textual 'puzzles' into a committed voyage through the key issues of twentieth-century literary criticism.

The result is that, whilst, for reasons of space and also because it has been very well done by others elsewhere, I may not rehearse at length the theories of silence, interpretation, autobiography, gender studies, psychoanalysis and the role of the unconscious in literary creativity, nevertheless all these areas of study are relevant to the discussions in this book and will supply points of reference throughout. My study argues that there is a difference between traditional literary techniques and omission: the former allow a writer subtlety of expression but are used, let us say, actively to underline certain points the writer wants to make; and the latter, omission, is where the silence itself is of significance and where an element the writer ostensibly elides emerges none the less. There is some area of overlap: a writer may have aimed for only partial concealment or intended to deceive readers seeking the obvious, while planting clues for others. In times of formal censorship this is a useful technique since it allows writers to deny anything other than a literal reading of their texts. I decided not to cover the era of Fascist censorship in Italy, since this would be a different kind of study altogether. I felt instead that when censorship does not apply and when society is accepting of most subject-matter, as is true of the latter half of the twentieth century in Western Europe, what writers choose not to say becomes particularly interesting.

There is a clear link with autobiography, the genre *par excellence* that manipulates truth and suppression so that the reader is unable to disentangle them. In fiction the truth is an abstract reality, with the written word presented as false in the literal sense. In autobiography we are invited to believe that everything written is true in every sense. In reality, as the by now vast body of research on this subject attests, autobiography can tell blatant untruths, but it can also distort by means of its structure, its focus, above all by leaving out what does not fit in with the writer's agenda. As Paul John Eakin has it:

The autobiographical pact, which posits for the account of a life, some basis in potentially verifiable fact, seems upon examination to promise a rendering of biographical truth impossible in practice to fulfill. Why, we might well ask, with its pretensions to reference exposed as an illusion, does autobiography as a kind of reading and writing continue and even prosper? Why do we not simply collapse autobiography into the other literatures of fiction and have done with it?[2]

Some of my examples are presented by their authors as fiction, some as a hybrid form, but all are based so closely on the 'truth' or at least on the writer's perception of his or her life, that we often find ourselves comparing what the writer has expressed in non-fictional contexts in order to understand the reasons for the missing elements and the significance of their elision.

Nevertheless, the book concentrates on texts, not biographies. The central chapters consist of a series of case studies of well-known Italian authors, all of whom, I argue, are characterized by the power of the unsaid in their work.

Primo Levi (1919–1989) makes explicit in journalism and interviews his desire not to distress the reader, and his writings on the Holocaust are notable for their restraint.[3] The notion of silence and the unspeakable is, of course, central to all discussions about this horrific and pivotal episode in twentieth-century history. I focus on Levi's style, discerning a poetics based on respect for the reader, pinpointing *ritegno*, or restraint, as the specific element that makes his work particularly approachable for a wide readership. *Ritegno* is seen to be not only a feature of style but also a state of mind, for both Levi and the reader, and is connected closely with the *vergogna* experienced by the innocent victim. Levi's restraint when dealing with harrowing subject matter meshes with the psychological response of his reader, which is that of the helpless observer of atrocities, a natural sense of recoil, described by Levi himself as *ritegno*. *Ritegno* as defined in this chapter is partially responsible for Levi's reputation for calm and objectivity, despite passionate outbursts in his texts. It sometimes leads to surprising ellipses in his writing and may be implicated in the initial rejection of Levi's first book by publishers and public.

Cesare Pavese (1908–1950) did not join the anti-Fascist partisans in the latter part of the Second World War. He did join the Communist Party after the war, but journals suppressed after his suicide have emerged recently and show that he entertained Fascist sympathies at the most savage point in the civil conflict. I suggest that he is a highly confessional writer and that an apologia for these attitudes is encoded in one of his best novels, *La casa in collina* (1948).[4] Pavese's last novel, *La luna e i falò* (1950) is also examined for its political message, an aspect that I argue is a continuation of the apologia contained in the earlier book.

Natalia Ginzburg's book *Lessico famigliare* (1963) is a curiosity, an autobiography that the writer insists should be read as a novel and that elides its first-person narrator.[5] I point out how the family 'language' implemented so innovatively in this text acts like background music, which at moments of great tragedy falls silent. The second section of the chapter examines elements in the text that are political and 'feminist' in effect, despite Ginzburg's professed reservations about the feminist movement. There are therefore three areas of silence in the book: the silence that surrounds tragedy (and Ginzburg is explicit that certain things cannot be described in words); the silence of the central figure, which is the result, I feel, of insecurities, reticence and self-effacement typical of the female; and finally the reluctance to speak out on women's behalf, also the result of insecurity and ambivalence regarding women's 'place' in society and modern culture. Ginzburg (1916–91) in this way provides a link with the final part of this section of the book, which is devoted to the area of women's writing.

Francesca Sanvitale is a living author, born in 1928. Her novel *Madre e figlia* (1980) is an overtly semi–autobiographical depiction of the relationships between women.[6] Women's silence is a very strong motif culturally: I note the importance of the incidence of speechlessness in fairy-tales, since these influence our collective psyche. They often describe a female as silent when wronged, only regaining her voice when the offence is righted. The issue of the 'gaze' and its effect on women's behaviour and self-perception is current in feminist and film theory and sharply relevant to the way women portray themselves. I focus on Sanvitale's remarkably honest and vivid book to illustrate strategies female writers find to reveal themselves without the exposure this implies.

In a concluding section, I examine the publishing phenomenon of Einaudi in the context of post-war attitudes and tastes in literature, bringing together many of the authors and issues discussed earlier in the study. I compare the self-laceration of Pavese's fiction and the self-pitying bitterness of his diaries with the autobiography of Tina Pizzardo, a major political and personal figure in Pavese's life.[7] Her account displays the shifting nature of autobiographical 'truth' and is a product of attitudes inculcated in the author in the Fascist years, even though the book was not published until 1996. Pavese's diary, *Il mestiere di vivere*, which he left for publication after his suicide, is paradoxically less self-revealing in certain important ways than his fiction because of cuts made not only by the author but also by the editors, Natalia Ginzburg and Italo Calvino, both influential writers and editors at Einaudi in the post-war years.[8] In this context, it is notable that Ginzburg was one of the editors who rejected Levi's manuscript on behalf of Einaudi in the late 1940s; and it was Ginzburg and Calvino who concealed Pavese's incriminating secret journals, which remain hidden to this day. In keeping with the thematics of suppression, I examine what insights their editorial decisions give into social and moral attitudes in Italy in the 1950s and how these attitudes affect the way writers present themselves both in fiction and autobiography.

Notes to Preface

1. Stefan Collini, Introduction to Umberto Eco with Richard Rorty, Jonathan Culler and Christine Brooke-Rose, *Interpretation and Overinterpretation* (Cambridge: Cambridge University Press, 1992), 13. The germ of some of the arguments in this interesting collection of essays is already present in Susan Sontag, *Against Interpretation* (London: Eyre and Spottiswoode, 1967), 10, 14.
2. Paul John Eakin, *Touching the World: Reference in Autobiography* (Princeton: Princeton University Press, 1992), 27.
3. Primo Levi, *Opere*, ed. Marco Belpoliti, 2 vols. (Turin: Einaudi, 1997).
4. Cesare Pavese, *La casa in collina*, idem, *Prima che il gallo canti* (Milan: Mondadori, 1967), 137–281.
5. Natalia Ginzburg, *Lessico famigliare* (Milan: Mondadori, 1974; orig. pubd Turin: Einaudi, 1963).
6. Francesca Sanvitale, *Madre e figlia* (Turin: Einaudi, 1980; repr. 1994).
7. Tina Pizzardo, *Senza pensarci due volte* (Bologna: Il Mulino, 1996).
8. Cesare Pavese, *Il mestiere di vivere* (Turin: Einaudi, 1952; repr. 1990).

CHAPTER 1

Theoretical Approaches to the Unsaid and Cultural Background

'Silence' as both Thematics and Style

Throughout the discussions in this book I use the terms 'the unsaid' and 'silence' as interchangeable. The question whether there is any difference between the two terms is, however, interesting and encourages the reader to consider what exactly is happening when ellipsis is perceived in a text. Perhaps one could define 'the unsaid' as referring specifically to everything that is not articulated. 'Silence' instead can be a condition, and therefore can be the theme of a text, related to 'ineffability', or else it can be the muteness of a character, central to the plot (such as Dacia Maraini's silent duchess)[1] or, for instance, the inability of the victim to voice his or her pain, particularly relevant to any discussion of Holocaust literature. Perhaps one term suggests a gap that is more deliberate, more willed than the other, but it would be arbitrary and somewhat artificial to say which. Therefore, although I will be considering many different kinds of silence in literature, these two words will remain interchangeable for me.

The notion of the unsaid is central to traditional discussions of literature. One of the definitions of poetry might be the use of as few words as possible to convey as vivid a meaning as possible. Clearly, the best prose too suggests more than it specifically says. The techniques of suggestion are familiar to all those interested in the study of literature: imagery, ellipsis, symbols, semantic associations. Effective writing is at least as evocative as it is specific; perhaps this is the distinction between the clarity of a 'functional' text, a legal document for example, and the almost infinite interpretative possibilities offered by a verse of poetry. In between, there is a gamut of combinations of these two styles, and to some extent we expect certain kinds of narrative to veer towards one or the other. It is felt that 'facts' or 'truth', both concepts that have always been at the heart of philosophical enquiry but nevertheless still resist definitive pigeonholing, should be expressed in the plainest, clearest, most unadorned language, whereas fiction can have free rein stylistically. This perceived appropriateness can in itself be a creative tool, as when fiction uses the tone of a factual account for specific effect; however, when a factual account uses figurative language the writer risks exciting a sense of disbelief in his reader, the suspicion that somehow the 'truth' is not being told. Autobiography can combine adventurous style with perceived 'truth' without necessarily alienating the reader, but when history collides with personal experience, as in accounts of historical events, then suspicion may be engendered by a literary style that the account is not 'true'. These issues will be important when discussing individual writers.

However, my study is not specifically about silence as part of the subtlety of style, although this aspect naturally informs some of my discussion. I am concerned with those moments in a text when the silence conveys something other or more than economy of style. In other words, where ellipsis is used as a conventional stylistic technique, the author suggests, through other means rather than explicit words, concepts he intends to convey to his reader. The author's 'intentions' are of course infinitely debatable, as many critics and commentators have pointed out. Nevertheless, there are occasions when a writer omits elements that emerge none the less. Often there is an overlap between these two situations: a writer offers a hint of something he or she preferred not to articulate fully, but more meaning is conveyed than perhaps was intended. There may be deliberate concealment, intending nothing to come through, or partial concealment intended to deceive readers looking for the obvious but allowing for different interpretations. It can sometimes be useful for a writer to deny that certain meanings were intended: in times of censorship this is clearly the case.

In all nuances of this tapestry of omission/articulation, an element of self-deception is possible and indeed inevitable. It is well known that the text can move beyond what the writer consciously intended. Here I can cite no less an authority than Umberto Eco, who, in his response to Stefan Collini, assures us that he did not 'intend' many of the meanings and connections perceived by readers in *Il nome della rosa*.[2] However, he is obliged to admit, however humorously, that these readings are pertinent and intelligent: 'Text plus standard encyclopedia knowledge entitle any cultivated reader to find that connection.'[3]

Modern literary theory is not a major part of this book; nevertheless it is extremely helpful when examining the unsaid, in so far as it encourages us to view language as far less under our control than we might once have thought. Language is shifting, unreliable and ideologically bound. Traditional 'style', as literary critics have understood it, might be thought of as the conscious application by the author of structures perceived by writer and reader alike as absolute and whose function is clear and predictable. Structuralism and post-structuralism have thoroughly undermined this notion, separating author and text irrevocably and extending the interpretative scope of the reader. Once it has been established that language is not totally reliable and transparent, it has been a natural progression to give at least as much importance to the unsaid as the stated, and the unsaid has been debated by many eminent theorists.[4] As Sanford Budick and Wolfgang Iser have it:

What allows the unsayable to speak is the undoing of the spoken through negativity. Since the spoken is doubled by what remains silent, undoing the spoken gives voice to the inherent silence which itself helps stabilize what the spoken is meant to mean. This voicing of the unsayable is necessarily multilingual, for there is no one language by which sayings of things can be undone.[5]

The Theorists

Oswald Ducrot's *Dire et ne pas dire* provides an interesting discussion of the linguistic devices available for concealment, that is, the basic tools of the language of concealment, to be used consciously or unconsciously. He points out that there are often circumstances when one needs to be able to say things but to be able to act as if one hasn't said them. Departing from the linguistic reality that everything that is stated can be contradicted, he points out that it is sometimes useful not to be explicit, so that an idea can be expressed covertly without attracting comment or contradiction. We can go further and suggest that in these cases the idea passes into the reader's or listener's subconscious and is more likely to be accepted as 'true', which is the basis of the notion of the subliminal message. In this way the unsaid can be extremely powerful, influential and indeed dangerous. In this connection Ducrot describes the function of unarticulated messages in advertising. The relatively harmless ones encourage us to buy one product rather than another, but others may attempt to forge our attitudes by reinforcing prejudices. Advertising, by its nature, must prefer one element over another and must seek out persuasive and preferably unconscious means to convince the consumer. Syllogism is often a significant part of this process. Ducrot gives a simple example, where a minor premiss is stated, followed by a conclusion that suggests a major premiss: for example, she knows best, she buys X, therefore X is best.[6]

In a complex and extended narrative this very basic technique can acquire great subtlety. In Primo Levi's work, for example, discussed fully in a later chapter of this book, there are many examples. For instance, the episode concerning Henri in *Se questo è un uomo*, where the narrative, when analysed in terms of a simple syllogism, states: Henri was a civilized person whose company was a pleasure; one always felt uncomfortable after an encounter with him and I (Levi) prefer never to see him again; therefore (not stated) he was guilty of something terrible. Another example is contained within the chapter describing the hanging of a rebel: we witnessed a hanging; we were ashamed and angry; therefore what we saw (not described in detail) was particularly horrible.

Jacques Derrida has offered some stimulating ideas about the nature of the unsaid. His isolation of the notion of 'undecidability' offers a category for the unsaid or at least a framework within which to consider the status of the unsaid.[7] The unsaid is discernible, we can locate it, the fact that it is implied means that it cannot be defined as total silence; and yet it is not words either. It is undecided, in Derrida's terminology. His discussions of writing as 'pharmakon' are also thought-provoking in this context: writing is the *pharmakon*, both cure and poison, inasmuch as writing replaces memory inadequately and imperfectly. This has wide-ranging implications in any discussion on autobiography or the relationship between a narrated account and the 'truth'.

Here we are reminded of Frank Kermode's reflections when discussing history and fiction in the context of readings of the Bible in *The Genesis of Secrecy*, where he reflects that all narrative is subject to 'shaping' of some kind. He says, 'historians as well as novelists (traditionally) place [...] value on "followability"'; we remember a plotted narrative and believe it. This imposed structure he refers to as 'occult figurations'. He adds that 'too strict a distinction between meaning and truth would leave few historical narratives capable of interesting us'.[8] This separation of event from its narration, and the implication for 'truth' and 'meaning', is highly significant when we consider what is left out in a narrative and why the writer has made particular omissions. Kermode's comments continue to elucidate this link with modern theorists when he says that presuppositions are part of our linguistic apparatus, but they militate against the meaning of the text (what is actually written) as opposed to the truth of the text (what it is written about). He goes on to mention the 'occult sense' of a text and how this can be interpreted in Freudian, biblical or literary terms. The slippage between meaning and truth is arguably the most fertile area of a text, and the writerly skill involved in creating this gap, whilst at the same time suggesting what it must be filled with, is one of the most subtle and complex at the writer's disposal.

Derrida, in his provocative discussion of phonocentrism and logocentrism, also suggests that speech and thought are more closely linked to one another than thought and writing, arriving at his conclusions by way of Aristotle and Rousseau. He refers to a history of silence, the repression of writing while speech is favoured.[9] It is interesting to consider what happens to the suppressed thought or the unexpressed thought in this process and where such thoughts can be placed in this hierarchy. It could be argued that the technique of the unsaid finds a place for these anomalous constructs of the mind, codifying them in writing, whilst not actually writing them down. In this way, the fleeting thought in our minds, which we do not always bring to the fore and make whole either in our heads or in speech, can be trapped permanently on the page, in writing, in the form of the unsaid. This occurs often via the 'trace', as Derrida defines it: if language is a system of signs that depends on a word selected not being the word that is not selected (a notion derived from Saussure's assertion that language is purely differential), then every word suggests the others that are not there. Clearly this could generate a meaningless cacophony of unspoken words, but by a process of association, the words selected tend to suggest only a small proportion of other possible expressions. When we consider the meaning of what is not said, this shifting terrain offers enticing open-endedness, but the text that is there provides guidance and some limits, avoiding loss of meaning.

Mikhail Bakhtin's literary and phenomenological discussions also offer useful insights into how to approach the unsaid.[10] He has stressed that language is not fixed in meaning, but meaning changes according to the cultural context of the reader or listener, and in this sense the reader becomes the author. This is particularly productive in the context of the unsaid, because the reader in a profound sense becomes the author of what must be supplied to fill the silence, without creating confusion by distorting the language that is supplied. In the context of the unsaid, Bakhtin's reader-author is an extreme case. A great deal more of what Bakhtin has to say helps with our understanding of specific areas of literature: the author–hero relationship in autobiographical accounts, the concept of Carnival and the emphasis on the body and the grotesque has been revealing when examining women's writing, where the body often features as a cumbersome, bleeding, leaking entity in its own right. In these cases, the literary tools provided by Bakhtin give an insight into why narrative focus shifts in certain kinds of writing. His discussions in *Esthétique et théorie du roman* regarding how the author's voice becomes the narrator's are also relevant in any examination of autobiography and autobiographical fiction.[11]

Roland Barthes offers further observations which pertain to the definition and use of silence. In *Essais critiques: Le Bruissement de la langue*, he says that the voice is the substance of life, and so we might infer that silence is a negation of life.[12] This, however, needs to be considered in conjunction with his observations on tense, whereby the past tenses are fixed but the future is fluid, alarming and silent. Silence is often the space left by a gap in the text, and I suggest that any shifting of tense leaves space for gaps: if we say or write, 'I feel this now, but I felt that then and I may feel differently in the future', the 'truth' defined by the text becomes infinitely flexible and detached from any fixed 'reality'. A fixed tense, like the traditional third-person past narrative, suggests a finished quality, immovability, 'truth'. By introducing shifting tenses, a writer draws attention to the slipperiness of language and its arbitrary attachment to actual events. The identity of the author is called into question, too: who is the author? Is it the person writing now or the one about whom we are reading? Any uncertainty of this kind allows for gaps.

Barthes's frivolous theory of the erotic gap is pertinent here: the gap between the shifting meanings of language, which he defines as erotic, are the moments when the text gapes in silence. As Ann Jefferson points out: 'it is intermittence which is erotic'.[13] Indeed, erotica, as opposed to pornography, relies on the unseen and the unsaid for its effect: its sense of tension and expectation and leaving of space for the imagination allows the individual's preference to come into play. The erotic possibilities of silence are strikingly illustrated by the omission in Lampedusa's *Il gattopardo* of an extra chapter, recently found, in which the Prince beds his nephew's intended bride. Peter Schwenger's theory of textual envisioning would imply that the 'fantasm' of this episode is present in the published text even though the chapter is omitted.[14] The status of the text as it stands is called into question in a most unsettling but stimulating way.

It is in the field of writing about the Holocaust that the issue of speech versus silence has been most passionately discussed. Maurice Blanchot has said that in any literary work the most admirable element is the decision to remain silent.[15] In 'Le Paradoxe d'Aytrí', he states that silence is itself a means of expression and that the writer always departs from the position of being without words:

L'écrivain [...] ne peut guère songer à commencer autrement que par une certaine incapacité de parler et d'écrire, par une perte de mots, par l'absence même des moyens dont il surabonde. Ainsi lui est-il indispensable de sentir d'abord qu'il n'a rien à dire.[16]

He finishes the essay with the statement:

le silence du langage créateur, ce silence qui nous fait parler, n'est pas seulement une absence de paroles, mais une absence tout court, cette distance que nous mettons entre les choses et nous, et en nous-mêmes, et dans les mots, et qui fait que le langage le plus plein est aussi le plus poreux, le plus transparent, le plus nul, comme s'il voulait laisser fuir infiniment le creux même qu'il enferme, sorte de petit alcarazas du vide.

So for Blanchot, the word of the creative artist is specifically a means of escaping the void of silence, but that void is always present, it is the absolute, the given, which words temporarily fill. This idea, in the context of my study, lends particular resonance and weight to the silences perceived within the works of the writers examined.

Jean-François Lyotard suggested that after the Holocaust only 'negative testimony' is possible, in other words, he declared that it is not possible to say what happened.[17] He states that if we transcribe the Holocaust into words we risk making it an 'ordinary' event. This has affinities with Primo Levi's insistence that the Holocaust is not an event to be 'understood', since this might in some sense appear to justify and rationalize it.[18] If Lyotard proposes that the only alternative to silence is constant repetition of our failure to tell the story, I would argue that the poetics of the unsaid overcomes this impasse, permitting communication whilst abiding by what Lyotard has implied is a form of propriety. Levi provides a superb example of this, maintaining the principle of negative testimony by means of his *ritegno* and omissions, and at the same time being supremely communicative and even analytical.

Finally, Harold Bloom has pointed out how intertextuality aids the efficacy of the unsaid.[19] Allusion is unavoidable. As the body of literature grows, we need to say less because we can draw on our knowledge of other texts. Every gap or silence therefore invites us to supply not only our own ideas but also fragments of other literatures, prompted either deliberately or unconsciously by the patterns of words around those silences. The silences become ever richer and more unpredictable.

If I end my brief excursion through some of the theories pertaining to the unsaid here, it not because I feel I have come to any conclusion. However, this is not necessarily a bad thing: the most stimulating aspect of modern literary theory in connection with this study has been its tendency to widen the field of perception, open the mind and alter perspectives, rather than in the provision of fixed rules and guidelines. The field of discussion remains broad. Budick and Iser's collection of essays offers a selection of some of the approaches, but the range of scholarly material available is an indication of the enduring importance and interest of this topic.

Psychology and the 'Unsaid'

As readers, scholars and human beings, we are all aware of the drive towards 'telling', and narrative is a uniquely human activity as far as we know. The telling of fictional stories has performed different functions in society, acting as an instrument of education, propaganda, even subversion. Every conversation in which we refer to a past event, however recent, is a form of narrative and involves shaping, deletions and often distortions. The conscious mind is aware both of itself and the world around and constantly seeks to make sense of its environment by imposing a narrative structure on events. When we decide to leave an element out of a narrative or when we read an account with gaps (which actually means all narrative, to a greater or lesser extent), what happens in the mind, what becomes of that vacant space?

This is a question that has particularly interested scholars working on the literature of the fantastic.[20] All reading encourages us to create 'fantasms' in our minds, relying on the suggestion provided by selected details for us to create complete pictures for ourselves, in the hope that these pictures will be specifically meaningful (and different) for each individual. This becomes particularly important in the literature of the fantastic, where often the power of the text lies in the fact that we each conjure up our personal nightmare. Todorov, for example, when discussing Henry James, speaks of an 'absence' at the centre of a tale. It is precisely this that gives his stories their power: 'Le secret du récit jamesien est donc précisément l'existence d'un secret essentiel, d'un non-nommé, d'une force absente et surpuissante.'[21]

Schwenger's book on this 'textual envisioning' is admirably clear. In his introductory essay, 'Entering the Book', he points out that a reader supplies much more than 'meaning' to a text, as reader-response theory would have it, but actually supplies visual and other details. The author has a full image in his or her mind, not all of which will eventually find its way in words onto the page, but the curious and seductive idea expressed in Schwenger's book is that in some way these unspoken aspects are nevertheless conveyed. This is borne out by writers' accounts of their methods. Schwenger quotes Hemingway: 'you could omit anything if you know that you omitted ... and make people feel something more than they understood'.[22] Novelists often have a biography worked out for each of their characters containing minutely detailed material that will never find its way into the final text, but nevertheless they feel it is essential to 'know' the character in this way, as this wholeness of conception emerges in the eventual depiction of the character. So, the writer's imagination prompts our visualization, which is a stimulus for our unconscious. Schwenger calls on Lacan's theory of the signifying chain functioning in a vertical arrangement, which operates 'to signify something quite other than what it says'.[23] Psychology and linguistics come together: imagery and metaphor suggest the complete image held in the writer's mind, but by means of the 'polyphonic poetry' of the word and all its associations the unconscious mind of the reader is linked to that of the writer. Lacan calls these metonymy and metaphor, but together they express the unconscious and return us to Freudian territory. So language can suggest and create images that are only linked with difficulty to the actual words on the page.

George Steiner argued passionately in his essay 'The Hollow

Miracle' that the German language had been tainted in its entirety by its misuse during the Nazi era:

Everything forgets. But not a language. When it has been injected with falsehood, only the most drastic truth can cleanse it. Instead, the post-war history of the German language has been one of dissimulation and deliberate forgetting.[24]

Steiner would probably agree that this judgement (written in 1959) has now been superseded by German efforts to acknowledge and make amends for the Nazi past, but the general principle of the nature of language, he insists in his own footnote, remains sound.[25] We can see clearly how the use of language can affect content and distort meaning in each individual instance of usage, but it is a more challenging notion that the language retains a taint of this distortion in the period following widespread misuse and that it needs to be consciously purged. We tend to view language as a tool of the intellect, but Steiner's assertion, with reference to George Orwell of course, tells us that thought is restricted by the words available and the superficial meanings ascribed to them and that language operates independently of the user. I suggest that the unsaid is surely an antidote to this dangerous exploitation of language, in that meanings suppressed still hover in the spaces left behind.

In the context of the psychological processes of the writer, it is of great importance why certain things are left unsaid. The reasons can include fear of social opprobrium, political repression, expediency, cultural factors. Recurrent motives for omissions in texts seem to be linked to guilt and victimhood. For instance, the central first-person narrator in Ginzburg's novel/autobiography (her own designation), *Lessico famigliare*, is so far effaced as even to suggest psychological problems in the writer. However, there is undoubtedly a strong cultural link with the motif of the silent woman at the centre of many traditional narratives. This is particularly evident in folk-tales, as Marina Warner has pointed out (*BB*), and as I will discuss in a later chapter of this book. This image in itself is connected with the traditional image of the virtuous and desirable woman being silent, a requirement which is obviously inhibiting and damaging for the woman writer generally, and more so when writing about herself in autobiographical fiction or autobiography.

Levi, as I point out in a later chapter, makes the reasons for his reticence explicit: he does not wish to distress or alienate his reader.

However, there is also a strong possibility that he is psychologically unwilling or even unable to articulate certain episodes. The utterance of words is felt to have a talismanic effect, and there is strong cultural resonance behind this idea. Rites and rituals involve the speaking of words, the calling up, with the voice, of spirits or the calling upon of deities; the naming of gods and devils can have dire consequences; words have power. This is reflected in folk-tales across all cultures, of which the Grimm version of 'Rumpelstiltskin' is the best-known in Europe, where the naming of the wicked dwarf robs him of his power.[26] As is well documented, humiliation and torment by oppressive regimes often involve forcing victims to utter degrading insults against loved ones or other objects of respect, and even though everyone involved knows the words are extracted under duress and cannot be construed as 'true' (the whole point of the humiliation being to make someone say things they find hateful), nevertheless the fact of having uttered the words engenders shame in the victim and satisfaction in the tormentor. As Bruno Bettelheim wrote in his study of the psychological effects of living under Nazi terror: 'They were forced to curse their God, to accuse themselves and one another of vile actions, and their wives of adultery and prostitution. I never met a prisoner who had escaped this kind of initiation.'[27]

Some of the writers I have chosen, notably Levi and Ginzburg, I believe sometimes remain silent when they are afraid to make horrific events more concrete by naming them. In Sanvitale's *Madre e figlia* there is a significant passage where she says explicitly that even objects have no reality unless their names are uttered aloud, nor can anything exist unless it is described. I would argue that the unsaid undermines this concept, whether it is a hope or a dread, because objects do exist independent of language, terrible things happen whether spoken of or not; but the articulated word, spoken or written is indeed powerful, so powerful that its resonance spills over into silences left by us all.

If we return to Lyotard, who argues that transcribing the Holocaust into words renders it 'ordinary', and to Levi's reluctance to 'understand' the Holocaust because it will make it seem 'normal', we deduce that understanding tends to come through expression and discussion, words in fact, and that both commentators are in agreement that speaking of something pins it down. Some writers see this as possibly cathartic and capable of reducing the power of the trauma described. Levi, for instance, has stated as much, so he would seem to be advocating an ideal middle way, which offers the relief of unburdening but does not revitalize horrors in the witness's mind by articulating them. It becomes clear that the choice between speaking and not speaking is delicate and sophisticated.

The psychological implications of women's silence are wide-ranging and merit separate treatment in a dedicated chapter. Our collective psyche sees the silent or quiet woman as desirable, well-behaved. The Italian literary canon is notably lacking in female writers before this century, and new work on rehabilitating 'forgotten' or ignored female writers from the past does not alter the fact that women's voices have been silenced over the centuries nor that there exists the legacy of that silence in terms of the way modern women write. Folk-tales from all cultures often portray a wronged woman as silent until the wrong is righted, but they also depict women being deprived of speech as a punishment for behaviour deemed unacceptable by society (sometimes, indeed, as a punishment for speaking). Even the 'New Woman' in current society, as depicted in the media at all levels, only seems to have a voice if she takes on traditionally masculine traits of independence, aggression and sexual predatoriness; in other words, if she acts like a traditionally 'masculine' man, she acquires the male right to speak. Women fulfilling trad-itionally 'feminine' roles are still not expected to speak. Paradoxically, it is acknowledged that women have a greater facility with language at an earlier age in a cross-section of the population, and also find it easier to learn foreign languages at later stages in their development. It would seem, therefore, that there is an uneasy contradiction between society's tendency to silence women and women's natural propensity for language.

The body of recent research on the genre of autobiography is highly significant for anyone considering writers' decisions, creative or otherwise, to alter, arrange or reshape their own experience when depicting it for others. As autobiography claims to be more 'true' in some sense than 'fiction', these decisions become extremely highly charged for the author of autobiography or semi-autobiographical fiction.

Rather than attempt to examine the entire field, I have decided to concentrate on the links between women's fiction and women's autobiography, still a broad canvas, but a well-defined area of research. The 'identity crisis' peculiar to the woman writer, whether of fiction or autobiography, was significant in the effect it has had on the style of women's writing. It seemed that the various and conflicting self-images available for women have resulted in certain literary tendencies, which included motifs and tropes of silence or muteness, the displacement of the female figure from the centre of the narrative even when a text was ostensibly about a woman, and strategies for talking about the female 'self' that involved concealment. Film theory was particularly helpful in analysing the processes at work in women's autobiographical writings. All these elements are approached in a later chapter in this book.

Interpretation and Overinterpretation

Finally, I am of course aware of the dangers described by Richard Rorty in the 'The Pragmatist's Progress' in *Interpretation and Overinterpretation*, where he warns against 'the notion that there is something a given text is *really* about, something which rigorous application of a method will reveal'.[28] In none of the texts I have chosen would I suggest that the work is entirely 'about' one particular thing, revealed by the areas of silence that I pinpoint. However I do insist that examination of the 'unsaid' has the function of 'bringing to light connections or implications not previously noticed or reflected on', as Jonathan Culler points out in 'In Defence of Overinterpretation'.[29]

The whole debate of the intention of the author (*intentio auctoris*) versus the use to which the text is put by the reader (*intentio lectoris*) is particularly pertinent in the area of the unsaid. The kind of authorial silence in the texts I examine can fall into different categories: intended reticence (Levi), psychological reticence (Ginzburg), disguised statements (Pavese), self-delusion (Pizzardo), self-effacement and communication by means of the visual rather than the abstract (Sanvitale). Of course there is overlap between these broad distinctions; for instance, Levi chooses to restrain his emotions but possibly would be by nature unable to be more outspoken owing to his upbringing or the psychological syndromes suffered by victims of great trauma. The degree of the author's intention to suppress must vary in all the texts. I do not wish to fall into the trap of speculating what the author's intention might have been, only what emerges from the text as it stands. I would disagree with Rorty's implication that an analysis or 'overinterpretation' of a text detracts from the reader's emotional and personal response. I would argue that the emotional response comes first and that literary criticism is partly the result of curiosity to see 'how it works', how that response is elicited, in exactly the same way that we might take a piece of machinery to pieces to see how it works. Admittedly, this can affect the illusion temporarily, but my experience is that on rereading after analysis the original emotion not only endures but is enhanced by a sense of greater understanding of the mechanics of the text. Eco makes this same point:

> Did this kind of theoretical awareness reduce the pleasure and the freedom of my further readings? Not at all. On the contrary, after this analysis I always felt new pleasures and discovered new nuances when re-reading *Sylvie*.[30]

In conclusion, it seems there are at least two sides to the way in which the unsaid manifests itself in texts. The first aspect to consider is how the unsaid is embedded in the actual expression, which is the tendency of words to act independently of their surface meaning (as described in the theoretical writing of Lacan, Derrida and many others) as well as traditional imagery, metaphor and symbol. The second aspect for consideration is governed by the psychological imperatives of the writer, who does not wish or cannot bring him- or herself to articulate certain things, but these elements emerge nevertheless, usually by means of the mechanisms listed above. In this book I will be unravelling these two aspects, focusing on individual case studies of writers selected for their historical, literary and personal importance.

Notes to Chapter 1

1. Dacia Maraini, *La lunga vita di Marianna Ucrìa* (Milan: Rizzoli, 1990).
2. Eco, *Interpretation and Overinterpretation*, 45–88.
3. Ibid., 82.
4. See Simon P. Sibelman, *Silence in the Novels of Elie Wiesel* (New York: St Martin's Press, 1995), 11–30, for an excellent introduction to theoretical approaches to silence.
5. Sanford Budick and Wolfgang Iser, *Languages of the Unsayable: The Play of Negativity in Literature and Literary Theory* (New York: Columbia University Press, 1989), p. xvii.
6. Oswald Ducrot, *Dire et ne pas dire: Principes de sémantique linguistique* (Paris: Hermann, 1972), 5–7.
7. Jacques Derrida, *Writing and Difference*, trans. Alan Bass (Chicago: University of Chicago Press, 1978).
8. Frank Kermode, *The Genesis of Secrecy* (Cambridge, MA: Harvard University Press, 1979), 113–14.
9. Derrida, *Writing and Difference*, 34–5.

10. Mikhail Bakhtin, *The Dialogic Imagination: Four Essays*, ed. Michael Holquist, trans. Caryl Emerson and Michael Holquist (Austin: University of Texas Press, 1981).

11. Mikhail Bakhtin, *Esthétique et théorie du roman* (Paris: Gallimard, 1978), 22–8. See also Ann Jefferson, 'Bodymatters: Self and Other in Bakhtin, Sartre and Barthes', *Bakhtin and Cultural Theory*, ed. Ken Hirschkop and David Shepherd (Manchester: Manchester University Press, 1989), 152–77, for a very clear summary of Bakhtin's ideas.

12. Roland Barthes, *Essais critiques: Le Bruissement de la langue* (Paris: Éditions du Seuil, 1985), 212.

13. Jefferson, 'Bodymatters', 171.

14. Peter Schwenger, *Fantasm and Fiction: On Textual Envisioning* (Stanford: Stanford University Press, 1999).

15. Maurice Blanchot, *L'Espace littéraire* (Paris: Gallimard, 1955), 18.

16. Maurice Blanchot, 'Le Paradoxe d'Aytré', idem, *La Part du feu* (Paris: Gallimard, 1949), 66–78.

17. Jean-François Lyotard, *Le Différend* (Paris: Minuit, 1983).

18. Levi, Appendix to *Se questo è un uomo*, *Opere*, i. 197.

19. Harold Bloom, *The Anxiety of Influence* (New York: Oxford University Press, 1973).

20. See e.g. Christopher Collins, *The Poetics of the Mind's Eye: Literature and the Psychology of the Imagination* (Philadelphia: University of Pennsylvania Press, 1991); Tzvetan Todorov, *The Fantastic: A Structural Approach to a Literary Genre*, trans. Richard Howard (Cleveland: Press of Case Western Reserve University, 1973); Schwenger, *Fantasm and Fiction*.

21. Tsvetan Todorov, *Poétique de la prose* (Paris: Éditions du Seuil, 1971), 153.

22. Ernest Hemingway, *A Moveable Feast* (1964), 75, quoted in Schwenger, *Fantasm and Fiction*, 3.

23. Jacques Lacan, 'The Agency of the Letter in the Unconscious', idem, *Écrits: A Selection*, trans. Alan Sheridan (London: Routledge, 2003), 161–97 at 172.

24. George Steiner, 'The Hollow Miracle', idem, *Language and Silence* (London: Faber & Faber, 1967), 117–32 at 131.

25. Ibid., 117–18.

26. See *BB* 134 for the origins of this tale.

27. Bruno Bettelheim, *The Informed Heart* (London: Penguin, 1986; first pubd 1960), 124.

28. Rorty in Eco et al., *Interpretation and Overinterpretation*, 102.

29. Culler, ibid., 110.

30. Eco, ibid., 148.

CHAPTER 2

'Il ritegno':
Writing and Restraint in Primo Levi

The notion of something held back, left 'unsaid' in Levi's work is not new in itself.[1] In 1985 Irving Howe singled out this aspect of Levi's style. He commented on 'an emotional restraint and a steadiness of creative purpose that can seem almost indecent to demand from survivors' and a 'kind of muted tactfulness that Levi shows in his work', adding: 'He recognises that there are some things that can be said and some that cannot', and 'with some subjects writers need a pledge of stringent omission'.[2] Marco Belpoliti, in his edition of Levi's complete works (1997; i. 1376), speaks of 'un virile pudore' in his writing, whilst Bryan Cheyette, in a valuable study (1998) identifying 'ethical uncertainty' in Levi's narrative approach, touches on the notion of restraint in the introduction to his discussion.[3] Robert Gordon, in his new monograph (2001), has a chapter entitled 'Discretion, or Language and Silence', where he also notes the word *ritegno* and defines it as 'discretion as prudence or tact, on the one hand, and discreteness or discrimination, on the other, in the acknowledgement of difference and the capacity to distinguish that is at the core of our engagement with others and with the world'.[4] Two lengthy biographies published simultaneously, by Ian Thomson and Carole Angier (2002),[5] are testament to the respect accorded to Primo Levi by the English-speaking world and continuing and increasing curiosity about the man and his work. However, despite this huge critical interest in Levi in recent years, the significant aspect of his 'restraint' has not been explored fully, nor its importance, for both Levi and his readers, properly emphasized.

The success of Levi's work world-wide, in particular the reception of the second version of *Se questo è un uomo* (1958) and *Il sistema periodico* (1975),[6] whose success in translation in the United States introduced all Primo Levi's work to a much wider audience, and the fact that in Italy *Se questo è un uomo* is a secondary-school text, suggest that something about his shaping and expression of the facts makes unbearable material approachable for a wide range of people, including potentially problematic or resistant audiences, such as Germans in the immediate post-war years, or the young. I suggest that the element of *ritegno* or restraint is a singularly powerful influence throughout Levi's writing career. It represents an important aspect of his personal poetics, already signalled clearly in the opening chapter of *Se questo è un uomo*, where, in the moving passage describing the last hours before departure for the camp, Levi states (i. 10): 'Molte cose furono allora fra noi dette e fatte; ma di queste è bene che non resti memoria'; or where he records his farewell to the woman with whom he made the hideous journey (i. 13): 'Ci dicemmo allora [...] cose che non si dicono fra i vivi'. *Ritegno* continues to exert its influence as a stylistic element in all Levi's essays, narrative works and journalism, but it is important to remember that it is an emotion too, emerging time and again, as will become clear in this chapter.

It has become a critical commonplace that Primo Levi is a controlled, non-judgmental, even passionless writer, for example: 'Ciò che colpisce di più quando si legge *Se questo è un uomo* è il tono pacato, spassionato del libro';[7] 'distacco intellettuale [...] incredibile equanimità [...] imparzialità, serenità, preoccupazione di essere correttamente informato, controllo sui propri ricordi [...] razionalità intrepidamente chiara e distinta';[8] 'insistence on lucid objectivity'.[9] He has been portrayed as the scientist conscientiously recording data as if for scientific or technical purposes, dispassionately noting events and observations, with no artistry and little emotion involved in his accounts. In fact this image of Levi is not accurate at all; his style, whether in testimony, fiction, essay or narrative, is measured, but hardly 'pacato' or 'spassionato'. Judith Woolf points out in her chapter 'The Pardoner' just a few of the examples of passion, anger, disgust and condemnation in Levi's writing.[10] There are many more that could be quoted, for instance, in the afterword to *Se questo è un uomo* Levi stresses, 'gli esecutori di ordini *non sono* innocenti! [...] non si può comprendere, anzi, *non si deve* comprendere, perché comprendere è quasi giustificare' (i. 197; Levi's emphasis), showing that he has not forgiven or even understood; in 'Vanadio' in *Il sistema periodico* he distinguishes between forgiving and even loving the enemy who has genuinely repented, 'e cioè quando cessino di essere nemici', but adds of the unrepentant enemy 'è nostro dovere guidicarlo, non perdonarlo' (i. 932–3); also, in an interview with Risa Sodi:

I don't really know what forgiveness is. It's a concept that's outside my world. I don't have the authority to bestow forgiveness. If I were a rabbi, maybe I would; if I were a judge, perhaps. I believe that if someone has committed a crime, he has to pay. It's not up to me to say, 'I exempt you from punishment.' The authority does not rest with me.[11]

Furthermore, the artist/scientist contrast is generally illusory in any case; apart from highly-specialized writing for technical journals, a literary element to any account is inevitable, and indeed many scientists have written 'artistically' about science.[12]

Belpoliti comments in 'Io sono un centauro', introducing a collection of interviews with the writer:

I libri di Levi sono, seppur in misura diversa, pregni di quella 'finzione' che è propria della letteratura (in quasi tutte le interviste si sofferma spesso su questo, vuole spiegare quali avvenimenti reali si celino dietro ai racconti, compresi anche quelli di cui è venuto a conoscenza da altri).

On the question of fiction versus history Belpoliti adds:

Levi dimostra, rispetto ad altri narratori del genocidio ebraico, di sapere quanto problematico sia il rapporto tra narrazione e realtà [...] in altre conversazioni, sottolinea il fatto che c'è sempre una discrepanza tra quello che lui ha narrato e ciò che è accaduto nella realtà.[13]

This issue of narrative versus 'fact', central to all discussions about the literature of the Holocaust, is too large to approach here in any detail.[14] Nevertheless it is important to clarify in all discussions of Levi's testimony that at no point is the essential truth of the events related being brought into question.[15] On the one hand, Levi insists on the truthfulness of his testimony, on the other, he admits to artistry; but the second aspect does not cancel out or contradict the first.

Since Levi has left us with several statements concerning the creative process, it is useful to put some of them side by side in order to build up a satisfactory picture of his method for our analysis. He admits that a myth has grown up, with his connivance, that the genesis of *Se questo è un uomo* was completely natural and unstudied. In an interview with Germaine Greer (1985) he says:

Ho costruito una sorta di leggenda attorno a quest'opera, affermando che l'ho scritta senza alcuna pianificazione, di getto, senza meditarci sopra. [...] In realtà, la scrittura non è mai spontanea. Ora che ci penso, capisco che questo libro è colmo di letteratura [...].

He also states in the same discussion that it is impossible to portray real people accurately or satisfactorily:

È sempre rischioso trasformare una persona in un personaggio. A prescindere dalle buone intenzioni dell'autore, dalla sua cura nell'evitare ogni distorsione dei fatti, dal suo tentativo di migliorare il personaggio rispetto all'individuo in carne e ossa, di renderlo piú nobile o piú affascinante, la persona reale rimane sempre e comunque delusa.[16]

In this way, we understand that *Se questo è un uomo* is not untruthful, but it is a work of art and follows the rules of narrative.[17]

However, the especially harrowing nature of Levi's subject-matter demands exceptional and appropriate treatment: an extremely significant feature of his style, the aspect to which I wish to draw attention in this chapter, is a notable reticence, or *ritegno*, which consists in omitting what could become oppressive detail. Levi writes a personal and truthful account but exercises restraint in what he tells us. He encapsulated his technique when he said (*Opere*, i. 1377) of the writing of *Se questo è un uomo*, 'Quello che mi importava era mettere giù, più che i fatti, le impressioni legate ai fatti.' There is ample evidence that he implemented consistently this policy of separating event and response and suppressing brutal facts in order both to spare and engage the reader.

In 1947, Levi wrote of *Se questo è un uomo* in 'L'Italia che scrive' (*Opere*, i. 1384):

Ho evitato i particolari crudi e le tentazioni polemiche e retoriche. Chi leggerà potrà avere l'impressione che gli altri, ben piú atroci, resoconti di prigionia abbiano passato il segno; non è cosí, tutte le cose che si sono lette sono state vere, ma non era questa la faccia della verità che mi interessava. Neppure mi interessava raccontare delle eccezioni, degli eroi e dei traditori, bensí, per mia tendenza e per elezione, ho cercato di mantenere l'attenzione sui molti, sulla norma, sull'uomo qualsiasi, non infame e non santo, che di grande non ha che la sofferenza, ma è incapace di comprenderla e contenerla.

In an interview with Roberto di Caro (1987) he uses the revealing metaphor of constructing a laboratory instrument in order to confirm the practical, precise element of the writer's craft and how, crucially, it involves economy of style:

Non c'è molta differenza tra costruire un apparecchio per il laboratorio e costruire un bel racconto. Ci vuole simmetria. Ci vuole idoneità allo scopo. Bisogna togliere il superfluo. Bisogna che non manchi l'indispensabile. E che alla fine il tutto funzioni.

Then, in response to the question whether writing is less technical than factory and laboratory work, he adds: 'Al contrario, per me è un lavoro molto preciso.'

Next, he clarifies that much of that process is one of deletion:

Ci sono delle frasi storte, fatte male, che vanno tolte e sostituite. Appena scritto, un testo è illeggibile, non ha senso, è come guardarsi allo specchio e vederci sempre la stessa faccia. Bisogna lasciarla riposare, giorni o settimane, e poi riprenderlo. Allora un po' di martello funziona. Meglio ancora: funzionano le tronchesine. Per questo il Macintosh è uno strumento meraviglioso: perché taglia via tutto senza pietà, non rimane traccia di una sola cancellatura.[18]

Later on in the same interview he adds:

Mi sembra che l'elemento decisivo del procedimento narrativo debba essere un accorto bilancio fra il necessario e il superfluo. Io leggo un po' di tutto ma preferisco gli scrittori che non indulgono troppo al superfluo [...] I miei libri, credo di potermene vantare, non contengono niente di superfluo. Mi viene spontaneo e naturale astenermi dall'adornamento, dall'aggiunta messa lí solo affinché la pagina sia 'bella'.

Finally, another interesting comment is:

Qualche volta mi capitano per le mani dei manoscritti non disprezzabili, di gente che non sa scrivere ma che ha delle cose da dire. Verrebbe voglia di prenderli e riscriverli.[19]

So, in summary, his view of testimony is that the truth must be told, certain things must be said, but literary style and restraint are both important factors. The events themselves, plainly transcribed will not be sufficient to do their work of informing and convincing the reader.

In *La chiave a stella* (*Opere*, i. 943–1105) Levi's narrated self is a scientist debating whether to move into writing as a full-time activity, and the narrator's comments on how a story is constructed tie in with Levi's remarks in interviews about his own writing methods. Two of the most interesting in the context of this book are as follows:

Uno dei grandi privilegi di chi scrive è proprio quello di tenersi sull'impreciso e sul vago, di dire e non dire, di inventare a man salva, fuori di ogni regola di prudenza. ('Tiresia', *Opere*, i. 988)

Ho promesso a Faussone che [...] in nessun modo avrei ceduto alla tentazione professionale dell'inventare, dell'abbellire e dell'arrotondare; che perciò al suo resoconto non avrei aggiunto niente, ma forse qualche cosa avrei tolto, come fa lo scultore quando ricava la forma del blocco. ('Il ponte', *Opere*, i. 1048)

Here, in the first extract, he is stating the writer's right to embellish and invent, but also to leave things out. In the second, he promises not to embellish or invent, but again reserves the right to leave things out.

In *L'altrui mestiere* (1985; *Opere*, i. 629–856), he discusses the difference between writing factual accounts and fiction and admits that there is some overlap, with creative and artistic considerations being involved even in the presentation of things one has witnessed.

Scrivere di cose viste è piú facile che inventare, e meno felice. È uno scrivere-descrivere: hai una traccia, scavi nella memoria prossima o lontana, riordini i reperti (se ne hai il talento), li cataloghi, poi prendi una sorta di macchina fotografica mentale e scatti: puoi essere un fotografo mediocre, o buono, o magari 'artistico'; puoi nobilitare le cose che ritrai, o riportarle in maniera impersonale, modesta e onesta, o darne invece un'immagine distorta, piatta, sfuocata, scentrata, sotto o sovraesposta, ma in ogni caso sei guidato, tenuto per mano dai fatti, hai terra sotto i piedi. ('Scrivere un romanzo', *Opere*, ii. 741)

In another article, 'Perchè si scrive?', a light-hearted discussion of the writer's craft, amongst many possible reasons why anyone might write, he makes this statement:

Perchè si scrive? [...] Per liberarsi da un'angoscia. Spesso lo scrivere rappresenta un equivalente della confessione o del divano di Freud. Non ho nulla da obiettare a chi scrive spinto dalla tensione: gli auguro anzi di riuscire a liberarsene cosí, come è accaduto a me in anni lontani. Gli chiedo però che si sforzi di filtrare la sua angoscia, di non scagliarla cosí com'è, ruvida e greggia, sulla faccia di chi legge: altrimenti rischia di contagiarla agli altri senza allontanarla da sé. (*Opere*, ii. 617)

It is important to note that this restraint exercised in writing is not only an artistic decision but a personal psychological response, as is clear from a discussion with Virgilio Lo Presti (1979), when Levi makes a poignant confession of how it has been impossible to talk about his experiences with his children, though they are clearly aware of what happened to him and have read what their father has written. He says:

Io non so dire, ognuno vive delle esperienze a modo suo, certo che in molte famiglie effettivamente 'gli altri', i non superstiti, i non reduci, si sono opposti a questo raccontare. Il perché, varrebbe la pena di saperlo. In molti casi perché il reduce è scomodo e noioso.... Ravviva le sofferenze, vuole infliggere le sue sofferenze, vuole prevalere su un altro infliggendogli le sue soffrenze e questo può disturbare. È l'esempio dei miei figli, Renzo compreso, che non ha mai voluto che io ne parlassi.[20]

On the same matter, in his interview with Milvia Spadi (1986) he says:

Io penso che teoricamente vada raccontato tutto. La mia esperienza con i
miei due figli è stata completamente diversa. [...] Sanno benissimo tutto,
hanno letto i miei libri, però non mi hanno mai permesso di parlarne. [...]
Mi vietano di parlarne in casa. Mi vietano con i fatti. Mi rendo conto
perfettamente che è *unanständig* (indecoroso, sconveniente) da parte mia il
forzarli su questo argomento.[21]

The notion of holding something back when speaking or writing
of experiences occurs again in an interview with Marco Vigevani
(1984), when Levi asserts that 'un testimone è tanto piú attendibile
quanto meno esagera o quanto meno rischia di essere scambiato per
uno che esagera'.[22] He adds that he was unaware of much that went
on the camp and meticulously only narrated what he actually saw:

Io volevo raccontare quello che avevo visto. E in piú vorrei aggiungere che
qui c'entra anche una questione di temperamento, di stile; non mi piace
parlare forte e, me ne sono accorto dalle innumerevoli testimonianze che ho
ricevuto, questo ha incontrato il consenso. È piú efficace una testimonianza
fatta con ritegno che una fatta con sdegno: lo sdegno dev'essere del lettore,
non dell'autore e non è detto che lo sdegno dell'autore diventi sdegno del
lettore. Io ho voluto fornire al lettore la materia prima per il *suo* sdegno.[23]

This last comment is fundamental to Levi's method: he speaks of the
use of *ritegno* to spare his readers, but nevertheless to awaken in them
an awareness of the enormity of what (paradoxically) is not described.
Later in the same conversation he says of the dehumanization of
victims and their tormentors: 'È un argomento delicato e di cui si
parla troppo e in modo sgarbato, mentre va trattato con estrema
cautela.'[24] Here he again states clearly that one can say too much and
uses the curious and arresting adjective *sgarbato* to characterize
accounts that are overly explicit. He feels, with justification, that
certain things enter the realms of the obscene and therefore cannot be
discussed even in a serious forum; they need to be kept off the main
stage, though possibly implied by what is to the fore of the scene. The
choice of vocabulary, *ritegno*, *sdegno*, *sgarbato*, the rejection of 'parlare
forte', all construct a poetics made up of dignity, politeness and
consideration of the feelings of others. This is strikingly at odds with
the subject described and with the harshness of the language of the
camps (to which he has alluded only seconds before in this
conversation), and, I would suggest, offers a kind of deliberate
resistance and partial antidote to their brutalizing effects. It is not

therefore surprising that Levi reserves particular disdain for books and films exploiting or distorting the suffering of those who endured the camps, in terms expressing a sense of outrage or violation (*Opere*, i. 1268): 'son cose nostre, intime, e ci dà disagio vederle manomesse'.

If the need for reticence or *ritegno* as part of the creative process is, then, clearly signalled by Levi, the word *ritegno* also appears in other contexts, not only discussions of literary method. As I have suggested, *ritegno* is both a stylistic technique and an emotional response. The following examples show how *ritegno* can be a reaction of the observer of atrocity, of the narrator of that atrocity or of the person reading about an atrocity; and how it can even become a reluctance to face up to the knowledge of such atrocity altogether.

In *La tregua* (*Opere*, i. 203–397) Levi describes the reaction to what they find of the young Russian soldiers who were the first to enter the camp after the departure of the Germans (206):

> Non salutavano, non sorridevano; apparivano oppressi, oltre che da pietà, da un confuso ritegno, che sigillava le loro bocche, e avvinceva i loro occhi allo scenario funereo. Era la stessa vergogna a noi ben nota, quella che ci sommergeva dopo le selezioni, ed ogni volta che ci toccava assistere o sottostare a un oltraggio.[25]

The 'confuso ritegno', that almost embarrassed sense of recoil felt by the just observer of some great cruelty, mirrors the illogical sense of shame of the innocent victim. Levi's evident *simpatia* for the Russians, which emerges throughout *La tregua*, is partly inspired by respect for their first, instinctive response of *ritegno* and *vergogna*, 'la vergogna che i tedeschi non conobbero, quella che il giusto prova davanti alla colpa commessa da altrui' (*Opere*, i. 206). On occasion, this *vergogna* on the part of the narrator, victim, listener, reader or observer becomes a conviction that certain matters are an inappropriate subject for discussion, '*unanständig*', as Levi himself described his attempted conversations with his own children. A vivid image of the post-war turning away from testimony and how it was linked with a sense of what was felt proper or seemly, is given in a fictional context in *Se non ora, quando?* The returning partisans have been invited to an elegant party in Milan, where they are respected and welcome; but they make the error of talking about their experiences without *ritegno*, and it is presented (with great authorial irony) as an error of taste as far as the hostess is concerned (*Opere*, ii. 501):

> Ma era in ansia anche per un altro motivo: era una signora fine e bene

educata, e alcune cose che i cinque raccontavano le ferivano gli orecchi. Pavel e Gedale, in specie, non avevano ritegno. Si sa, queste cose esistono, sono avvenute, la guerra non è uno scherzo, tanto meno è stato uno scherzo la guerra che hanno fatto questa povera gente; ma in un salotto, via nel suo salotto... Sí, va bene per gli atti di valore, le rappresaglie contro i tedeschi, i sabotaggi, le marce nella neve; ma dei pidocchi si può anche fare a meno di parlare, e delle pezze da piedi, e degli impiccati nelle latrine...[26]

George Steiner suggested that this reluctance to face the worst has been even more resilient amongst the British in his comments about British responses to accounts of the Holocaust in his review of the English translation of *I sommersi e i salvati*:[27]

No ash from the chimneys of Treblinka floated on an English wind. Witness the non-event of the brief showing in this country of Claude Lanzmann's *Shoah*. Not our patch. This abstention from public and private encounter tells of a continuum of sanity, of liberal imagining in British politics. It embodies a pragmatic resolve to maintain certain decencies and restraints even in fantasy and metaphysical speculation. The abyss can dizzy. It can also exercise a subtle, self-dramatizing flattery (some, notably in America, have turned the Auschwitz experience into eloquent kitsch).

In Levi's gentlemanly determination not to be *sgarbato* with his readers, he consistently avoids graphic detail in his writing. An example of an obvious kind is when, describing the treatment of would-be escapees in *I sommersi e i salvati*, he says they were subjected to 'un cerimoniale vario da volta a volta, sempre di ferocia inaudita, in cui si scatenava la crudeltà fantasiosa delle SS' (*Opere*, ii. 1114) without giving specific details. This discretion is undoubtedly a relief for the reader, whilst not detracting from the power and suggestion of the statement.[28] Many others of this nature could be quoted. However, there are subtler ways in which 'ritegno' shapes a text. In discussing *Se questo è un uomo*, Judith Woolf cites Elie Wiesel's *La nuit* as an example of hindsight in narrative and exploitation of the reader's prior knowledge of the circumstances described, from documentary evidence and other literary or even fictional accounts,[29] in contrast to Levi, who always narrates from the standpoint of his own ignorance at the time of the events described. Wiesel also is harsher than Levi, more specific in descriptions, though paradoxically his name is associated with silence and the whole debate of silence and the Holocaust.[30]

The descriptions in Levi's account in *Se questo è un uomo* and in

Wiesel's of a public hanging give an example of the difference in style between the two writers, who were in Auschwitz at the same time, though they never met there.[31] Levi's concentrates on the effect the spectacle had on the men, not on what they saw, whereas Wiesel, in two accounts of an execution, confronts us with the shock of what he actually saw. Levi (*Opere*, i. 146) limits himself to:

La botola si è aperta, il corpo ha guizzato atroce; la banda ha ripreso a suonare, e noi, nuovamente ordinati in colonna, abbiamo sfilato davanti agli ultimi fremiti del morente.

Describing a similar scene, Wiesel writes:

Sur un signe du chef de camp, les trois chaises basculèrent.
    Silence absolu dans tout le camp. A l'horizon, le soleil se couchait.
    — Découvrez-vous! hurla le chef du camp. Sa voix était rauque. Quant à nous, nous pleurions.
    — Couvrez-vous!
    Puis commença le défilé. Les deux adultes ne vivaient plus. Leur langue pendait, grossie, bleutée. Mais la troisième corde n'était pas immobile: si léger, l'enfant vivait encore....
    Plus d'une demi-heure il resta ainsi, à lutter entre la vie et la mort, agonisant sous nos yeux. Et nous devions le regarder bien en face. Il était encore vivant lorsque je passai devant lui. Sa langue était encore rouge, ses yeux pas encore éteints.[32]

Both writers end the account with a reflection of how the prisoners felt that evening. Wiesel's is dramatic:

Derrière moi, j'entendis le même homme demander:
    — Où donc est Dieu?
    Et je sentais en moi une voix qui lui répondait:
    — Où il est? Le voici — il est pendu ici, à cette potence...
    Ce soir-là, la soupe avait un goût de cadavre.[33]

Levi's account concentrates on the effect on the prisoners, their sense of being 'domati', 'spenti, degni ormai della morte inerme che ci attende', wholly in accordance with his declared intention to convey 'più che i fatti, le impressioni legate ai fatti'. We should note that there then follows a moment of the purest anger, including a direct address to the German nation generally, with the force and resonance of a biblical admonition, a powerful example of the kind of passion that effectively belies Levi's literary image as a controlled and unemotional observer (*Opere*, i. 146):

Distruggere l'uomo è difficile, quasi quanto crearlo: non è stato agevole, non è stato breve, ma ci siete riusciti, tedeschi. Eccoci docili sotto i vostri sguardi: da parte nostra nulla piú avete a temere: non atti di rivolta, non parole di sfida, neppure uno sguardo giudice.

However, whilst Wiesel's ending is figurative and openly dramatic, attributing 'un goût de cadavre' to the soup, Levi's account ends with a subdued return to the routine of the day, focussing on the physical ravages of hunger and again the emotional effects of what has happened (ibid.):

Abbiamo issato la menaschka sulla cuccetta, abbiamo fatto la ripartizione, abbiamo soddisfatto la rabbia quotidiana della fame, e ora ci opprime la vergogna.

He ends this distressing chapter with the weight of that word *vergogna* and thereby gives it enormous emphasis. By filtering our response to this terrible spectacle through his own response, Levi spares the reader the brutality of exposure to crude description of what he saw, but his method does not weaken the moral impact of the scene he depicts, indeed the opposite is true. Avoiding extensive passages of pathos or violence leaves a space for the imagination of the reader and invites our own response of *vergogna* and *ritegno*. *Vergogna* and the instinct for *ritegno* are closely linked, both for Levi and, significantly, for the reader.

The issue of restraint or *ritegno* has some bearing on the form of the original version of *Se questo è un uomo* and the reception of that book. There are many different possible reasons why the first version of the book was not acceptable to Einaudi and then not particularly widely read in its published De Silva edition. This has been discussed fully elsewhere, most recently in Belpoliti's scholarship, as noted above; but in summary, the reasons are likely to be a combination of two main elements: firstly, a general feeling that it was time to put the shattering events of the war aside and look to the future; and secondly, something about the style of that early version.

It is this second aspect to which I would like to return here. If post-war sensibilities meant that the narration of atrocity, however truthful, was nevertheless unseemly, it might be that the first version of the book was unacceptable partly because it was too harrowing, and one might therefore logically expect it to be longer and to contain more distressing detail than the more successful later one. The first version is in fact shorter than the second. However, this does not invalidate my argument that the first version was less 'restrained'. *Ritegno* does not necessarily mean leaving things out, although this is often what happens; it can also entail adding appropriate material to 'soften' an account.

It is well known that Levi wrote the first version quickly, the result of an 'impulso immediato e violento', as he says in his preface to *Se questo è un uomo* (*Opere*, i. 5–6). The 'literary' features nevertheless clearly discernible in the text are there because he was steeped in a classical and literary tradition as a result of his schooling at a *liceo classico*. However, the instinct for restraint has a significant influence on this first work: the form of the first version arises from a combination of urgency of purpose and the writer's reluctance or even psychological inability to reveal more than an outline of what he actually experienced. Levi, a young man only just emerged from his nightmarish experience, has a story he urgently needs to tell, but he confines himself to recounting fragments of his tale, leaving out the most horrifying details. Nevertheless, paradoxically, precisely the starkness of the account renders it still too harsh for post-war sensibilities.

This is confirmed by the fact that many of the additions in the later edition are indeed 'softening' elements. In his analysis of the variants of this text (*Opere*, i. 1380–1408), Marco Belpoliti compares the chapters of the text that appeared initially in journals, the notebook found by Tesio containing a hand-written version of the book, the De Silva first edition and the final Einaudi edition of 1958. Here we are most concerned with the differences between the De Silva edition and the Einaudi edition, though all changes seem to be based on similar stylistic decisions: the insertion of explanatory material, brief digressions of a moral nature and the addition of literary imagery.[34] Belpoliti summarizes the various changes to the opening of the book as follows: precise explanation of the circumstances of the writer's arrest combined with an element of hindsight, of looking back at himself. The other changes to the first chapter are the addition of a meditation on the reactions of people going to their death, of literary elements and the final sentence ('La cosa suscita in noi collera e riso e uno strano sollievo'), which Belpoliti even describes as 'al limite dell'umoristico'.

These are all elements that 'reassure' the reader: events are put in context; any form of analysis of those events, however sombre, begins to make them seem containable, manageable; literary elements inevitably distance the events from reality, however powerful the imagery, whilst the effect of the final sentence arouses the same 'strano sollievo' in the reader; the horrors and uncertainties have already been rendered less threatening. The 'rounding out' that Belpoliti documents makes the text more of a work of art, less a cry of protest or pain, by alleviating the harshness of its original bald narrative.[35]

If we now go back to the dual nature of Levi's assertions as to the way the book was written, both 'di getto' and yet wrought as a work of art, we see that both are possible. The first drafts, whether handwritten or typed up almost word-perfect, could well have been written quickly, shocked snapshots of episodes the writer urgently needed to express. His instinct for restraint, however, made him tend towards brevity, sparseness, but this resulted in a harsher text, modified by additions in the later version. In this way, Levi's eagerness not to be *sgarbato* with his reader can lead equally to both omissions and additions. We can deduce that the first outpouring, the De Silva version with its 'maggior cupezza', as Belpoliti notes (*Opere*, i. 1400), was a list of moments that were most starkly important in the writer's mind, whilst nevertheless to some extent already unconsciously shaped by his literary schooling. The result was perceived by contemporary readers as harsh, because not rounded out by the kind of details added later.[36]

However, there is another important aspect to this method that may have affected the reception of both versions of the book, which is that the text may not have been entirely clear to its first readers. We later readers have a vast array of documentary information upon which to draw, as well as other biographical accounts or fictionalized accounts, on film or in writing, all of which we have internalized, so that however brief or elliptical an account we read now, we can supply the missing elements for ourselves. The post-war response to the horrors and devastation of the war was to get on with life and leave these matters behind, so that, after the newsreel showing footage of the liberation of the camps had been shown, the general public in the West was not exposed to much more of this information immediately, only gradually over a number of years.[37] So the way to make the new version of *Se questo è un uomo* more successful than the first was to make it less harsh but clearer to the uninformed reader, a paradox Levi solved by adding 'innocuous' detail that might involve the reader but not distress him, and sometimes explanations to clarify the situations described.

Nevertheless, in the Einaudi version of *Se questo è un uomo*, there remains a striking example of ellipsis based on *ritegno*. I suggest that, in the chapter 'I sommersi e i salvati', Levi's instinct for *ritegno* has led to a gap so wide between what he says and what he implies was actually happening that there is some loss of comprehension for the reader. In the final part of the chapter, the enigmatic personality of Henri is described in detail and with apparent sympathy. We know that he is intelligent, well-educated, *civile* but also *consapevole*. He has suffered emotional loss, the death of his brother in the camp the year before, and Levi signals this event as emotionally cauterizing for Henri: 'da quel giorno Henri ha reciso ogni vincolo di affetti; si è chiuso in sé come in una corazza'. Henri's methods of survival are specifically described as functioning without him being obliged to compromise his humanity, being 'i metodi che l'uomo può applicare rimanendo degno del nome di uomo', so that he assumes a special significance in relation to the title of the book.[38] His success at acquiring food is indicated with humour and his methods are listed as 'l'organizzazione, la pietà e il furto'; but when Levi describes Henri's exploitation of *pietà*, he introduces specifically homosexual overtones, likening Henri's looks to 'San Sebastiano del Sodoma'.

There follows a general comment about human nature, typical of Levi's avowed intent (*Opere*, i. 5) to furnish 'uno studio pacato di alcuni aspetti dell'animo umano' in this book, when he states that *pietà* is a basic human instinct and can be found even in the hearts of the most brutal oppressors. This is a surprising revelation and is not developed further in this text. For a fuller analysis of the concept the reader needs to wait until Levi's last published work, *I sommersi e i salvati*, the collection of meditations revisiting the issues first touched upon in *Se questo è un uomo*, where *pietà* is defined as a momentary impulse, a primitive response, not indicative of the evolved personality as a whole.[39]

Henri, having discovered this curious quirk of human nature, exploits it, but in the young man's desperate circumstances the ploy strikes the reader as acceptable. Nevertheless, an unattractive simile follows: 'Come l'icneumone paralizza i grossi bruchi pelosi, ferendoli nel loro unico ganglio vulnerabile, cosí Henri valuta con un'occhiata il soggetto, "son type".' This comparison to a predatory insect negates the earlier fundamental association with humanity. A list of his conquests follows. Levi stresses how pleasant ('gradevole') it is to spend time with Henri, how he feels a closeness with him; but then abruptly, Henri distances himself and becomes 'duro e lontano, chiuso nella sua corazza, nemico di tutti, inumanamente scaltro e incomprensibile come il Serpente della Genesi'. The Serpent is the great betrayer, a deceiver, Evil incarnate (the Devil) and is traditionally associated with sexual 'knowledge'. Levi explains he always feels as if he has been used in some way by Henri.

The chapter ends on an unequivocal statement: 'Oggi so che Henri è vivo. Darei molto per conoscere la sua vita di uomo libero, ma non desidero rivederlo.' In the strong position as the last words of a chapter devoted to the evocation of specific individuals, such a statement comes as a shock. On the evidence we have here, surely Henri is not so despicable that he warrants this condemnation. After all, there are very few people that Levi states categorically he would prefer not to meet again, and the reasons are usually clear enough. For instance, one example is the German chemist, Muller, in 'Vanadio' in *Il sistema periodico*, Levi explains carefully why he would prefer not to agree to meet him (*Opere*, i. 928):

Dell''auspicabile incontro' non parlai. Inutile cercare eufemismi, parlare di pudore, ribrezzo, ritegno. Paura era la parola [...] non mi sentivo capace di rappresentare i morti di Auschwitz, e neppure mi pareva sensato ravvisare in Müller il rappresentante dei carnefici. Mi conosco: non posseggo prontezza polemica, l'avversario mi distrae, mi interessa piú come uomo che come avversario, lo sto a sentire e rischio di credergli; lo sdegno e il giusto giudizio mi tornano dopo, sulle scale quando non servono piú.

Later (*Opere*, i. 932) he repeats: 'Non lo amavo, e non desideravo rivederlo'.

It could be that in using particularly human qualities to exploit other human beings Henri after all devalues his own humanity, but it is probable that there is a gap here: as a result of his policy of *ritegno* Levi has avoided mentioning specifically what terrible thing it is that makes Henri so unacceptable to him. There is obviously a homosexual element, and we have to ask ourselves whether Levi is condemning the young man so utterly for his implied homosexuality alone.

Sexuality in the camps is an area which Levi prefers not to discuss. He leaves it aside in *Se questo è un uomo*, for reasons which are clear from one of his comments in his interview with Risa Sodi, discussing Liliana Cavani's film *Il portiere di notte*, when he says: 'For common prisoners like me, sex wasn't a problem. It was completely forgotten, even in our dreams.'[40] Elsewhere, Levi consistently argues that restraint is desirable when discussing this aspect of camp life. He justifiably despises the commercial exploitation of this subject matter. For instance, in a book review originally published in *La Stampa* (10 March 1978) he angrily asserts 'quanto furfantesca e bugiarda sia l'operazione che allaga tutti gli schemi sotto l'alluvione dei film sesso-nazisti'.[41] In an article in 1979 occasioned by the television serial 'Holocaust' of which, on the whole, he does not disapprove, he says 'esistevano bordelli in alcuni lager: ma stuoli di corvi se ne sono cibati, riempendo gli schermi di mezzo mondo con una valanga di film indecenti'.[42] However, the interview with Risa Sodi stands out as an anomaly, for Levi's comments are far less clear and logical than is usual in the many 'conversazioni' recorded with him. He describes Cavani's film as 'profoundly false' (the interview is reproduced in English) and goes on to describe the situation in the camps regarding prostitution. It is worth quoting this passage at length in order to be able to examine the logic of it:

The SS had nothing to do with the Lagers. [...] I'll grant you that there was prostitution. Himmler himself decided at a certain point (I think in '42) that each Lager should have a brothel. He had two reasons: first of all, he was a moralist, he knew there was homosexuality in the camps, and so he said, 'Let's provide them with women so that the men will go with women instead of with other men.' In any case, he didn't have the Jews in mind (who had no need of women anyway). No, he was thinking of the political prisoners and the German criminals. He held it was, well, logical, that they have this brutish outlet. I learned much later that there was even a brothel in my camp, but it was 'staffed' with non-Jewish women.

Now, the heap of lies that has been built up around this absurd topic is overwhelming. First of all, the prostitutes were well off and, second of all, they were professionals. They were mostly professional prostitutes who were arrested as such and plied their trade in the camps ... and they were envied by all. I know of a Jewish girl who was able to pass as Aryan in order to work as a prostitute. That way, she ate a little more (they were paid in kind), and the clients who, as I said, were well-fed—being political prisoners and common criminals—paid her with butter, oil, bread, sweets and even stockings. There was another reason to encourage prostitution: obviously in those circumstances, the prostitutes and their clients formed deeply emotional bonds, and the clients in particular felt strong ties to these women. They confided their secrets to them—and many of the prostitutes were Gestapo agents.

So the motives involved in camp prostitution were very complex. The cliché of the innocent woman forced to be a 'Soldatenhure' (a 'soldiers' whore'), condemned to prostitute herself against her will, is absolutely false. It was a different thing altogether. I remember clearly, even after all this time, seeing the SS promenade through the paths of the camp, arm in arm with the prostitutes on Sunday afternoons. The prostitutes were not only their friends, they were often their colleagues.

This is of course an interview, so is relatively spontaneous, possibly edited and presumably conducted in English which, though Levi spoke the language well, might have made clarity of expression more difficult for him; nevertheless, even taking all this into account, there is such confusion in the sequence of ideas, such contradiction of what Levi has said elsewhere, that it reflects profound unease with the topic as a whole. All he needed to say, in order to debunk the premiss of Cavani's film and others exploiting this subject, was that prostitutes were not, generally speaking, drawn from amongst prisoners. Instead, from his reply, it is not clear what exactly Levi was aware of at the time of being a prisoner, nor what his attitude was to prostitutes, either as a prisoner, or indeed at the time of the interview.

His view of Himmler, instead, is clear: Himmler is treated with evident irony, a 'moralist' and 'logical', his distaste for homosexuality giving him in his own view a moral superiority unassailed by his role in mass murder. His assessment of human nature is also seen as suspect, since Levi later states that the sexual instinct was irrelevant in the circumstances of the camp. This irony conveying a moral point is entirely in keeping with our experience of Levi's writing.[43] The assertion that the SS had 'nothing to do with the Lager' is downright puzzling. Levi himself mentions the presence of the SS in too many places to quote exhaustively.[44] Presumably his statement 'I learned much later' must mean later on, whilst he was still a prisoner (not after his release, as it seems to imply), since, in *Se questo è un uomo*, Levi actually mentions the existence of a brothel in the chapter 'Al di qua del bene e del male', and the point made about it not being for Jews echoes part of what he says in the interview and therefore seems to suggest the same memory source (*Opere*, i. 76):

È successo un altro periodo di rialzo dovuto a una singolare ragione: il cambio della guardia al Frauenblock, con arrivo di un contingente di robuste ragazze polacche. Infatti, poiché il buono-premio è valido (per i criminali e i politici: non per gli ebrei, i quali d'altronde non soffrono della limitazione) per un ingresso al Frauenblock, gli interessati ne hanno fatta attiva e rapida incetta.

We must assume also that he encountered the Jewish girl who became a prostitute only after his release from the camp; but having learned of her circumstances, in retrospect, might he not suppose by the time of this interview that other prostitutes were also in some way constrained to do what they did? It seems unlikely that all the 'robuste ragazze polacche' were professional prostitutes. Finally, his dismissal of all the prostitutes as particularly loathsome spies and willing associates of the hated SS, suggests distinct revulsion for the women involved and no sense of the 'zona grigia' that he describes so meticulously in *I sommersi e i salvati*, written shortly before this interview.

My reason for dwelling on this matter is that in searching for the missing element to explain Levi's distaste for Henri, the thing he could not bring himself to mention, I feel it must lie in this area of the exploitation of sexuality. It seems probable that Levi suspects Henri of operating at least some of the time as a homosexual prostitute. If we turn to Wiesel's account again, he mentions the sexual exploitation of children by homosexuals.[45] It may be that Levi thought Henri was involved in this traffic. Whilst his stance against racial prejudice is well-documented and to be expected (the clearest and most detailed expression of it being 'L'intolleranza razziale', *Opere* i. 293–311), we cannot know whether it is anachronistic to assume he would not be prejudiced against homosexuals. He has a natural reluctance to discuss sexuality openly, in keeping with the time of his upbringing, shared for instance with Italo Calvino, who excised elements of sex and violence from his youthful works.[46] We have seen that he feels unease and confusion in discussing matters to do with sexual exploitation in the camps, even in the context of an indifferent film more than twenty years later, that he prefers discretion when writing about people's sexuality, as is confirmed by the kind of corrections he made to his typescripts, so the enigma connected with Henri is most probably connected with sexual exploitation or sexual orientation.

I would stress that in the context of this study we do not need to know what the specific 'truth' is, only that Levi feels reluctance to discuss something he finds particularly distasteful or ugly, and that this leaves a gap in logic in his text. This is an example of *ritegno* becoming so imperative that it both overrides the writer's objectivity and blocks understanding for the reader. Usually *ritegno* protects readers; here it confuses their response. In his account of Henri, it would seem that Levi experiences an exceptionally strong reaction of *ritegno* (and *ribrezzo* and *sdegno*) and, in the same way, he recoiled from discussions on similar matters in his interview with Risa Sodi much later, in 1987. There are two important points here: firstly that *ritegno* sometimes causes lack of clarity, and secondly that Levi once more is proved to be far from consistently calm, objective or 'scientific' in his responses.

A further question needs to be posed: whether the elusive source of 'guilt' of Henri is in fact a creation of Levi's imagination. Recently a memoir was published by a man who felt he recognized himself as the Henri in Levi's text. Paul Steinberg narrates his own terrible experiences as a prisoner in Auschwitz, some of the episodes clearly parallel to Levi's account, for instance a chemistry 'examination' followed by work in the laboratory. In his memoir Steinberg refers to Levi's book briefly at various points, but there is one main passage of analysis:

I am astounded to find that he speaks at some length about me, changing a few details. He calls me Henri, for example. He says I was twenty-two years old, when I was barely eighteen, and he mentions my vast literary and scientific knowledge, which is an exaggeration, to say the least.

All the rest is there and leaves no room for doubt. Beardless, polyglot: French, English, German, Russian. Having special dealings with the British prisoners-of-war. My brother, who died in the camp during the winter of 1943–44: Philippe. My intrigues to establish useful contacts for myself among the senior block inmates and other *Prominenz* of the camp.

How strange it is to see oneself at a distance of fifty years through the eyes of a neutral and surely objective observer, with whom I would have had no special relationship.

He paints a picture of a rather unlikable fellow, something of a cold fish, whom he found pleasant company, it's true, but never wanted to see again.

He seems to know that I survived; I wonder how he found out.

He must have been right. I probably was that creature obsessed with staying alive. 'Enclosed in armor', he says; someone who knew how to attract the benevolence and compassion of the powerful, in case of need, 'by displaying ... the sores on his leg'. A solitary fighter, cool, calculating, who possessed 'a complete and organic theory on the ways to survive in the Lager'.

He was a neutral observer, that's how he saw me, and I was surely like that, ferociously determined to do anything to live, ready to use all means at hand, including a gift for inspiring sympathy and pity.

The strangest thing about this acquaintance that seems to have left such precise traces in his memory is that I do not remember him at all. Perhaps because I hadn't felt he could be useful to me? Which would confirm his judgment.

Now I feel a sharp sense of regret. Primo Levi is gone, and I'd never realized what he thought of me. He said he 'would give much to know about [my] life as a free man'. Maybe I could have persuaded him to change his verdict by showing that there were extenuating circumstances...

I'll never know whether I have the right to ask clemency of the jury.

Can one be so guilty for having survived?[47]

Steinberg's account is full of the kinds of disturbing details that Levi leaves out, the 'extenuating circumstances' he mentions in ironic understatement, which certainly convince the reader that the 'methods' employed by Paul/Henri to survive do not deserve such condemnation. This passage demonstrates Steinberg's bewilderment at the dislike Levi displays towards him, harrowing to read and parallel to our own puzzlement at the Italian author's harsh judgment. In it, he points out that Levi did not know him well and that there are factual discrepancies and inaccuracies. However, it is striking that Steinberg appears unaware of the homosexual implications in Levi's account of him, or at least chooses not to mention them. His memoir gives no indication of homosexual activity in the camp, and his own life, as outlined on the dustjacket, is as a heterosexual, married with two daughters.

There are several ways of interpreting this important difference in the pair of accounts of apparently the same person. One possibility is that it is simply not the same person at all and any similarities are merely a remarkable coincidence. Another is that Steinberg's account has deliberate omissions. Another is that Levi's account is not objective after all: he could have simply misjudged the young man and assumed him guilty of unspoken crimes. Most likely of all is that Levi has created a composite 'character', made up of Steinberg and someone else, real, imaginary, or composite yet again, and that this 'character' represents actions Levi finds particularly loathsome, at which he only hints, with his habitual *ritegno*. Marco Belpoliti has pointed out that Levi conflates portraits of real people to make a single, more rounded *personaggio* and that this naturally invites disquieting questions regarding the 'truth' of the accounts. In any case, as noted at the beginning of this chapter, Levi admitted it is difficult to portray real people accurately and 'la persona reale rimane sempre e comunque delusa'.

Certainly, the existence of Paul Steinberg's memoir adds to the puzzle of the portrait of Henri and once more undermines the assumption that Levi is the objective scientist describing what is empirically there, rather than the author of images based on reality but filtered through creativity. Paradoxically, Steinberg himself accepts the myth of this quality of objectivity and accuracy in Levi, with the tragic result that he torments himself with questions as to why he has been judged so harshly, compounding his feelings of guilt at survival.

In conclusion, it seems inescapable that Levi's *ritegno* is a major factor in his 'acceptability' as a commentator. I would suggest that this aspect of Levi's style taps into a strong psychological reflex in his readers. At the heart of his appeal to wide and diverse audiences is a dovetailing of his method and our naturally evasive response to evidence of harrowing reality. No person with normal psychological impulses actually relishes reading about real-life horrors. This is not the place to discuss in any depth what can be considered 'normal' in psychological terms, but I suggest that it is not 'normal' to confuse reality and fiction, nor to be entertained by factual accounts of horrific material. I accept that this may mean that large numbers of people are not 'normal', nevertheless, all researchers in the field admit to feeling depressed and burdened by the knowledge of the details of these events. Our recoil, our distaste, the obscure feeling of being tainted that we experience on reading about atrocities, is a mild and distant relation of the *vergogna* Levi describes after the execution in *Se questo è un uomo*, and of the response of the Russian soldiers entering the camp at the beginning of *La tregua*.

Just as there is a tension between Levi's avowed need to testify and his reluctance to shock or disturb, so readers' curiosity and sense of duty in wanting to know what happened is in conflict with their reluctance and distress at actually being told more than is bearable. 'Obscene' is a term that has been weakened by casual use, but Levi's method means he avoids the fundamentally obscene, refrains from turning the reader into a voyeur and does not foist his nightmares onto others. Readers feel secure that they will not be bludgeoned with detail that eventually numbs the mind and actually prevents analytical thought. Vast numbers are difficult to envisage, the personal may convey the horror of events effectively, but too much horror may actually prevent people listening. So readers feel protected by this benign narrator, able to respond intellectually and emotionally to what they are being told.

There is a further effect: undoubtedly we as readers sense the 'correctness' of this style, the concept of there being a polite, considerate way of telling this particular story, which is the opposite of *sgarbato* and *unanständig*. This same sense of an incongruous but essential propriety being observed could also lie behind the willingness of Germans to face Levi's words and respond to them, even in the immediate post-war years. Levi had an understandably hesitant relationship with the German nation, in which *ritegno* plays a large and ambiguous part. When the word is used in connection with encounters with Germans it is always closely linked with fear or disgust. The prospect of meeting Müller in 'Vanadio' led the writer to admit he uses it as one of many euphemisms for *paura* (*Opere*, i. 928): 'Inutile parlare di pudore, ribrezzo, ritegno. Paura era la parola.' It surfaces again as a reaction to the idea of writing a preface specifically for the German translation of *Se questo è un uomo* (*Opere*, ii. 1129): 'Provavo un ritegno confuso, una ripugnanza, un blocco emotivo che strozzava il flusso delle idee e dello scrivere.' In 'Auschwitz, città tranquilla', Levi writes of a German chemist called Mertens, who worked in the laboratories in Auschwitz, and examines the issue of 'ordinary' people working side by side with such horrors, apparently squaring their consciences because they were not actively involved in the cruelties or could not prevent them.[48] In his concluding paragraph he says: 'Non ho mai cercato di incontrarmi con Mertens. Provavo un ritegno complesso, di cui l'avversione era solo una delle componenti.' Levi was acutely conscious of the Germans as a potential readership throughout his post-war life. We know from the final chapter of *I sommersi e i salvati* ('Lettere di tedeschi', *Opere*, ii. 1124–48) that in 1959 he was particularly concerned about the impact of the German translation of his book, suddenly realizing (ibid., 1125) that 'i suoi destinatari veri, quelli contro cui il libro si puntava come un'arma, erano loro, i tedeschi'. In 1979, commenting on the television series 'Holocaust', he said:

Quanto alla Germania, è evidente l'urto che il filmato deve aver esercitato su questo paese, in cui ancora oggi vivono impuniti, e protetti da una vasta omertà, migliaia dei burocrati-assassini di allora, e centinaia di migliaia di cittadini ossequienti alle leggi (a quelle di oggi come a quelle di allora!) che si sono salvati l'anima rifiutando ostinatamente di sapere e di capire quanto avveniva intorno a loro, e tacendo con altrettanta ostinazione, anche ai propri figli, quanto casualmente avessero saputo o capito. È probabile che se questo filmato fosse stato trasmesso in Germania quindici anni fa invece che oggi, esso avrebbe rimbalzato contro la spessa parete di sordità volontaria dietro a cui si difende la generazione dei responsabili, ed il suo successo sarebbe stato assai minore.[49]

From this extract it seems Levi felt that even as late as 1964 most

Germans would be reluctant to face the truth. However, in the event, his book was read in Germany: I would argue that his restrained method of presenting the facts with discretion, his *ritegno* in short, avoided alienating either the innocent or the guilty. Levi's great artistic and moral triumph was in succeeding in transmuting his emotional response of *ritegno*, the fear and revulsion engendered by his terrible experiences, into the *ritegno* of style. This *ritegno* is at the heart of his appeal to a wide audience, his ability to make people think about and address painful issues without feeling voyeuristic or tainted; it is also largely the source of his paradoxical reputation for calm, objectivity and lack of emotion, despite his own assertions to the contrary and obvious departures from control and objectivity in *Se questo è un uomo* and elsewhere. Levi's *ritegno* is a complex response, not always easy to isolate or define, a shifting concept and emotion, whether our own or the writer's, but it is essential it should be taken into account in any appraisal of Primo Levi's work.

Notes to Chapter 2

1. The definitive edition of the writer's works is now Primo Levi, *Opere*, ed. Marco Belpoliti, 2 vols. (Turin: Einaudi, 1997) to which I will refer by volume and page number in this chapter. It includes conversations, interviews and journalism as well as published texts, extensive notes by the editor and an excellent introduction by Daniele del Giudice, covering many different aspects of Levi's work. For bibliography, see Marco Belpoliti, *Primo Levi* (Milan: Mondadori, 1998); Judith Woolf, *The Memory of the Offence: Primo Levi's 'If This is a Man'* (Hull Italian Texts; Market Harborough: University Texts, 1995). Woolf's study offers a thoughtful and detailed analysis of *Se questo è un uomo* (hereafter abbreviated *SQ* in notes). Also useful on *Se questo è un uomo* is Alberto Cavaglion, *Primo Levi e 'Se questo è un uomo'* (Turin: Loescher, Il passo del cavallo, 1993). Another excellent, comprehensive study on the author, with a full bibliography is Mirna Cicioni, *Primo Levi: Bridges of Knowledge* (Oxford and Washington: Berg, 1995).
2. Irving Howe, 'How to Write About the Holocaust', *New York Review of Books* (28 Mar. 1985), 14–17 at 15–16.
3. Bryan Cheyette, 'The Ethical Uncertainty of Primo Levi', *Modernity, Culture and the Jew*, ed. Bryan Cheyette and Laura Marcus (Cambridge: Polity Press, 1998), 268–81.
4. Robert S. C. Gordon, *Primo Levi's Ordinary Virtues: From Testimony to Ethics* (Oxford: Oxford University Press, 2001), 73–88 at 84–5.
5. Ian Thomson, *Primo Levi*, (London: Hutchinson, 2002); Carole Angier, *The Double Bond: Primo Levi, a Biography* (London: Viking, 2002).
6. *Se questo è un uomo*, *Opere*, i. 3–201; for the complex publishing history of the text, see Belpoliti's notes to the text, i. 1375–91, and his article on the reception of the first edition, 'Levi: Il falso scandalo', *La rivista dei libri* (Jan. 2000), 25–7.

Il sistema periodico, *Opere*, i. 739–942; first pubd Turin: Einaudi, 1975. Trans. Raymond Rosenthal as *The Periodic Table* (New York: Schocken Books, 1984).

7. 'Conversazione con Daniela Amsallem', *Primo Levi: Riga 13*, ed. Marco Belpoliti (Milan: Marcos y Marcos, 1991), 55.

8. Pier Vincenzo Mengaldo, 'Ricordando con lucidità gli orrori del lager', ibid., 140.

9. Woolf, *The Memory of the Offence*, 25.

10. Ibid., 65–78.

11. Risa Sodi, 'An interview with Primo Levi', *Partisan Review* 14 (1987), 355–66 at 364.

12. For examples, see John Carey, *The Faber Book of Science* (London: Faber & Faber, 1996).

13. Primo Levi, *Conversazioni e interviste, 1963–1987*, ed. Marco Belpoliti (Turin: Einaudi, 1997), pp. xiv–xv.

14. For a bibliography concerning the literature of the Holocaust and the surrounding debate, see Cicioni, *Primo Levi: Bridges of Knowledge*.

15. All history has been subject to narrative shaping. As Frank Kermode, *The Genesis of Secrecy* , 113, 114, points out, 'historians as well as novelists (traditionally) place such value on "followability" [...] Too strict a distinction between meaning and truth would leave few historical narratives capable of interesting us.'

16. Levi, *Conversazioni*, 55–76 at 65, 69.

17. For detailed analysis of Levi's literary techniques, see Woolf, *The Memory of the Offence*, chap. 4, 'Fictive Shaping', 39–50. However, see also Levi's comment in his interview with Risa Sodi, 366, when he feeds the 'leggenda' again and says, 'At that time, I didn't pay any attention to style. I wrote *Survival in Auschwitz* without giving it a second thought.'

18. Levi, *Conversazioni*, 195–205 at 195–6. This was the last detailed interview Levi gave.

19. Ibid., 200–1.

20. Levi, *Conversazioni*, 48–57 at 51.

21. Ibid., 242–59 at 256.

22. Ibid., 213–22 at 213.

23. Ibid., 214.

24. Ibid., 216.

25. Although *La tregua* was published in 1963, this passage was written in 1947, shortly after the events described and around the same time as the composition of the first version of *SQ*. See *I sommersi e i salvati*, 'La vergogna', *Opere*, ii. 1096–7.

26. This attitude might even provide a clue to a curious subtitling error in the BBC 'Bookmark' television documentary (1987) showing an interview with Primo Levi in his home shortly before his death. The following dialogue occurs when Levi and his mother recall the moment he arrived home after his ordeal: '*Signora Levi*: Poverino, lui era pieno di pidocchi.... e non vedeva l'ora di andare a farsi.... *Primo Levi*: Mi sono spogliato prima di entrare...!' The underlined words are mistakenly subtitled as 'Poor thing, he was surrounded by upstarts...' (presumably derived from misapplication of the idiom 'pidocchi rifatti'). It seems as if even in the late 1980s a kind of absurd drawing-room sensibility led a subtitler to disbelieve the possibility that the great writer might have once had lice.

27. Trans. Raymond Rosenthal as *The Drowned and the Saved* (London: Michael Joseph, 1988); review in *The Sunday Times* (10 Apr. 1988), §G (Books), 1–2.
28. I would argue that the widespread popularity of 'horror' genres does not invalidate this point: whilst individual tastes vary and there are differing views of what constitutes 'entertainment', most people are able to differentiate between reality and fiction and their response adjusts accordingly.
29. Elie Wiesel, *La nuit* (Paris: Minuit, 1958).
30. Woolf, *The Memory of the Offence*, 41. Note e.g. the titles of two recent books on Wiesel: Sibelman, *Silence in the Novels of Elie Wiesel* (1995); Colin Davis, *Elie Wiesel's Secretive Texts* (Gainesville: University Press of Florida, 1994).
31. See also Cicioni, *Primo Levi: Bridges of Knowledge*, 29, where other aspects of the two descriptions are usefully discussed.
32. Wiesel, *La nuit*, 104. An account of an earlier hanging (ibid., 101–2) also describes the dead man in graphic detail: 'Puis le camp tout entier, bloc après bloc, dut défiler devant le pendu et fixer les yeux éteints du mort, sa langue pendante.'
33. Ibid., 105.
34. As a supplement to this examination of Levi's style and how alterations he made to earlier drafts can give the reader insight into what the writer intended to achieve by his style, I add these observations on corrections to two texts from the Einaudi archives, *Il sistema periodico* and *L'altrui mestiere*, which I had the opportunity to examine recently. There is no possibility of viewing manuscripts, and these may not exist in any case: Levi's comment about the advantages of the Macintosh, quoted earlier, suggests he preferred not to preserve previous drafts. However, the few corrections made by the author to the typescripts fall into four broad categories: he changes words that might seem exaggerated or overly dramatic, makes alterations that are concerned with numerical or 'factual' accuracy or clarity, excises detail that might be considered 'indelicate' and makes changes that conceal or disguise real people's identity, particularly when the situation is sensitive. For instance, the seducer in 'Potassio', known in the published version as 'l'Assistente', is named in the typescript.
35. See also Belpoliti's comments on the effects of the corrections in his notes to *SQ*, *Opere*, i. 1403: e.g., regarding the corrections to 'Il canto di Ulisse', 'se la versione dattiloscritta conserva una maggiore immediatezza, quella a stampa sviluppa un distanziamento'.
36. See also Belpoliti, 'Levi: Il falso scandalo', where he suggests that both versions of *SQ* had a strong flavour of the literary style taught in *licei* during the Fascist era and that the book was therefore unappealing to readers turning their backs on the recent experiences, for stylistic as well as emotional and ideological reasons. Natalia Ginzburg, one of the editors who turned down the first version of *SQ* is of course known for her innovative, 'non-literary' style.
37. Today's reader may need to be reminded that, when the television series 'Holocaust' was broadcast in the United States and in Britain in the late 1970s, its detail regarding what had happened, even though much attenuated in order to make it broadcastable (indeed not *unanständig*), came as a surprise for many people of all ages, including some who had lived through the war years but were fortunate enough not to have been in occupied countries. The modern reader now knows the 'story'. The word 'Auschwitz' is sufficient to conjure up a

battery of images, whilst, as Levi has pointed out himself, there was a time when it had no particular meaning. In England 'Belsen' was a more evocative name in the post-war years, presumably owing to newsreel footage of the camp's liberation by Allied soldiers.

38. One possible alternative title for *SQ* was *I sommersi e i salvati*, which reinforces the suggestion that this chapter is one of those fundamental to the message of the book as a whole (*Opere*, i. 1380). Whilst Levi also favoured *Sul fondo* as a possible title, it is clearly significant that he took *I sommersi e i salvati* as the title for his last work, revisiting issues raised by his first book.

39. In the chapter 'La zona grigia', whilst discussing an account of a young girl found still alive when bodies were being removed from a gas chamber, Levi speaks of the phenomenon of *pietà* co-existing with cruelty (*Opere*, ii. 1033): 'Pietà e brutalità possono coesistere, nello stesso individuo e nello stesso momento, contro ogni logica; e del resto, la pietà stessa sfugge alla logica. Non esiste proporzionalità tra la pietà che proviamo e l'estensione del dolore da cui la pietà è suscitata: una singola Anna Frank desta piú commozione delle miriadi che soffrirono come lei, ma la cui immagine è rimasta in ombra.' He goes on to express disgust at the idea that small acts of charity could ever atone for sustained cruelty in the same individual.

40. Sodi, 'An interview with Primo Levi', 360.

41. 'Donne da macello', *Opere*, i. 1227–30 at 1230.

42. 'Le immagini di *Olocausto*', *Opere*, i. 1272–80 at 1273. Levi seems to have appreciated the *ritegno* displayed by the makers of 'Holocaust': in this discussion he calls it 'decoroso' and adds 'soprattutto [...] non abusa del materiale incandescente su cui è stato costruito: gli autori hanno conosciuto la misura, e non hanno ceduto alle sollecitazioni del macabro, del turpe e dell'orrido,benché l'orrido, notoriamente, "paghi"' (ibid., 1274). Conversely, in 'Un olocausto che pesa ancora sulla coscienza del mondo' (*Opere*, i. 1264–7), Levi criticizes some aspects of the book on which the film is based, saying it is 'ingenuo' and 'sinistramente comico' to suggest for instance that prisoners were allowed to keep personal belongings from home, such as photographs. Restraint or softening techniques are not the same as inaccuracy.

43. See Robert Gordon, '"Per mia fortuna ...": Irony and Ethics in Primo Levi's Writing', *Modern Language Review* 92 (1997), 337–47.

44. A few examples will suffice, but many more can be found. *SQ, Opere*, i. 155: 'Si udí un fremito di motore, ed ecco, una SS in motocicletta entrò nel campo. Come sempre, quando vedevamo i loro visi duri, mi sentii sommergere di terrore e di odio.' Clearly they were frequent visitors ('come sempre'). 'Il comandante di Auschwitz', *Saggi, Opere*, ii. 923: '[...] Questo denaro veniva versato ai nostri padroni, e cioè alle SS reggitrici del campo. [...] La loro gerarchia era oscura per noi: SS, Gestapo, Servizio del lavoro, Partito, fabbrica, tutta l'enorme macchina stava al di sopra di noi, e ci appariva appiattita, senza prospettiva; empireo di notte e di nebbia di cui ignoravamo la struttura'. The prisoners may have been unsure of the management structure of the camp, but they definitely knew that the SS were involved in it. The role of the SS in tormenting escapees as described in *I sommersi e i salvati* has already been quoted in this chapter.

45. Wiesel, *La nuit*, 80: 'Les enfants faisaient ici l'objet, entre homosexuels, d'une véritable traite.'

46. See Martin McLaughlin, *Italo Calvino* (Edinburgh: Edinburgh University Press, 1998), 149–54.

47. Paul Steinberg, *Speak You Also: A Survivor's Reckoning* (London: Allen Lane, 2001), 129–31.

48. *Opere*, ii. 873–7. Originally an article in *La Stampa* (8 Mar. 1984), it is amongst the material held by Einaudi for *L'altrui mestiere*, arranged for publication by the author, and should have been printed between 'Le parole fossili' and 'Il teschio e l'orchidea'. Clearly it was omitted, though no reason is indicated in the file. It appears in *Opere* under 'Racconti', somewhat oddly, prompting the question why it was not categorized as one of the 'Saggi'.

49. 'Perchè non ritornino gli olocausti di ieri (le stragi naziste, le folle e la tv)', *Opere*, i. 1269; orig. pubd in *La Stampa* (20 May 1979). This passage is yet another example contradicting Levi's reputation for calm or as Améry's 'Pardoner'; see *I sommersi e i salvati*, 'L'intellettuale ad Auschwitz', *Opere*, ii. 1091–1108.

CHAPTER 3

Cesare Pavese and the Need to Confess: Politics in Pavese's Key Works

From 'La famiglia' to the Secret *Taccuino*, *La casa in collina* and *La luna e i falò*

Many critics have written about Pavese's *La casa in collina* (1949).[1] Along with *La luna e i falò* (1950),[2] it represents the best of Pavese's output. Indeed, no less an authority than Calvino considered the earlier work the greater masterpiece.[3] However, even if one accepts the critical consensus that *La luna e i falò* is the superior work, *La casa in collina* is of major interest, for it is one of Pavese's most mature works, containing the familiar themes reworked so poetically in *La luna e i falò*: *città campagna*, childhood/adulthood, the role of myth and universal human experience. *La casa in collina* also tackles the issue of political commitment and gives a valuable insight into the psychology of a political 'refuser', all the more significant in the light of the document unearthed relatively recently, Pavese's *Taccuino*, which indicates that the writer's political allegiance at least as late as 1943 was not actually with the anti-Fascist struggle.[4]

Quite rightly then, criticism based on *La casa in collina* has concentrated on these Pavesian themes and on the protagonist's lack of *engagement* that it exemplifies. There seems to be general critical agreement that the book is confessional and autobiographical, a chronicle of the war but ultimately more concerned with the narrator's response to the war.[5] However, no-one has yet examined in depth the relevance of an earlier work, 'La famiglia' (1941), which undoubtedly served as a preliminary sketch for *La casa in collina*.[6] The primary aim of this chapter is to demonstrate how an analysis of 'La famiglia' throws light on crucial aspects of *La casa in collina* and to point out new links with some of the more controversial material that has emerged in the *Taccuino* and with *La luna e i falò*.

The three texts, 'La famiglia', the *Taccuino* and *La casa in collina*, have in common a narrative of guilt. In the two fictional works, the protagonist suffers guilt, agonizes over his responsibilities, offers self-justification—implicit rather than explicit—and by the end of the narrative is only partially vindicated in the path of action he chooses. In the non-fictional *Taccuino*, Pavese does not express feelings of guilt, but does express thoughts that he realizes will excite criticism and about which we can assume he later feels guilty; at the very least he feels vulnerable to attack for having expressed them, to the extent that he does not offer this text to posterity for publication as part of his diary, *Il mestiere di vivere* (1952).

All writers inevitably draw on their own experiences in their work, even if only to use their perception of reality in order to imagine other worlds. I do not intend to suggest that Pavese's fiction is purely autobiographical, nor that its importance lies primarily in any autobiographical aspect, but it is true that some writers are more overtly autobiographical than others, and Pavese almost always writes about himself, however obliquely. His protagonists are portrayed with a particular kind of gruelling psychological honesty that often makes them not particularly admirable and occasionally even repellent. The same kind of honesty pervades the published diaries, to similar effect. *Il mestiere di vivere* provides a commentary on Pavese's work and ostensibly clarifies the relationship between his writing and his life, but the diary is itself a literary artefact, prepared by the author and left specifically for publication as a postscript to his suicide.

A particular aim of this chapter is to draw attention to the confessional aspect in the two fictional works, 'La famiglia' and *La casa in collina*, and relate them to the revelations in Pavese's secret notebook of 1943, a document so authentically confessional that Pavese excluded it from immediate publication, whilst clearly choosing not to destroy it. I discern a particular progression between the short story and the novel, which takes into account the content of the *Taccuino*: 'La famiglia' expresses guilt over a personal dilemma, *La casa in collina* admits guilt regarding a similar personal matter as well as guilt concerning the far wider-reaching socio-political issue of commitment to the Resistance. I intend to demonstrate that within this admission of guilt in the later work, Pavese deals specifically with the revelations in the *Taccuino* and offers a kind of justification for the views he expressed there.

'La famiglia' (written in 1941 and published posthumously in the collected *Racconti*)[7] tells, by means of a first-person narrator, of the meeting one summer between the protagonist, Corradino, and an old flame, Cate, who now has a child, Dino. Corradino discovers that the child is his and contemplates rekindling the relationship with Cate, but she is now independent, working as a cabaret singer, with a likeable, responsible man as protector and partner, and finds Corradino immature, too similar to the person she knew in the past.

In *Il mestiere di vivere*, in the entry for 6 July 1939, Pavese recommends the recycling of personal experiences in art: 'L'atto dimenticato per la sua banalità, risorge come miracolo, come rivelazione, ed ecco lo slancio creatore.'[8] Possibly 'La famiglia' is the first exploitation of such an episode, but whether or not he had such an experience himself is not really relevant; what is known is that the theme of unresolved paternity recurs in his writing. In the case of *La casa in collina*, he takes the same material he used in 'La famiglia' and blends it into a work of far greater resonance.

If we compare 'La famiglia' and *La casa in collina*, we see that there are certain obvious differences: the short-story form versus the novel, the protagonist as third-person versus first-person protagonist–narrator, a simple, 'banal' narrative versus wider political, religious and existential themes. All these I shall touch upon, though an exhaustive analysis will not be possible within the bounds of the purposes of this chapter. However, I hope to show how certain elements Pavese has retained from the earlier work, considered together with those he has altered or discarded, must influence our interpretation of the later book, in particular our perception of the degree of 'guilt' of the protagonist and to what exactly he is confessing.

There is a nucleus of a trio of characters in both works: the protagonist, Cate and Dino. In both works, Pavese gives the son the same name as his protagonist. This has two likely functions: firstly, as a simple feature of the plot, a prompt to alert the wantonly *incosciente* protagonist to the possibility of his paternity; and secondly, in terms of the overall significance of the texts, to suggest an abstract relationship, Dino representing the child that Corrado/Corradino was and the child within him still. It is interesting that Pavese retains all the names of the characters in these two works. Names chosen for his characters are not arbitrary, as Pavese himself noted (*MV* 354, 8 Oct. 1948): 'Strano. Le donne sofferte e odiate [...] cominciano per E.; quelle vagheggiate e intangibili per C. Elena Elvira; Concia Cate.'

The presentation of Cate is an important key to our response to each of these stories. In 'La famiglia', as in *La casa in collina*, she has two separate personae, the Cate of the past and the Cate of the present narrative. The Cate of the past appears to be a lesser person, at least in the eyes of the protagonist. One assumes that the snobbery and misogynistic cruelty exhibited by the protagonist in both works, blind him to the true qualities of Cate. In 'La famiglia', the younger Cate was an 'impiegatuccia' (*Racconti*, 375), lacking style and, though shy and self-effacing, free enough with her favours to have been the lover of one of Corradino's friends beforehand. Nevertheless, his memory of her is as 'umiliata e in silenzio' (379), a response, it is fair to assume, to his own off-hand treatment of her. By the time he meets her again, she has thrown off this timidity and become a forceful, open character, with many attractive qualities, attractive to the reader and also to the protagonist. However, she only just falls short of a kind of vulgarity. Her chosen métier as a singer confers glamour on her but also that element of disreputability that ties in with her easy morals in the past. She has 'una franchezza, un'energia, una prontezza aggressiva che appunto sapeva di palcoscenico' (379).

We and Corradino learn the details of her background: a violent father and a mother who died as a result of the husband's viciousness; a hard life, reflected in a determination in her character and her slightly colourful speech and manner: 'Caro te, che vitaccia' (*Racconti*, 380). This Cate is 'esperta del mondo' (381); she flirts with Corradino (381–2): 'Sussurrò "Caro" all'orecchio. [...]. Davanti al banco delle calze, Cate fece aprire un pacco e gliene sciorinò una sulla mano. — Ti piace? — gli disse.' Nevertheless, by the end of the story, it is clear that there are two main strands to the character of the new Cate, an enviable confidence and openness coupled with the dignity of a good mother: 'franchezza' (379), 'semplicità' (385), 'ingenuità' (391), 'schiettezza, quel bastare a se stessa' (396) and '"Faccio la mamma" [...] un guizzo, un rossore negli occhi di Cate che imponevano silenzio' (385), 'rossa e orgogliosa' (386). Her slight vulgarity perversely consoles the snobbish protagonist. One of the last observations he makes in this story is 'notò con piacere che aveva insomma un sorriso volgare' (402).

So in 'La famiglia' we are invited to admire Cate's progress and development, whilst at the same time we might be justified in having some reservations about her: she has a louche side and we cannot be sure of her precise motivation in any of her actions, since we have to rely on the account of the protagonist, as recounted through another narrator. I will return to the question of this ironic perspective shortly.

When Pavese transfers this character to *La casa in collina*, he makes changes that are immediately apparent. The Cate of the present narrative in *La casa in collina* has developed positive qualities well beyond mere *ingenuità* and *franchezza*. From the very first meeting in the darkness she is seductive, but restrained, dignified, utterly in control of the situation (*CC* 146). Even the fact that Corrado uses *Lei* to address her lends her dignity, and this formal address persists until halfway through their next encounter. Any suggestion of easy virtue is dropped: there is no hint of other lovers before Corrado, and no definite admission that there may have been someone else since. In the course of the book, she will be revealed to be a self-made woman, a nurse, a committed socialist, courageous to the point of insouciance, responding thus to the narrator's warnings of danger (*CC* 235): 'Lei sorrise e mi disse "Lo so."' These in fact are her final words to us and Corrado (a very different last image from the final 'sorriso volgare' of 'La famiglia'). The opportunity to compare this ennobled Cate with the earlier version reinforces the already very clear impression in *La casa in collina* of a strong, respectworthy female character, quite out of keeping with the misogyny expressed elsewhere in the novel and in many of Pavese's other works, including his diaries and letters.

The similarities between the two characters repay some examination. In *La casa in collina*, Cate is described as she was in the past, awkward and poor, but without the family background of the Cate in 'La famiglia': 'una figliola beffarda e disoccupata, magra e un poco goffa, violenta' (*CC* 148). This last adjective is incongruous in context, not at all in keeping with the Cate of the present narrative. In the past, as a young girl, she had displayed 'degli sciocchi entusiasmi, delle brusche resistenze e ingenuità' (*CC* 149), qualities which the mature Cate in 'La famiglia' still exhibits, but the mature Cate in the later novel has left far behind. The adjective 'violenta' could be intended as an indication that the Cate 'rivoluzionaria' (*CC* 180) would be capable of violent action in battle, but all other evidence suggests that her skills would be as a healer and she never displays even verbal aggression. It is tempting to wonder whether this 'violenta' is not left over from the earlier version of the character, with her violent father and deprived background.

The first meeting between the protagonist and the mature Cate displays striking similarities in both works. In 'La famiglia', Corradino is at a dance and is convinced that someone, a woman, has looked at him, perhaps obliquely in a mirror. Haunted by the suspicion of a gaze, irritated even, he eventually turns and 'Ecco quegli occhi' (*Racconti*, 378). He is drawn by the eyes and in some sense recognizes them before actually recognising the woman. He is still obsessed by the eyes and needs to know before anything else whether Cate was indeed 'la donna dello specchio'. Later these same eyes continue to exert their power: 'nel modo come lo fissò c'era un raccoglimento, un'insistenza che metteva a disagio [...] sotto quegli occhi [...] gli occhi di Cate costrinsero [...]' (389) and 'si sentiva sorvegliato dagli occhi di Cate'(391).

This emphasis on 'lo sguardo' disappears entirely in the later work, but it is replaced by something else. When Corrado in *La casa in collina* first approaches Le Fontane, at the end of the first chapter, he describes insistently how he is drawn by voices: 'saliva dalla costa un brusio di voci frammisto di canti' (*CC* 142), 'perfino una [voce] di donna [...] magari sono gente che conosci [...] lasciandomi guidare dalle voci [...]' (*CC* 143). Then, in darkness, he is face to face with Cate, but it is the voice he recognizes: 'Una voce mi disse [...] Riconobbi la voce [...] scabra, provocante, brusca' (*CC* 145). In both cases, the woman has a sensuous power beyond the natural, quite remarkable in works that are otherwise very realistic, if one may use the term loosely.

The substitution of the voice for the eyes in the second work, I think, removes any element of flirtation, which is in keeping with the move towards a Cate of far greater 'seriousness', and whilst the device irresistibly recalls the fact that the Cate of the earlier work was a singer, Pavese nevertheless chooses a kind of singing and a setting that avoids completely the artificiality and tawdriness of the stage. Later in the book, we are told the companions sing 'vecchie canzoni di ieri—; Dino attaccò *Bandiera rossa*' (*CC* 195). We can therefore guess that the songs he hears in this first contact are likely to be folk-songs or revolutionary hymns and so serve to enrich the dual myth of *paesaggio* and war. In both works, the writer wishes to introduce Cate in some way other than by her physical appearance; the hero has to sense her presence, the result of a kind of instinctual memory he has of her. His eventual preference for the voice rather than the eyes may be accounted for by this passage from *Il mestiere di vivere*, written not long before beginning work on *La casa in collina* (*MV* 308, 13 Feb. 1946): 'Tu ricordi meglio le voci che non i visi delle persone. Perchè la voce ha qualcosa di tangenziale, di non raccolto. Dato il viso, non pensi alla voce. Data la voce — che non è niente — tendi a farne persona e cerchi un viso.'

In both works, the second chance at the relationship between Cate and the protagonist is a gentler encounter than the initial crude adventure. The similarities between the love-affair with the younger Cate are plentiful, but the mature relationship is far more sophisticated in the later book. The events described in 'La famiglia' take place over a matter of days, whilst those described in *La casa in collina* cover a period of about eighteen months (summer 1943 to winter 1944). The tense, frantic, superficial nature of the encounter in 'La famiglia' is replaced in the later work by a gradual dawning of respect and understanding between the characters, particularly on Corrado's part towards Cate. Although this implies a deeper, calmer relationship, paradoxically it can lead to readers discounting the power of the love-affair, and subordinating it entirely to the political content of the novel. I think an awareness of the rawness of the emotions and their dominance over the protagonist described in 'La famiglia' is helpful so that we do not lose sight of the importance of the love-story contained in *La casa in collina*.[9] In general terms, Pavese has made the love-affair and the loved one more substantial and worthy of our respect owing to the association of the woman with the Resistance. The result is that the love-story has more emotional impact, but also the two strands of commitment, to a person and to a cause, are inextricably linked, and to discount the strength of the love-story weakens the impact of the novel as a whole. I shall return to this point later.

The character of the protagonist is, of course, of prime importance in both works. There is a fundamental difference in presentation, inasmuch as the hero in 'La famiglia' is written about by another person whereas *La casa in collina* is in the first person with the narrator as protagonist. The narrative voice in 'La famiglia' appears to be something of an experiment, and perhaps the strategy is not entirely successful. There is a main narrator, a friend of Corradino, who speaks in the first person but principally about Corradino, who remains the protagonist of the tale. Sometimes the narrator draws on the testimony of another friend, Giusti, and on one occasion we hear Corradino's voice directly, through a letter; otherwise we have to assume that all the direct speech is a reasonably accurate report of what was said. The limitations of this method are obvious: there is no omniscient narrator, yet the first-person narrator, in his account of his friend Corradino, finds himself recounting thoughts, conversations and encounters of which he could not have personal knowledge. This leads to some very awkward expedients, interjections such as 'tutti lo sapevamo' (*Racconti*, 369), 'così ci disse quella sera' (372), 'Corradino sostiene che in quel momento capí [...] Ma — dice — in quell'attimo Cate decise' (382). Corradino is described as naturally solitary ('un desiderio di solitudine antico', 372), yet in order for the narrative to be possible he must have related all his most intimate moments in gossipy sessions with his friends, which he himself would probably have described as 'womanish' or as a 'discorrere tra loro di cose futili' (396). However, the choice of this kind of narrative was definitely made with some care, and Pavese wanted to create many different levels of narrative point of view. In *Il mestiere di vivere*, the entry for 4 April 1941 explains this (*MV* 221):

la ricchezza del punto di vista [...] c'è un modo tecnico di comporre un punto di vista che consiste nel disporre varî piani spirituali, varî tempi, varî angoli, varie realtà — e derivarne proiezioni incrociate, gioco d'allusioni, ricchezza di sottintesi, cui tende tutta la tua preparazione e il tuo gusto. Un buon esempio potrebbe essere la scoperta di stamattina che la storia di Corradino si può sí raccontare in terza persona ma circondando i fatti di un'atmosfera in prima plurale che non solo dà un ambiente e uno sfondo al troppo gratuito Corr., ma inoltre — massimo pregio — permette di ironizzarlo.

The theory is good, and there are some very well-realized passages, such as a description of the rapid mood-swings and the minute mental dissection of events typical of someone in love, a once-removed *style indirect libre*, with no self-awareness on the part of Corradino and no apparent deliberate irony on the part of the narrator, though obviously a great deal on the part of the author (*Racconti*, 381):

Adesso era lieto di non aver cercato di abbracciare Cate, non perchè temesse di venir respinto ma perchè tutto il caso di quella sera si era svolto sotto un segno di franchezza e di fiducia ch'erano tanto più straordinarie se si pensava al passato. E ancora al mattino svegliandosi, sorrideva. Ma poi la telefonata di Giusti — Giusti non telefonava mai, proprio quel giorno doveva venirgli in mente —, e per compenso il silenzio di Cate, lo misero di malumore, tanto che non ebbe voglia di andare al Sangone. Un saluto di Cate, anche soltanto per telefono, quel mattino gli avrebbe significato molto... Ma già la notte stessa rientrando, pensò che non aver smesso d'amarlo toccava se mai a Cate, e si coricò soddisfatto. L'indomani, il silenzio del telefono gli gelò il contento in faccia, e la rosea giornata che aveva sperato cominciò al solito angosciosa.

However, it seems that Pavese realized that on the whole the technique was cumbersome; indeed, an editor's note in the *Racconti* (508) states: 'Delle prime pagine esistono stesure posteriori [...] con correzioni a penna (dalla terza persona si passa alla prima)', suggesting that Pavese was already moving towards the straightforward first-person narrative to be used in *La casa in collina*, a method that in any case certainly does not preclude irony.

The question of irony is important in both works. As mentioned above, when reading 'La famiglia' we need to ask ourselves how we should interpret Cate, since she is perceived through Corradino's report, in its turn one stage removed through the narrative of a friend, someone close enough to the events perhaps to add his own gloss. My personal view is that the irony arises from the protagonist's viewpoint and is largely at his expense. For example, the image of Cate presented to the reader changes radically midway through the story. Up until this point, all descriptions of Cate portray her as a beautiful, confident, well-dressed woman: 'donna adulta e compiacente [...] calze sottili [...] unghie e labbra scarlatte [...] Corradino le cercò in viso i segni degli anni, ma ci vide soltanto un rossore di gaiezza' (*Racconti*, 378–9). Time and again there is emphasis on her smile, her gaiety, her attractiveness, and there is no reason to imagine she is anything other than 'davvero una bella donna' (382).

However, an abrupt change in the picture presented takes place on the day the protagonist takes Cate out on the river: he notes that the evening before he had found her 'assai truccata e con un nuovo cappello' (a hat of which he clearly disapproves) and comments on 'la faccia del mestiere, quei lineamenti consunti e troppo vistosi che sanno di luci false e di vita notturna' (*Racconti*, 388). From now on all remarks about her looks are pejorative, and all are based on a suggestion that she is tired, aging, worn, secondhand. The episode that marks the sudden reversal is the revelation that she has a son. We can safely assume that she has not suddenly changed in appearance, but that the protagonist changes attitude towards her and that the narrative is probably always coloured by his viewpoint. The mere fact that she has a child sullies her in his eyes, regardless of whether or not he is the boy's father, as at this stage that question has not arisen. By the end of the story, the same aspects of Cate that provoked appreciative comment at the beginning have become elements to criticize, so that the smiling gaiety so admired in the early part of the story has soured to the final 'sorriso volgare' already noted. (In *La casa in collina*, Cate's role as a mother never provokes anything other than the highest respect.) In this way, then, Pavese uses the irony of the protagonist's viewpoint in 'La famiglia' in order to reveal far more about him than about the woman described and eventually denigrated.

In *La casa in collina*, ambiguity, the difficulty of interpreting the 'truth' of the narrator's situation, plays a very significant role in the book and is one of the elements that make it such a rich novel. Indeed, this pervasive irony is too large a topic to cover in much detail here. However, the question of Corrado's paternity can serve as a useful point of comparison as to how the text is deliberately made unreliable in both works and particularly so in the very sophisticated later novel. In 'La famiglia', Cate introduces a tenuous element of doubt in two instances towards the end of the tale, when she says: 'Io non potrei mai darti la certezza che Corrado è tuo figlio. Ho fatto male a parlartene' (*Racconti*, 392), and 'Tu non credi che Dino sia tuo figlio e hai ragione. Sono stata stupida a parlare quel giorno' (401), but on the whole the protagonist (and, I think, the reader) seems to accept without serious question that the child is his. In *La casa in collina*, instead, Corrado never explicitly accepts his paternity, though there is complex textual evidence that can be used to suggest that he is the boy's father.[10] The richness of suggestion and irony in *La casa in collina* allows this smudging of the issue of Corrado's paternity to be incorporated fully into the later book, and it is very important, since the uncertainty involved is an integral part of the dilemma of decision, concerning both the protagonist's responsibilities towards Cate and his responsibilities towards political activism. In the one case, is the boy really his son? In the other, is violence and bloodshed really an appropriate response for Italians who want the best for their fellow men?

It is reassuring to know from Pavese's diary entry cited above that Corradino in 'La famiglia' is meant to be a somewhat unappealing character, and there are remarkable similarities between this 'troppo gratuito' Corradino and the Corrado of *La casa in collina*. Both have an ambiguous attitude towards women and sex, desire mixed with revulsion; both are drawn by the idea of paternity but reluctant to assume any responsibilities; both are solitary by nature, though the earlier creation fears solitude whilst the later Corrado accepts it as an uncomfortable necessity; both suffer a kind of depression; both get involved half-heartedly, in the past or currently, with a middle-class woman; both are selfish and inclined to emotional cruelty. The Corradino of 'La famiglia' loves nature, but in a rather banal way, as a background for love-making in boats and getting a sun-tan in peace; in *La casa in collina*, of course, nature has taken on the symbolic role so fundamental in Pavese's mature work and Corrado's refuge in nature is part of wider themes, such as nature and the *selvaggio*, discussed fully and very eloquently elsewhere.[11]

The main addition to the character of the protagonist, the aspect that makes him into a rounded character and one worth pursuing through a full-length novel, is his internal debate regarding political commitment and action. The germ of this exists in 'La famiglia', where Corradino feels belittled by the responsible, mature other man, Pippo, who is taking care of Cate and Dino, and who is 'preoccupato di una questione di protezione sindacale degli orchestrali' (*Racconti*, 399). Even if this is Fascist union activity, a possibility, as the story has a contemporary setting, the important point is that Pippo is presented as a rounded personality, someone with mature interests and preoccupations. No political point is intended, and we do not need to know what Pippo's politics are. Politics have no role at all in this story, unlike the later reworking.

At this point, the progression regarding the kind of guilt examined in the two works becomes clear. In 'La famiglia' we do not condone Corradino's withdrawal from responsibility for Cate and Dino, yet, even though we are more or less certain that he is the child's father, and we recognize that Cate has matured into a strong personality, we do not feel so distressed by the protagonist's behaviour that the story becomes tragic. This is because Cate is presented as only partially respectable (today's reader might not feel that Cate's sexual mores and general lifestyle detract from her *gravitas* as a character, but a contemporary reader, and certainly the misogynistic and embittered Pavese that emerges from the pages of *Il mestiere di vivere*, would have judged her more harshly), she is cared for adequately by another man, and the protagonist, though 30 years old, is still unformed and immature, so the reader's distaste for him is tempered by tolerance. In *La casa in collina*, the guilt under scrutiny is far more intense. Here, Cate is morally beyond reproach, fully mature and worthy of total respect. The protagonist this time is 40, a thoughtful, educated man who should be able to make mature judgements.[12]

Now, the central dilemma of whether to commit oneself or not is extended from the personal issue of whether to be committed to the mother of one's child, to the wider socio-political issue of commitment to a cause. Comparison with the earlier work serves to emphasise how the two questions run parallel. There is a point in *La casa in collina* where the two strands intertwine in a single sentence. At the beginning of chapter 14, Corrado says he no longer visits Cate at Le Fontane because German anti-partisan activity is becoming more menacing. He says 'Compromettersi per gioco è troppo stupido' (*CC* 222). Here there is an unmistakeable double entendre, where both a romantic entanglement and political involvement are meant.

It is also very striking in this book that Corrado's response to the traumatic realization that he could be a father is described in very similar terms to his response to the sight of the arrests at Le Fontane: 'M'incamminai con un senso di nausea. Da quel momento la mia vita rovinava. Ero come in rifugio quando le volte traballano' (*Racconti*, 171); 'Provai un senso di nausea, di gelo, tentai di dirmi ch'erano gli uomini di Fonso, mi parve che il sole si fosse coperto' (*CC* 236). In both episodes, the narrator feels nauseous, then has a thought that ranges beyond the immediate, then expresses his fear in an image linked with the idea of disaster raining down from the sky. A similar link between the two situations occurs in 'La famiglia', and it is expressed openly when Corradino is debating with himself whether to ask Cate to marry him and thus shoulder responsibility for the child, and he expresses that sense of inevitable and undesirable involvement thus: 'tutto succede come alla guerra' (*Racconti*, 395). This brief simile contains the only mention of the war in this story, even though Italy had already been at war for over a year at the time of its composition, and it occurs in connection with the fear of enforced moral responsibility.

The titles of the two works indicate a similar preoccupation with the issue of commitment. 'La famiglia' is a curious title for the novella, but it seems most likely to refer to the idea of the outsider, the loner, excluded from the family unit, or included only on the fringes, never quite part of it precisely because he is unable to commit himself. (Even 'La feria', the alternative title, conjures up for the unattached the spectre of lone bank holidays, when families close ranks.) Similarly, the 'casa' in *La casa in collina* is a place of warmth, refuge, of involvement, in which the protagonist is an outsider owing to his inability to commit himself emotionally (Elvira's home); the other 'casa' is the community at Le Fontane, and in this case he is excluded owing to his inability to commit himself both emotionally and politically. Once again, there is a very close link between the two psychological stances. Clearly, the guilt associated with the rejection not only of a good, decent human being, but also of an ideal—these two concepts here represented by Cate as revolutionary—is a far heavier burden than the guilt engendered by a domestic betrayal in ambiguous circumstances (as in 'La famiglia').

The most interesting development between the two works takes place concerning the character of Dino. In 'La famiglia', the boy Dino is a normal, healthy, rowdy, active child. He is crucial to the drama inasmuch as the fact of his existence imposes on the hero guilt, a crisis of conscience and a decision whether or not to assume responsibility for Cate and the boy. The character's importance is stressed by the build-up to the child's appearance: 'tutto in quel giorno congiurava' (*Racconti*, 384), and by the protagonist's immediate psychological agony on learning of his probable fatherhood: 'è come ricevere un mattone in testa' (390), but there is not much more detail about Dino; his function relates entirely to the mechanism of the plot. The only hint of any role beyond this is one quite striking moment, when the protagonist asks himself 'È un vigliacco, com'ero io?' when he sees the boy apparently avoiding a fight (395). The image of Dino as 'vigliacco' will definitely not feature in the later work.

In *La casa in collina* Dino is by no means a straightforward character, clearly not just a child, sometimes not even a satisfactorily-realized child.[13] Critics have seen him as representative of childhood and of the child that the narrator once was. However, this seems to me to be reading backwards from *La luna e i falò* and superimposing what we know about the narrator in that book, divided between the adult self of the present and the child self of the past, with Cinto as the medium providing free access between these two elements.[14] Although Dino in *La casa in collina* can fulfil a similar symbolic role, acting as a rough-hewn equivalent of Cinto and Anguilla as child, and representing the myth of the *selvaggio* in general terms, we lose some of the important aspects embodied in the figure of Dino if we see him anachronistically merely as a more clumsily realized version of the later creation.

The Dino of *La casa in collina* bears a more sombre significance than Cinto or Anguilla, which I feel has not been adequately explained in mainstream criticism so far. Most critics have agreed that ultimately he is representative rather than realistic, and that he stands for a generalized concept like 'il mito della giovinezza' or the narrator's self as a boy, but I suggest that, more precisely, he offers the key to

Corrado's political refusal. There is ample evidence in the text that Dino stands for thoughtless, conscience-free violence: not just the savage inherent in nature and in man, which has already been pointed out by many critics, but, in this book, specifically the capacity for violence that sometimes passes for courage amongst both the Fascists and the partisans, and therefore, somewhat controversially amongst the narrator's friends and of course Pavese's friends.

In *La casa in collina*, the idea of a boy, a son, is anticipated in the very first chapter: 'si direbbe che sotto ai rancori e alle incertezze, sotto alla voglia di star solo, mi scoprivo ragazzo per avere un compagno, un collega, un figliolo' (*CC* 142). Corrado then imagines himself alone with this boy, talking, rediscovering 'le scoperte selvatiche d'allora'. We can take it that this boy represents the child alter ego within every adult, again a familiar and well-researched interpretation. When Dino actually makes an appearance, there is initially a great similarity with the first appearance of the boy in 'La famiglia': 'un ragazzetto girò l'angolo correndo e si fermò' (*CC* 159); 'un ragazzino che fuggì liberandosi con uno strattone' (*Racconti*, 384).

But there the similarity ends. The boy in the earlier story runs off to play, whilst the description in *La casa in collina* goes on (*CC* 159): 'Era un bianco ragazzo, vestito alla marinara, quasi comico in quello scialbo di luna. La prima sera non l'avevo notato.' This presents a ghostly image, a child that is almost invisible and can go unnoticed, and to me the curious 'bianco ragazzo' implies a supernatural element. I hope to show in what follows that in this introduction to Dino as a white, ghostly, sometimes invisible figure, we are being prepared for the creation of a character who, whilst having much in common with Cinto and Anguilla the child in *La luna e i falò*, has a more specifically sinister side to him, a side disturbing enough in its implications to have been presented in a cryptic form.

Initially, Dino appears to be a fairly normal small boy. His interest in violence is soon apparent, but his fascination with war and love of war-games seem ordinary manifestations of the temperament of small boys. At the same time, at this stage in the book (chap. 6), he shows characteristics that link him to the pacifist intellectual father-figure of the narrator: for example, he enjoys a pastoral interlude when he shares the narrator's interest in nature and love of the countryside (*CC* 175: 'Dino arrivò col suo bastone, zufolando, preceduto da Belbo'). However, as the novel progresses, there is a discernible movement in the presentation of this character. In chapter 8, Dino is still childlike, finding it difficult to stay awake late at night (CC 186: 'Dino che mi trottava davanti assonnato'), he has enjoyed studying flowers with Corrado (CC 189: '"Quando tu gli spiegavi dei fiori era felice" disse Cate, "gli piace imparare"'), but the savage side to his personality is in evidence (CC 188: '"Strappa tutto. A scuola fa sempre la lotta con tutti"', though his mother does add to this statement: "Non è mica cattivo"), and Corrado warns that the boy's interest in flowers may mislead (CC 189): '"Non fidarti. In queste cose i ragazzi si divertono come a fare la guerra."' Ironically, Cate, the committed activist, wants Dino to become like the passive, dilatory narrator (ibid.): '"Vorrei che studiasse e diventasse come te, Corrado"', but the boy is moving in the opposite direction to pacifism.

By chapter 9, for Dino the woods are the settings for violent games, whilst the narrator sees the beauty of nature (CC 193): 'Dove per Dino era questione di tribú, d'inseguimenti, di colpi di lancia, io vedevo le belle radure, lo svariare delle versanti, l'intrico casuale di un convolvolo su un canneto.' As the war intensifies and violence comes closer, the narrator expresses irritation with Elvira and those like her, who seem unprepared for what must follow; he identifies more with the partisans, but only in so far as they, like him, know what to expect; and he adds that he prefers Gregorio who is like the earth and Dino, 'grumo oscuro d'un chiuso avvenire' (CC 198). Here, the myth of the *selvaggio* provides the link between the old farmer and the child, but the somewhat gruesome image of 'grumo oscuro' and the sinister connotations of 'chiuso avvenire' are also pointers to what Dino's kind of courage will entail. Now, at the end of chapter 10, children's games are to become a brutal reality, but will still be approached in the same spirit of bravado (CC 201): 'Sangue e ferocia, sottosuolo, la boscaglia: queste cose non erano un gioco? Non erano come i selvaggi e i giornaletti di Dino?' Here, despite the partisan context, there is a disturbing echo of a Nazi slogan, *Boden und Blut*, quoted enthusiastically by Pavese in the *Taccuino* (17):

Ora che nelle tragedie hai visto più a fondo, diresti ancora che non capisci la politica? Semplicemente ora hai scoperto dentro — sotto la spinta del disgusto — il *vero* interesse che non è più le tue sciocche futili chiacchiere ma il destino di un popolo di cui fai parte. *Boden und Blut* — si dice così? Questa gente ha saputo trovare la vera espressione. Perchè nel '40 ti sei messo a studiare il tedesco? Quella voglia [...] era l'impulso del subcosciente a entrare in una nuova realtà. Un destino. *Amor fati.*

It is interesting and unsettling to note also the appearance here of certain words that have particular resonance in Pavese's writing: 'subcosciente [...] realtà [...] destino'.

Gradually, Dino as political creature matures, becomes fully involved, there are 'bisbigli e ammicchi d'intesa' (chap. 12, *CC* 210) between the child and his partisan mother, Dino can supply information to the narrator regarding the activities at Le Fontane; then, 'Dino era anche lui parte del mondo stravolto; Dino era chiuso, inafferrabile' (*CC* 212), preferring the company of active fighters to the teacher and his books. Eventually the link between a boy playing rough games and hooligans roughing up innocent people is made explicit (*CC* 213): 'Per le strade di Torino la notte crepitavano fucilate spavalde, i "chi va là" dei ragazzacci, dei banditi che tenevano l'ordine; anche il gioco e la beffa ormai sapevano di sangue.' Dino now has the confidence of Fonso and Nando, 'lo staccavano da me e dalle donne' (*CC* 214), and he listens apparently tranquilly to accounts of atrocities. When Corrado is reproached by Cate for his passivity, he suggests, '"Manda Dino domani a casa mia ... gli insegnerò queste cose"' (*CC* 215), perhaps a hope that pacifism or even passivity could be taught in order to counteract natural savagery. However, it is too late for Dino, who is now thoroughly obsessed with the war, fascinated by the death of some spies (chap. 13) and the bloodstained pavement (chap. 14).

There is a striking correspondence between the idea of youthfulness ('ragazzi') and violence. This is linked with the Pavesian myth of duality—child/adult, savage/civilized—expressed so evocatively in *La luna e i falò*. In *La casa in collina*, the emphasis lies heavily on the savage element in the child and in man, with the innocent and the idyllic having a lesser role, which is only appropriate when writing of such a brutal episode in our recent history. The narrator comments (*CC* 217): 'Soltanto un ragazzo che di tutto si stupisce poteva viverci in mezzo senza stupore.' In *Il mestiere di vivere*, 8 February 1944, Pavese gives us a kind of definition of *stupore*, a key word which occurs in the diaries several times (*MV* 274): 'Lo stupore è la molla di ogni scoperta. Infatti esso è commozione davanti all'irrazionale.' Violence as mystery and ritual is a central theme in Pavese's writing, and here the notion of *stupore* confers on the boy's responses the connotations of a rite of passage.

However, the point here in *La casa in collina* is that the child looks upon horrific events with the same neutral interest as he regards any phenomenon in the world about him; all is new, all is marvellous. The child's lack of horror in the face of terrible acts, because of his lack of moral discernment, is similar to the impulses of certain adults in these circumstances. This is made specific in the next sentence (*CC* 217): 'Che io non fossi un ragazzo come Dino, era soltanto un caso; lo ero stato vent'anni prima.' The narrator is 40 years old at the time the novel takes place, so that he is stating that is possible to be 'un ragazzo' in this sense at the age of 20. Yet an adult ought to have moved beyond this stage and towards the civilized state. Instead, a man can be as wild and savage and uncomprehending as a child, and in the author's view this is indeed what political activists are like.[15] As if desperately trying to preserve the innocent child that must have existed alongside the savage, Corrado asks, '"Non metti piú quel vestito bianco alla marinara?"' (*CC* 217), recalling for us that first encounter with Dino.

From now on, Dino hardly functions as a child at all and becomes purely representative. The issue of Corrado's involvement is ever more urgent as danger closes in and action is demanded. At the end of chapter 13, Cate makes a gesture that is the closest she ever comes to promising Dino and herself to the narrator (*CC* 221): 'Forse un riflesso involontario, una promessa. "Se fai la tua parte" poteva aver detto, "c'è anche Dino..."' But Corrado's response comes immediately: '"Me ne infischio di Dino."' If this is taken at face value, it suggests a hideous meanness of spirit, but if it is understood that here Dino represents a kind of courage, and that Pavese intends us to understand that if Corrado can will himself to act he will recoup that part of himself that is courage, then the protagonist's reaction, instant rejection of the particular kind of courage that Dino represents, a blind, thoughtless bravery all too often resulting in savagery, becomes at least understandable.

This interpretation is even more convincing if we bear in mind that Natalia Ginzburg characterizes Pavese with the words '"se ne infischiava"' (*LF* 117–18). A few pages later, this kind of courage and the link with 'un ragazzo' is described specifically, when the narrator ponders Castelli's gesture (*CC* 225): 'Ecco, pensai, tutta la sera, chi arrischia, chi agisce davvero, è cosí, non ci pensa. Come un ragazzo che si ammala e non sa di morire.' The motivation of those who take brave, rash action is even called into question (ibid.): 'Crede di fare il suo interesse come tutti, come un altro.' Corrado makes a last attempt to alter the course of history; he offers Dino a gift of a torch and some books, probably crudely symbolic of enlightenment and education. Dino does not quite refuse the gift; he makes it clear he would have preferred a pistol and plays with the torch accordingly, 'puntando la lampadina come un'arma e accendendocela addosso' (*CC* 227).

Once the arrests at Le Fontane have taken place, the story of Dino becomes ever more improbable, if we were to view him as having any kind of naturalistic role in the narrative. It is odd, for instance, that he is not taken away by the Germans: he is definitely seen by them, 'i tedeschi non l'avevano lasciato salire' (*CC* 230), yet, as if to stress the strangeness of this clemency, we are told earlier of 'arresti di donne e bambini per prendere l'uomo' (*CC* 211). This should be read as a pointer to the idea that Dino has now moved beyond the boundaries of a normal character and has become an essence, the spirit of action and reaction in the face of atrocity. His behaviour, if he is to be perceived as a normal child, is scarcely credible, showing as he does no fear for himself, nor distress at the fate of his mother.

He now appears in the narrative from time to time, almost at random, a shadowy presence, disturbing the narrator's peace of mind in the school, finally disappearing to continue his mission with the partisans. At this stage he has become a symbol for fearless, but mind-less violence, tainting the peace of the monastery and disappearing offstage where great cruelties are being committed. If we accept that this is what Dino has come to mean, Corrado's rejection of him and horror at finding him amongst the children in the school becomes understandable. When presented with the idea of Dino being looked after within the monastery, Corrado's response is, 'La strana idea mi rivoltò, per il pericolo evidente' (*CC* 246). Corrado is indeed a coward, fearing on a practical level that Dino's presence might lead the Nazis to him, but Dino's presence incongruously brings the dark stain of violence, 'il grumo oscuro' cited above, into the ordered world of the monastery. This is the only way to make sense of the word 'strana' here, since placing the child in a church-run institution ought to be an obvious solution to his abandonment.

There is more evidence to suggest this direct link between the figure of Dino and an ultimately reprehensible kind of activism. The word 'ragazzo' occurs repeatedly in the text in ever more sinister circumstances. It acquires a dual meaning: it refers backwards in mythical time to childhood innocence (and this is the kind of *ragazzo* the narrator yearns to be again and towards which he journeys), but in *La casa in collina* it can also indicate violent adults and alerts us to their true nature, the savage, moral vacancy of the child. When we are required to admire an individual, he is described as 'un uomo'. In this novel *ragazzo* always implies *incoscienza*, sometimes an innocent *incoscienza*, sometimes mere blindness; *uomo* generates respect. The use of the two words is not schematic, and man and boy can and do exist within the same person, tying in with Pavese's ideas regarding the rational and the prerational in man. We can trace a development from boy to adult of certain of the characters. Fonso is described in chapter 7 thus: 'Era proprio un ragazzo' (*CC* 183) and 'Fonso ghignò, come un ragazzo' (*CC* 185), but by chapter 12 he has joined the partisan fighters and is described as 'un uomo occupato' (*CC* 213). We see a similar development with Giorgi, who in chapter 6 is 'un bel ragazzo magro e moro' (*CC* 176), but in chapter 10 (*CC* 198):

Che cos'altro poteva fare quel ragazzo? Come lui ce n'erano molti, che non credevano all guerra ma la guerra era il loro destino: dappertutto era guerra, e nessuno gli aveva insegnato a far altro. Giorgi era un uomo taciturno. Aveva detto solamente; 'Il mio dovere è lassú' e ripreso a combattere. Non protestava, non cercava di capire.

Here, 'ragazzo' links Giorgi with all the participants in war, the perpetrators and the victims of violence. However 'uomo' suggests a more mature spirit, 'taciturno' introduces the idea of a troubled heart, and the statement 'non cercava di capire' can be read as *style indirect libre*, implying doubts in the man's mind about his own actions, so that our final impression is of someone who does understand that what he is doing needs to be questioned but has little choice and fears examining the moral issues too closely. In chapter 21 we see him differently, a partisan now, and confident in his decision: 'un uomo alto [...] rivoltella alla cintola, parlava a una ragazza che teneva in braccio un bimbetto' (*CC* 267), where the manliness and maturity of the character is contrasted directly with the image of the girl and the child, femininity and youth. Nevertheless, he goes on to say, 'Finito il lavoro coi neri [...] si comincia coi rossi' (*CC* 269), a reminder that violence against one's fellow man, in whatever cause, is still violence and can be harnessed in any direction. This concords with the narrator's fundamental observation in the final chapter: 'ogni guerra è una guerra civile: ogni caduto somiglia a chi resta' (*CC* 281). The closest the narrator comes to suggesting a 'moral', is that there is no such thing as a just reason for killing, no politics that makes murder right.

I have suggested that an analysis of the way the term *ragazzo* is used throughout *La casa in collina* indicates that it almost always implies an element of *incoscienza*. Sometimes innocence is suggested and sympathy evinced, but very often *ragazzi* means men capable of unacceptable violence. The term begins to have some of the same connotations as the words 'our boys' when used in English: sympathy, empathy, but a whiff of jingoism. A few examples will suffice to illustrate this: we see the 'ragazzi di campagna', the Fascists in Borgo del Pino (chap. 6), 'tutti i Giorgi, tutti i bei ragazzi che avevano fatto la guerra' (chap. 7), the Tuscan soldier, the 'ragazzo' at Borgo (chap. 12), the description of the Fascist militia enemies as 'i giovani di leva [...] i ragazzi del Sud (chap. 18), the 'camion pieno di ragazzi col basco, di canne di fucile' (chap. 20), 'un'auto guidata da un ragazzo [...] una decina di ragazzi' (chap. 21), the dead ambushed Fascist soldier, 'ragazzo di cera incoronato di spine' (chap. 22) and 'gli eroi di queste valli sono tutti ragazzi, hanno lo sguardo diritto e cocciuto dei ragazzi' (chap. 23).

The association of *ragazzi* with violence is repeatedly made. Corrado rejects the savage side of the *ragazzo* and also the parallel role of innocent victim, and gradually attempts to regress to a state of true, prerational innocence and therefore invulnerability. The book opens with the idea of returning to 'dove giocai bambino' (chap. 1), but the narrator is caught up in events all requiring adult decisions and responsibilities. In fear and horror, he retreats, so that after the arrests at Le Fontane, his flight is towards childhood, where he seeks emotional rather than physical safety. (There is nothing to suggest that the narrator's refuge is physically safer than any other place; indeed, the final chapter points out that violence has touched the village.) There is progression in his journey: 'mi sentivo temerario, incosciente, ragazzo' (chap. 20), in the peace of the derelict church 'fumammo una sigaretta come fanno i ragazzi' (chap. 22), then when he reaches his home, 'Questa è la vita dei boschi che si sogna da ragazzi', 'la collina [è] un paese d'infanzia [...] di giochi', and the final simile, 'come un ragazzo che giocando a nascondersi entra dentro un cespuglio [...] e si dimentica di uscirne mai più' (chap. 23).

There are therefore two specific kinds of *ragazzo* depicted in *La casa in collina,* and the violent kind are not exempt from guilt, however *incoscienti*. The portrait of Dino as manifestation of violence and *incoscienza*, together with the various images of aggression linked with youth, make the novel a powerful condemnation of violence of any kind, including that perpetrated by the partisans. It is therefore not merely a refusal to take sides, not merely a depiction of the doubts and procrastinations of a pusillanimous man torn between conscience and cowardice. The narrative gives us firm moral grounds for his choice of neutrality, his rejection of comradely activism.

It is over this issue that the link between narrator and author becomes very important and that the novel should be read as both self-justifying and confessional. In 1943 Pavese secretly expresses sympathies for Nazism and antipathies towards the Italian resistance to Fascism; by 1948 Pavese is shocked by his own words in the secret diary and knows how damaging their revelation is likely to be; he now regrets any leanings towards Nazism but still stands by his reasons for rejecting partisan activity: *La casa in collina* represents the bridge between the rantings of the *Taccuino* and the subdued musing tone of *La luna e i falò*. In *La casa in collina* Pavese even tackles the question of to what extent the narrator has elements of savagery within himself, and I think it is not unreasonable to identify the author closely with the protagonist over this issue. At a point where clearly Dino is displaying attitudes very unlike the narrator, Corrado states, 'la stoffa di noi due era simile' (*CC* 248), but goes on to conclude, 'Nemmeno negli anni lontani, nemmeno bambino, avevo avuto il sangue ardito di Fonso. Ero diverso anche da Dino.' This confused attempt to make sense of his own misgivings and his guilt continues as a debate within the pages of the book, the most touching perhaps being 'Dino era un grumo di ricordi che accettavo, che volevo, lui solo poteva salvarmi, e non gli ero bastato' (*CC* 256). The use again of the word *grumo* is striking. Many references to Dino seem to express an ambivalence of response which concords with what we now know of Pavese's feelings towards the anti-Fascists. At this point, the combination of distance and immediacy conveys strongly the pain of the man writing so soon after the terrible events he describes.

The concluding chapter of the novel draws together the narrator's solemn meditations on the subject of violence, war and political activism: 'penso che soltanto l'incoscienza dei ragazzi, un'autentica, non mentita incoscienza, può consentire di vedere quel che succede e non picchiarsi il petto' (*CC* 278); 'la guerriglia, tutta quanta questa guerra, sono risse di ragazzi' (*CC* 281). As for Dino (*CC* 279): 'lui se n'è andato, e per fare sul serio. Alla sua età non è difficile.' Here the use of the word *serio* contrasts with all the allusions to children's games elsewhere in the novel, but the reference to his age and the facility of action at that age reinforces the idea of youth and violent action being naturally linked. However, he adds, 'Piú difficile è per gli altri, che pure l'han fatto e ancora lo fanno.' This last sentence is, I feel, Pavese's apology to 'gli altri', those who were not mindlessly violent, those who made a thoughtful decision, those who did sacrifice themselves for a principle. He acknowledges their courage and their choice, but his overwhelming thesis in this book is that generally commitment to the cause was not an informed decision but the result of an instinctual thrust towards violence, impervious to reason or morality, an expression of the natural savagery of man, akin to the thoughtless bravado and bloodlust of the child. It is hardly surprising that only two years after the end of the war Pavese chose to disguise such a harsh and provocative message, using Dino as the code.

The secret *Taccuino* indicates beyond any doubt that Pavese harboured Fascist sympathies in the period 1942–3. Later, in March 1944, in *Il mestiere di vivere*, the shock of Leone Ginsburg's death is registered (*MV* 276) but no further direct comment made in the months that follow. As Guglielminetti points out in his perceptive introduction to *Il mestiere di vivere* (p. xxvii), 'Il "sangue versato" è il retaggio di altre culture, le primitive e le selvagge; incredibilmente non gronda dall'attuale.' Guglielminetti clearly has suspicions that something is missing from the journal dealing with this period: 'Sono talmente enormi le reticenze da rendere sospetta la fruizione del diario di Pavese in termini di una confessione pubblica.' However, by the time Pavese writes *La casa in collina* (1947–8) he will have learnt all the bitter truth about Fascism, Nazism and the atrocities he mentions so lightly in the *Taccuino* (p. 16): 'Tutte queste storie di atrocità naz. che spaventano i borghesi, che cosa sono di diverso dalle storie sulla rivoluzione franc., che pure ebbe la ragione dalla sua? Se anche fossero vere, la storia non va con i guanti. Forse il vero difetto di noi italiani è che non sappiamo essere atroci.' It is fair to assume he genuinely regretted his views in those months or years, and part of his attempted reparation consisted in joining the Communist Party and working on its behalf after the war.

This reassessment of 'La famiglia' and *La casa in collina* has, I hope, shown that the progression between the works is connected with Pavese's instinct for confession. 'La famiglia' has little or no political content but does have a strongly confessional element that condemns the protagonist's emotional immaturity; *La casa in collina* addresses the political situation of those turbulent times, through the perspective of Pavese as he was then, though written with the wisdom of hindsight. In it he acknowledges his own error in despising the activists and

salutes the courage of those 'che pure l'han fatto', but, in charac-
teristically self-lacerating fashion, he still wishes to depict his error as
it was. The fact that he fictionalizes it in the figure of Dino suggests
his own guilt and unease at the time of writing and also acts as a
protection against the inevitable opprobrium such a confession would
attract. It has become a critical commonplace that *La casa in collina* is
a coded confession,[16] and even in this form it enraged the left wing at
the time of publication. We must remember that Pavese did not
destroy the *Taccuino*, merely separated it from the diary meant for
publication; so, in the same way, although he dreaded making known
the nature of his true feelings in the crisis years, nevertheless he felt
compelled in *La casa in collina* to leave us with the means to discover
them for ourselves.

The Concealed Political Agenda in *La luna e i falò*

Gian Luigi Beccaria, in a wide-ranging introduction to the most
recent Einaudi edition of *La luna e i falò*, reaffirms Gioanola's
statement that the political passages in the book are 'i momenti piú
deboli',[17] stressing the book's poetic rather than realistic qualities.
There is no doubt that the novel was conceived as a poetic work. The
evidence suggests that Pavese wrote *La luna e i falò* quickly, though the
ideas in terms of style and content had been maturing in his creative
consciousness for a long time. Beccaria (*LEF*, p. xxxiii) traces the
development from the 'classicismo rustico' mentioned in 1943 in *Il
mestiere di vivere* (255) to Pavese's great excitement at the inkling of
what he was about to write, on 17 July 1949, where he speaks of 'una
grande intuizione — quasi una mirabile visione [...] su ci dovrei
costruire una modesta *Divina Commedia*'.[18]

He began writing on 18 September 1949 and finished less than two
months later on 9 November. He defined it as 'il libro che mi portavo
dentro da piú tempo e che ho piú goduto a scrivere' (*Lettere*, 532, 30
May 1950). The book's great beauty lies to a large extent in its deceptive
ease of style, the melding of poetic and realistic, the 'simple' voice which
is nevertheless rich and complex. I am therefore entirely in agreement
with the general critical view that *La luna e i falò* is primarily the poetic
culmination of Pavese's long and well-documented interest in the
enduring power of myth in the human psyche. However, I would argue
that the book also contains the next 'instalment', as it were, of the
writer's apologia for his lack of political commitment, and that the

perception that the political aspects of the novel are the weaker ones underlines the writer's continuing unease with political matters.

In the entry for 17 November 1949 in *Il mestiere di vivere* (375), Pavese categorizes *La casa in collina* as 'resistenza' and *La luna e i falò* as 'post-resistenza', a clear indication that the focus as far as the writer is concerned is not on the war, but the Resistance. The novel bears this out as, though it covers the prewar years and the war in some detail; the ending of the book lays emphasis on Resistance issues and concludes abruptly with the stark death of Santa at the hands of Italian Resistance fighters. The summary nature of Santa's condemnation and execution, the incongruity of such brutality juxtaposed with her archetypal beauty and femininity, combined with the fact that her executioner Baracca also meets a summary and violent end, emphasize the horror and futility of violence. There is therefore a strong sense of continuity with the earlier novel, *La casa in collina*, in which similar disgust for violence of any kind is expressed.

The thematics of guilt and commitment already explored in the earlier novel are also evident in *La luna e i falò*. In Nuto we see a politically ambiguous figure, the narrator's alter ego, an apologist for Pavese's political stance, and therefore a direct descendant of Corrado in *La casa in collina*, rather than the Virgil to Anguilla's Dante that the notion of a new *Divina Commedia* might suggest. Nuto is evasive about any direct involvement of his own with the Resistance and states clearly that fear of reprisals stopped him being active. He is depicted as a holder of socialist/Communist principles, but essentially in their manifestation as attitudes of human decency. There are many examples of his egalitarianism and compassion, and he is clearly presented as an admirable character, but at the same time he denies active participation in the partisan struggle. He presents himself as a pacifist, replying to the narrator's 'Avevate il coltello dal manico' with 'Io non avevo che una pialla e uno scalpello', and gives a categorical 'No' to the question as to whether he fought in the hills: 'se ci andavo, mi bruciavano la casa' (chap. 4). This is repeated right at the end of the book in chapter 32, when, though Nuto is now 'deciso, lui stava coi disertori, coi patrioti, coi comunisti', nevertheless his practical involvement is still limited by fear and practical considerations: 'Non fosse stato della mamma vecchia e della casa che potevano bruciargli, Nuto sarebbe andato anche lui nelle bande.' So Nuto is not unlike the Pavese of those politically confusing years, someone without a history of commitment to a specific cause, but who would declare himself instinctively respectful of human life (and with a strong instinct for self-preservation too, if we can be blunt).

The rejection of a simplistic interpretation of political events and people's political adherences is also made clear in *La luna e i falò* in the opening to chapter 12, where latent Fascist attitudes come to the fore again amongst outwardly respectable villagers. Again the word *ragazzi* occurs, used first to mean those fighting on the Fascist side (*LEF* 64), then twice for those fighting on the other side (*LEF* 65, 66). The people in the village and, by implication, a proportion of Italians generally throughout the Fascist period and the war, are put in a dim light: they are described as 'tutta gente che si è messa il fazzoletto tricolore l'indomani', changing with the prevailing wind and unwilling to take moral responsibility for any of the preceding years. The placing of anti-Communist views in the mouths of these morally dubious characters can reasonably be interpreted as a pro-Communist statement on the author's part. In this way, the next instalment of the apologia for the uncommitted Pavese, takes the form of a pro-Communist declaration, the author justifying himself to his comrades in the postwar Communist Party and assuring them of his sincerity.

The ambiguous image of America in *La luna e i falò* is a fundamental part of this pro-Communist stance. Davide Lajolo suggests that Pavese's interest in American culture in the pre-war years became an anti-Fascist position and quotes from Pavese's journalism to support this view.[19] In *La luna e i falò* the same images of American life, derived from novels, are used with different emphasis. During the years of Italian Fascism before the war, Pavese was attracted by fictional accounts depicting the struggle for democracy of ordinary Americans; he saw American lives in terms of a fight for freedom and the literary style of his chosen American writers in terms of a defence against Fascist conformism and rhetoric. In post-war Italy, America's role was increasingly to combat the influence of Communism (Gioanola calls this 'antipaese'),[20] and so in *La luna e i falò* Pavese stresses the negative image of America as a place where poverty, alienation and injustice still hold sway.[21]

Though the narrator in *La luna e i falò* overtly suggests a socialist solution to Italy's post-war problems, there is a tension between his verbal expressions of political activism, coupled with his politically-committed past as a young man in Genoa, and the escapism of his emotional response to any statement of the harsh realities of political commitment. He listens to the priest's vitriolic, anti-Communist sermon in chapter 12, and far from being outraged, despite his disagreements with the villagers in the early part of the chapter, in which he declared 'non ero d'accordo', he now says: 'A me quel discorso non dispiacque.' Here he is not talking about the content of the sermon, but expresses a nostalgic and sentimental response: 'da quanto tempo non sentivo più la voce di un prete dir la sua'. He shifts to a childhood memory, the times of his innocence, 'credevo che la voce del prete fosse qualcosa come il tuono, come il cielo, come le stagioni', but now disillusionment has set in as he realizes 'che i morti servivano a lui'. This 'conoscere il mondo' is something he regrets.

Later, the evasion, the reluctance to face what war has brought to the *colline*, is even more subtle, and emerges through style in a very interesting way. We find that the Corrado of *La casa in collina* persists in the narrator of *La luna e i falò*, in Anguilla's determination not to face the reality of violence and his disgust and terror at the spectacle of violence. The narrator consistently does his best to avoid facing this brutal reality. At times, the reader is eager to know what happened in the past, but the narrator pulls back, with a reluctance bordering on the pathological. His eye travels to the countryside or to the idyllic, prelapsarian past, both things he clings onto in a vain hope that they can represent a partial reality of beauty, nostalgia, comfort, whereas Nuto forces him to see that they have intrinsic to them their dark seam.

For example, Nuto complains in chapter 13, of the priest's attitude to the discovery of the bodies of the Fascist spies: '"Se anche fossero stati fucilati per niente [...] toccava a lui fare la forca ai partigiani che sono morti come mosche per salvare il paese?"' (*LEF* 72), and the narrator immediately shuts out these violent, bitter images with 'Mentre parlava, io mi vedevo Gaminella in faccia, che a quell'altezza sembrava più grossa ancora, una collina come un pianeta, e di qui si distinguevano pianori, alberetti, stradine che non avevo mai visto. Un giorno pensai, bisogna che saliamo lassù.' He casually asks Nuto whether he was a partisan up in those same hills. Nuto's response is evasive and mentions the violent reprisals, 'c'era pericolo che una spia mandasse a bruciarti la casa', but the narrator sidesteps the questions begged by this statement and its implications with 'Studiavo di lassù la piana di Belbo, e i tigli, il cortile basso della Mora, quelle campagna — tutto impiccolito e stranito.' This juxtaposition of the beautiful setting and the savagery of what happened in it in this way is emphasized by the author and denied by the narrator in the same phrases.

A similar technique is used when the narrator's journey of self-knowledge comes to a climax at the end of the book, when Nuto forces him to face the evil of what has happened in the beloved 'colline'. In chapter 31, Nuto attempts to force the narrator to hear the story of Santa, and begins with 'Possibile che abbia fatto quella fine', but the narrator does not seize on this hint, as the curious reader is eager for him to do, instead his mind apparently drifts (*LEF* 165):

Mi fermai a guardare in giù nella valle. Fin quassù non ero mai salito da ragazzo. Si vedeva lontano fino alle casette di Canelli, e la stazione e il bosco nero di Calamandra. Capivo che Nuto stava per dirmi qualcosa — e non so perché, mi ricordai del Buon Consiglio.

He claims not to know why he conjures up this idyllic memory. I suggest it must be because he is still resisting knowing the truth, recoiling from the logical end of his search for self, the discovery of the *selvaggio* in men. Nuto drags him back to the reality he is describing: 'tanto vale che te lo dica'.

This technique of recoil from reality has its most striking manifestation in the positioning of chapter 30. Chapter 29 has ended with the shockingly flat, laconic and implacable revelation of the degeneration of the family at La Mora. Pavese now presents a final image of the rural idyll, the narrator's last luxurious plunge into nostalgia and, as we and he eventually realize, self-delusion. Chapter 30 is a diversion, a return in time to before the tragedies, and it is one of the most beautiful and evocative chapters in the book. After this chapter we return to the realities of the narrative of the 'present' and the brutal truths about the past. In this way, this 'escapist' technique is seen in both microcosm and macrocosm through the course of the novel.

We do not see the narrator again after the epiphany of the last paragraph, and this abrupt hiatus leaves us with a sense of silent shock, sharing with the narrator his desolation at the knowledge of what reality is. For Pavese, this reality was in part a psychological one, constructed of the guilty knowledge of the violence endured by his old companions and of his own deliberate turning away from recognition of responsibility. The cyclical inevitability conjured up by the final reference to the 'letto di un falò' can only add to this sense of despair: this is what nature is, this is what men are and the pattern will be ever repeated, rebirth leading to destruction and death.

Notes to Chapter 3

1. Page references are to the Mondadori edn in *Prima che il gallo canti* (1967), 137–281.
2. Page references are to the most recent edn, Cesare Pavese, *La luna e i falò*, introd. Gian Luigi Beccaria (Turin: Einaudi, 2000).
3. Italo Calvino, 'Natura e storia nel romanzo', *Una pietra sopra* (Turin: Einaudi, 1980), 19–38 at 35–7; 'Pavese: Essere e fare', ibid., 58–63.
4. The 'testo integrale' of the secret notebook, referred to here as the *Taccuino*, was published as *Il taccuino segreto*, *La Stampa* (8 Aug. 1990), 15–17, from photocopies ed. Lorenzo Mondo, with indications of its source. The original is yet to be uncovered. See also Carlo Dionisotti, 'Per un taccuino di Pavese', *Belfagor* 46 (1991), 1–12.
5. Aíne O'Healy, *Cesare Pavese* (Boston: Twayne, 1988), 119; Tibor Wlassics, *Pavese falso e vero* (Turin: Centro Studi Piemontesi, 1985), 148.
6. There are some useful indications regarding 'La famiglia' ibid., 147, 157–8. O'Healy, *Cesare Pavese*, 118, makes passing reference.
7. Cesare Pavese, *Racconti* (Turin: Einaudi, 1994). All references are to this edn.
8. Cesare Pavese, *Il mestiere di vivere*, ed. Marziano Guglielminetti and Laura Nay (Turin: Einaudi, 1990), 155. Page references are to this edn.
9. For example, Antonino Musumeci, *L'impossibile ritorno* (Ravenna: Longo, 1980), 101, goes so far as to say of Cate: 'La sua funzione non è sessuale, e la pressione che esercita su Corrado non ha alcun carattere erotico.' Of her voice he says: 'Cate [...] è senza volto. Corrado la percepisce come una semplice voce, prima ancora di riconoscerla visualmente.' I think Cate and her voice have a greater erotic charge than this suggests.
10. Wlassics, *Pavese falso e vero*, 156–7, supplies a detailed and, I think, convincing argument that there should be no doubt about the fact of Corrado's paternity in *La casa in collina*, based precisely on suggestion in the text.
11. E.g. by O'Healy, *Cesare Pavese*, 121–2.
12. The ages of the protagonists in the two stories correspond roughly to Pavese's age at the time of writing each, not a point to be belaboured but definitely contributing to the view that Pavese to a large extent identifies with his protagonists.
13. E.g., O'Healy, *Cesare Pavese*, 125, notes: 'In a child of seven or eight, Dino's sense of commitment seems utterly implausible. His actions are the symbolic projection of what the adult Corrado, trapped in his intimate quest for the past, is unable and unwilling to carry out.' Clearly Pavese is a poetic rather than a realistic writer, but there is no doubt that Dino is not the same kind of naturalistic creation as the other characters in *La casa in collina*.
14. E.g. Musumeci, *L'impossibile ritorno*, 107: 'Dino attualizza piú d'ogni altro nel presente l'infanzia di Corrado (come Cinto in *La luna e i falò*)'.
15. Musumeci, ibid., 102, comes close to a similar conclusion, but restricts his comment to an aside, when he says, 'Il fatto che Cate sia attiva nel movimento della Resistenza è forse di secondaria importanza per Corrado che considera aprioristicamente l'azione politica e sociale come un indaffararsi fanciullesco.' I think it is not Corrado but Pavese that regards political activism as 'un indaffararsi fanciullesco', but the link between the *fanciullesco* and the savage, so explicit in

La casa in collina, means that 'childish' actions and concerns cannot be taken lightly and are all the more sinister for being unrestrained by adult, civilized influences.

16. Wlassics, *Pavese falso e vero*, 148.
17. Elio Gioanola, *Cesare Pavese: La poetica dell'essere*, 2nd edn (Milan: Marzorati, 1972), 361.
18. Cesare Pavese, *Lettere 1945–50*, ed. Italo Calvino (Turin: Einaudi, 1966), 399.
19. Davide Lajolo, *Il vizio assurdo* (Milan: Il Saggiatore, 1960), chap. 8.
20. Gioanola, *Cesare Pavese: La poetica dell'essere*, 359.
21. See Paul Ginsborg, *A History of Contemporary Italy: Society and Politics, 1943–1988* (London: Penguin, 1990), for a survey of the political situation in post-war Italy and the country's relationship with America.

CHAPTER 4

Natalia Ginzburg's *Lessico famigliare*

In this chapter, I will examine the best-loved, yet least typical, of all the writings by Natalia Ginzburg, *Lessico famigliare* (1963).

Natalia Ginzburg is a rare figure in Italy's literary canon: despite being a woman in a male-dominated culture, she achieved considerable stature as a writer in the post-war years and also played a significant role as a founding member of the Einaudi publishing house. *Lessico famigliare* has tended to be viewed affectionately by public and critics alike as a gently comic portrait of a family and its community and the era in which they lived and that they, to some extent, exemplified. In this chapter I will indicate how the work expresses points of serious political, social, psychological and literary significance, but does so with such subtlety and lightness of touch that many readers have been able to avoid acknowledging their presence in the text. This very fact prompts the question why Ginzburg might have expressed herself with such a degree of self-effacement.

The first section of the chapter examines the technique of the 'lessico' in the book and how it relates to the general public reluctance to express suffering in the postwar years of recovery and boom. The second section considers Ginzburg as a feminist writer who expresses views to which she would be reluctant to lay claim openly, but which nevertheless emerge as 'unsaid' in the text.

Music and Memory in *Lessico famigliare*

Lessico famigliare has often been described by critics as Natalia Ginzburg's finest narrative work but at the same time the one most unlike all her other output and the most unusual too in terms of genre and expression.[1] Only relatively recently, however, has there been some close analysis that attempts to define the appeal of this text. Clara Borrelli provides a detailed and interesting examination of its poetic aspects. She supplies an excellent review of the history of the criticism of the book, summarizing the radically opposing views of its style, which has been judged either cold and detached, or lyrical, or an uneasy combination of the two. Whilst acknowledging infelicities of register and noting the two quite different kinds of style used by the writer, she is firmly of the opinion that it is above all a lyrical and musical text.[2] Giuliana Minghelli considers the book as an expression of the art of the *cantastorie* with a convincing analysis that tackles the question of which genre the book belongs to and attempts to account for the gaps in the narrative.[3] The question whether the book is to be considered *romanzo* or *autobiografia* is one the author herself has raised by the ambiguity of her introduction to the text, in which she states, 'non ho inventato niente', but insists that 'si debba leggerlo come se fosse un romanzo' despite its 'vuoti e lacune' (*LF*, 'Avvertenza', 3). This last point is surely one of the most striking aspects of the book and demands comment, especially as a central episode, central in terms of chronology and emotional and historical impact, the death of the author's husband, Leone Ginzburg, at the hands of the Nazis, is dealt with so summarily and so obliquely. A third study is also well worthy of note: Judith Woolf's brief but extremely pertinent introduction to her translation of the book, in which she draws attention, amongst other aspects of the narrative, to the centrality of Proust.[4] In my view, and as I shall discuss in this chapter, Proust's *A la recherche du temps perdu* is a far more influential model for *Lessico famigliare* even than Woolf claims.

My own contribution to recent work on the book is an attempt to elucidate a clear link between three fundamental and problematic aspects of the text: its deliberate bestriding or combining of genres (*romanzo-autobiografia*), its apparently irregular musicality and the lacunae at the dark heart of the narrative.

Natalia Ginzburg has famously claimed that the book virtually wrote itself: '*Lessico famigliare* è un romanzo di pura, nuda, scoperta e dichiarata memoria [...]. Scriverlo era per me del tutto come parlare.'[5] The text's originality lies in the fact that it is the first in Italian literature to use 'il parlato' consistently as a narrative style, so that this statement can be seen, in part, as a declaration of Ginzburg's poetics in the book. Such a statement leads one to expect a free, meandering, stream-of-consciousness effect. To some extent the text appears as such, with its apparently random breaks between loosely connected, unnumbered passages of prose of varying length, its vague chronology and its idiosyncratic selection of subjects considered worthy of narration. However, the alert reader soon recognizes that the book is highly structured. There are between forty-three and forty-seven unnumbered 'sections' set off by blank lines, of varying but not random length.[6] There is a basic chronology consisting of the life-stories of the 'nonni', the life-stories of Natalia's parents, the period of the author's childhood and adolescence, the years of Fascism and war, and the post-war era. The shifts in time in the narrative follow a pattern based on the natural itinerary of memory, as I shall explain below, but the most striking feature of the artistry of this work is the distinctive *lessico*, which, with its trivia and attendant anecdotes, is part of a stylistic device inspired by the idioms of music.

So many critics have had recourse to musical metaphors when discussing *Lessico famigliare*, that the musical metaphor is clearly instinctively tempting.[7] It is therefore necessary to look at the nature of this 'music'. It is not the euphony of poetry or poetic prose as we usually understand the 'music' of words to be, but the presence and mingling of two distinct and very different 'voices', one providing us with the *lessico* and the other speaking as the detached chronicler. Borrelli calls this other voice 'un linguaggio classico e netto [...] un tono di meditazione lirico'.[8] In other words, the music is created through the rhythms of the *lessico*, and its musicality convinces the reader instinctively, despite the narrating voice's denial of any musical ability or inclination (*LF*, 38: 'tutti noi mostravamo, nei confronti della musica, una sordità totale'), a disclaimer I suspect is presented with the same ironic detachment as the judgements on Proust delivered at various points in the book. In Borrelli's article, musical analogies are particularly numerous, not surprisingly, since the main theme of her essay is 'lirismo'. Her most interesting comment in the context of this chapter is one further developed by Minghelli:

Per ora vorrei concordare con la Borrelli quando riconosce che 'il dialogo si dissolve in musica sommessa, ora vivace ora lenta, fino all'adagio affettuoso delle ultime pagine', ma direi che, piuttosto che 'accompagnare' come un commento musicale la narrazione (pura scrittura sorda alla musica?), il dialogo intraprende con lei un contrappunto che nel suo insieme dà vita all'*allegro non troppo* del testo.[9]

We are offered the possibility of the 'dialogo' of the *lessico* as a varying accompaniment to the narrative, either as muted music (Borrelli) or as a counterpoint to the chronicle style of narrative (Minghelli).

Distribution of the *lessico* in *Lessico famigliare*

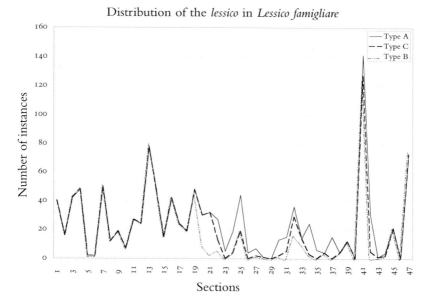

I would agree that the 'music' of the text lies in the interplay between the two kinds of style, but would place a different emphasis on the effect of the contrast: when the music of the *lessico* stops, logically there is silence, so that the passages of sustained narrative without *lessico* are the equivalent of silence, or take place against a background of silence.

In order to clarify this point, it is worth looking more closely at how the *lessico* is used in the text and above all how it is distributed. Every reader has an impressionistic understanding of the distribution of the *lessico*, but I have attempted in the accompanying graph to chart accurately the incidence of its use. It is difficult to be 'scientific' about this since personal judgement comes into selecting what constitutes a single usage. There is also a difficulty in grouping the examples, since there are no chapters, only somewhat ill-defined sections separated by blank lines. Sometimes a section might be half a page long or less (for example *LF* 122 on the arrival of German Jewish refugees fleeing Fascism), or else twenty pages long (*LF* 156–76, a section that will be discussed more fully later). In the light of this uneven structure, I have counted the occurrences of the *lessico* by page, a somewhat arbitrary measure, but one that can be remedied by then relating them to the kind of incident being recalled and the section of the narrative in which they fall.

Readers and critics alike again have an impressionistic and instinctive grasp of what actually constitutes the *lessico*.[10] Those examples that tend to come to the reader's mind first are the ones introduced at the beginning of the book, part of Natalia's childhood, connected with earlier generations of the family, usually generated by the mother's narratives, or else habitual utterances of her father. These I have called Type A. They occur at all stages in the book, sometimes marked with inverted commas, '"nuovo astro"' or '"di stufarsi"' (*LF* 13), sometimes merely part of dialogue. Each use of 'nuovo astro che sorge' is clearly a single use of the *lessico*, but I have also counted all the mother's assertions of boredom in conversation as individual recurrences of a Type-A item of the *lessico*, based on this early signalling. Clearly dialect-influenced or invented words ('sbrodeghezzi', 'potacci', *LF* 5) are obvious items of the *lessico*, but I have also counted as part of the Levi *lessico* the idiosyncratic use of 'skiare' and 'gli ski' rather than the more usual standard Italian *sciare*. This means that it occurs as a Type-A item in passages centring on Alberto and Miranda (who have their own lexicon, Type C, as explained below).

Nicknames pose no problem of categorization as belonging to the *lessico* ('il Demente', *LF* 21; 'il ferroviere', *LF* 112), but sometimes real names are used with such insistence that they acquire the obsessive, repetitive nature of the *lessico*. For this reason I have counted 'la Tersilla' (*LF* 172–3) as part of the *lessico* because, as she is part of the endless dressmaking cycle enjoyed by Lidia and Paola, her name represents domesticity and security for the family after the end of the war: '— C'è la Tersilla! — diceva la Paola, entrando nella stanza da stiro. — Che bellezza vedere la Tersilla! La Tersilla si alzava'. In the same way, the name 'Cafi' (*LF* 103) can be counted as part of Mario's *lessico*, as the author makes clear from the mother's comments (*LF* 105):

Sempre con quel Cafi! Cafi! Cafi! — diceva mia madre quand'erano di nuovo a casa e raccontando di Mario alla Paola e a me. Diceva 'con Cafi' come un tempo diceva: 'con Pajetta' lagnandosi di Alberto.

There is a second category of the *lessico* generated specifically by conditions in Fascist and wartime Italy: 'Erano entrate, in casa nostra, nuove parole.' These include 'compromettente', 'perquisizione', 'sorvegliato', 'pedinato' (all *LF* 97) but also the names 'Finucci' and

'Lutri' (*LF* 93), which become an integral part of the family episode of the father's imprisonment. These examples I have called Type B.

Finally, there is the *lessico* generated by other family units and other environments: the new families of the Levi siblings, the sayings from Natalia's period in the Abruzzi, Mario's French family, the Balbo family, the working environment at Einaudi, including a *lessico* linked with Pavese. I have grouped all of these together as Type C, though they might usefully be subdivided. It is significant that new episodes and characters generate new usages, and every family generates its own set of sayings, demonstrating the organic nature of the phenomenon alongside its static features of permanence and immutability, likened, of course, to Latin, 'il nostro Latino' (*LF* 23). When discussing the book, we tend to think only of Type A with its static function as a familial reminder, rather than the self-renewing and continuing nature of Types B (history) and C (new generations).

Other readers may not agree exactly with the way in which I have counted the *lessico*, but modifying the criteria does not significantly change the shape of the graph produced by the figures. The distribution or density of the *lessico* follows a distinct and logical pattern, in which normality is accompanied by a *lessico* and unusual events are not. Type A occurs thickly over the early, introductory part of the book. Counted in the way described above, there are about 376 instances in pages 5–64, averaging 6.37 per page, but at times with as many as 20 on one page. There is a sudden decline (average 4.14 per page) in pages 65–71 as we approach the episode where the Levi family take in and conceal the anti-Fascist Turati/Paolo Ferrari, with none at all on page 72 and only 4 over pages 72–5 when this episode is narrated. As soon as the drama is past, there is a recurrence of motifs of the Type-A *lessico*, with an average of 8.5 per page on pages 76–81 and then none on page 82 after the beginning of the new section where the family discuss politics (anti-Fascism). Similarly the account of Mario's arrest and escape starts with only one ('"la sua robina", come diceva la mia zia Drusilla'), but generates what promises to be a new (Type-B) one ('in acqua col paltò'). It is worth noting here a very particular use of the Type-A *lessico* when Mario writes from exile, '"Ai miei amici vegetali e minerali. Sto bene, e non ho bisogno di niente"' (*LF* 96), where his reference to a family game, having become part of the everyday *lessico*, acts as shorthand reassurance and a link with normality for the family.

Pages 82–151 have an average of 4.8 per page, but these are Type B, no longer strictly domestic or generated and repeated within the walls of the Levi household. For instance there are some connected with Natalia's friends ('Mi favò un bel pull-over', *LF* 127), her life in the Abruzzi as a married woman ('Stinchi Leggeri', 'quella vecchia', *LF* 148–9) and some connected with Pavese ('se ne infischiava' and variants such as 'me ne infischio', *LF* 117–18; 'non voglio idee', *LF* 143).[11] Leone's death is noted in section 35 (*LF* 144) almost as an aside and out of narrative sequence. There are now very few uses of the Type-A *lessico* until pages 163–4, when a sudden flurry occurs in connection with the description of Gino, who 'era di noi il più fedele alle antiche abitudini familiari', where the Type-A *lessico* is needed to reinforce links with the idea of the family as it was before the disruption of war. Pages 152–94 contain only new uses, Type C, connected with politics and Natalia's friends, the Balbo family. The occurrence of some Type-A examples on pages 170–5 indicates a return to normality after the war, but most striking is the reprise in large numbers of many of these 'original' elements of the *lessico* right at the end of the book (*LF* 195–8). One might expect a return of this *lessico* at the end for reasons of artistic symmetry with the opening of the book, but in these final pages they are also expressed with the *passato remoto*: instead of 'diceva', 'disse' etc. This has a dual effect: the Type-A *lessico* reinforces the impression of a return to normality for the Levi parents, but the *passato remoto* conveys a sense of the closing of that chapter of Natalia's life. She leaves her parents behind, contented, but static in their old life, whilst she embarks on an independent life of her own and no doubt a new personal *lessico*.

In graph form (see above), the distribution of the three types of *lessico* is very clear, showing the mingling and dominance of the 'melody' of each type at various stages in the novel. When all three 'melodies' are at zero, the most sombre events are being narrated. Leone's death occurs at the end of section 35 (*LF* 142–5), and on these two pages (*LF* 144–5) there are no instances of the *lessico* at all. The passage is inserted into a section dealing with the Einaudi publishing house and with Pavese, connected with whom there are inevitable associations with death, and there is no incidence of Type-A *lessico* to lighten the tone. Later, we are given a few more details of Leone's arrest (*LF* 156–7), and here again there are no instances of the Type-A *lessico* whilst the events are being narrated. However, these two pages are the first of section 36, the longest in the book, and one that also gradually builds up many Type-A elements, signalling a return to normality after the nadir of the abnormality of wartime. Placing the recollection of Leone's arrest at the beginning of this section indicates the author's desire to integrate it into normality, assimilate it and even elide it, part of the strange and disturbing silence surrounding this event.

If we return to the musical metaphor, then, the *lessico* is neither continual background music nor exactly a counterpoint. It should be seen rather as the themes or melodies of part of a larger piece of music: the book can be viewed as a concerto made up of words. The main melodies are presented in the early part of the book; variations based on new melodies appear throughout the course of the work; there is a 'largo' section where the melodies disappear altogether and a sombre mood takes over (wartime events and particularly Leone's death) and finally a 'coda' where the early melodies are played again with their final modulations (conveyed by the change to the *passato remoto*, which has the same effect as the resolving harmonies at the close of a piece of music). I would argue that, contrary to other interpretations of this 'music', the effect of the absence of the *lessico* in any of its forms is not only one of sadness and calm but actually of silence.

If it is true that in *Lessico famigliare* we have a piece of avant-garde 'music' that makes use of silent moments, this silence accords with the philosophy of silence that surrounds Natalia Ginzburg's approach to traumatizing events. In this context I draw attention to a key passage in *Lessico famigliare*, one that is fundamental when assessing Ginzburg's narrative intent: her discussion of the effect of the war on the style of post-war writing (*LF* 155–6):

C'erano allora due modi di scrivere, e uno era una semplice enumerazione di fatti, sulle tracce d'una realtà grigia, piovosa, avara, nello schermo d'un paesaggio disadorno e mortificato; l'altro era un mescolarsi ai fatti con violenza e con delirio di lagrime, di sospiri convulsi, di singhiozzi. Nell'un caso e nell'altro, non si sceglieva più le parole; perché nell'un caso le parole si confondevano nel grigiore, e nell'altro si perdevano nei gemiti e nei singhiozzi. Ma l'errore comune era sempre credere che tutto si potesse trasformare in poesia e parole, così forte che incluse anche la vera poesia e le vere parole, per cui alla fine ognuno tacque, impietrito di noia e di nausea.

From this important passage, it seems clear that Ginzburg was seeking a method of expressing what was, for her, inexpressible in words. The discussion bears striking similarities of approach to Calvino's discussion of post-war neorealism in his introduction to *Il sentiero dei nidi di ragno*. The novel was written in 1947, but the 'Presentazione' was added in June 1964, more or less contemporaneously with Ginzburg's *Lessico famigliare* (1963):

Durante la guerra partigiana le storie appena vissute si trasformavano e trasfiguravano in storie raccontate la notte attorno al fuoco, acquistavano già uno stile, un linguaggio, un umore come di bravata, una ricerca di effetti angosciosi o truculenti.

[...] Personaggi, paesaggi, spari, didascalie politiche, voci gergali, parolacce, lirismi, armi ed amplessi non erano che colori della tavolozza, note del pentagramma, sapevamo fin troppo bene che quel che contava era la musica e non il libretto, mai si videro formalisti così accaniti come quei contenutisti che eravamo, mai lirici così effusivi come quegli oggettivi che passavamo per essere.[12]

Both writers are troubled by the question of how to express harrowing, difficult experience; both see that there were two main approaches to this problem; both come to the conclusion that the problem cannot be overcome with words alone. Ginzburg declares that silence was one solution ('ognuno tacque'), describing an existential disgust ('noia' and 'nausea' are undoubtedly closest in meaning to the Existentialist terms 'ennui' and 'nausée'), whilst Calvino expresses himself in metaphors based on other artistic media: paint and music, with the music metaphor deriving from Vittorini's famous preface to *Il garofano rosso*.[13]

Calvino's respect for reticence is recognized, and the matter has been the subject of recent research, but his concern with silence also begins around this time.[14] In October 1962, he wrote to Natalia Ginzburg on the subject of the title of her collection of essays, eventually published as *Le piccole virtù*. In this letter he advises against the proposed title of *Silenzio*: 'il tuo libro è un libro positivo mentre *Silenzio* è un titolo negativo'. Furthermore, the marketing department at Einaudi seems to share this view and consider that the public would be put off by the title: 'l'ufficio commerciale, saputo del titolo *Le piccole virtù* anziché *Silenzio* ha subito triplicato la tiratura'.[15] There seems no doubt that silence was perceived generally at this time as a negative, dark quality.

The distribution of the *lessico* mimics the structure of a concerto, with a disturbing silence and stillness at its heart, but this very silence emphasizes the gravity and the pain of the events elided. The lack of detail and information is in itself troubling, but this effect is compounded by the absence of the 'melodies' of the *lessico*, achieving a silence of style as well as content. The same effect is achieved with all the narrative that is in the 'chronicle' style in *Lessico famigliare*, the direct narrative, but rather than it being a *contrappunto*, it is a silence; the music stops, and silence in a piece of music is far more shocking and striking than any other acoustic effect. So Ginzburg mirrors the idea of silence in testimony, later to become so central to all discussion of the literature of atrocity, with an imitation of silence as a musical effect. If we look at the passages where the music stops, if I may so express it, they are when the tragic events in the book are narrated. These passages have a poetry of their own, entirely in keeping with the subject matter. I do not concur with the view that they are cold or in any sense ironic.[16] Instead I would draw the reader's attention to the striking similarity of style between the presentation of the death of innocents in Ginzburg's book and the treatment of similar topics in Primo Levi's *Se questo è un uomo* (*Opere*, i. 14):

Cosí morí Emilia, che aveva tre anni; poiché ai tedeschi appariva palese la necessità storica di mettere a morte i bambini degli ebrei. Emilia, figlia dell'ingegnere Aldo Levi di Milano, che era una bambina curiosa, ambiziosa, allegra e intelligente; [...].

Compare this with the death of Miranda's parents in *Lessico famigliare* (166): 'Così i tedeschi se li portarono via, lei la madre piccola, candida e ilare, malata di cuore, lui il padre grande, pesante, tranquillo.' There is a lapidary quality about both, the resonance of an epitaph, which is poignantly appropriate, particularly set against silence.

Both Levi and Ginzburg express more than they say, and that is the principal strength of their style. Borrelli makes the point that Natalia Ginzburg's language 'spesso, più che dire, suggerisce, in quanto dietro di esso si intravede qualcosa di non detto, che pur esiste'.[17] Minghelli hints at this silence at the heart of Ginzburg's language too when she says, 'L'autobiografia [...] è quindi scritta attraverso un'operazione di si sottrazione, è creata attraverso la definizione di ciò che in disegno è chiamato spazio negativo, lo spazio che imprigiona la figura nel mondo.'[18] Cesare Garboli states, 'La Ginzburg è uno scrittore muto, per così dire, quanto più parla' and comments on 'la capacità della Ginzburg di far coincidere la sincerità, il massimo della sincerità, con la reticenza'.[19] Ginzburg was of course familiar with Levi's book, not only as a member of the reading public, but as the Einaudi editor who had rejected the original manuscript in 1947. There is of course notable irony in the phrase 'poiché ai tedeschi appariva palese la necessità storica di mettere a morte i bambini degli ebrei', an irony that differentiates Levi from Ginzburg very substantially.

The creation of a musical effect by means of words may be unconscious, but I doubt it. There are literary precedents (most notably Vittorini's 'operatic' *Conversazione in Sicilia,* written in 1938–9 but one of the key texts for all post-war neorealist writers, according to Calvino),[20] but the most obvious literary model for *Lessico famigliare* is Proust, with overt clues in Ginzburg's text, in particular references to 'la petite phrase' (*LF* 57). By the time of writing *Lessico famigliare,* Ginzburg had translated *Du côté de chez Swann* (1949) and therefore knew the text very well indeed. She must inevitably have assimilated elements of its style, some unconsciously, but the presence of references to Proust in the text suggests deliberate echoes of Proust's method.

Clearly this is not the place for a detailed discussion of Proust's *œuvre,* but *A la recherche du temps perdu* certainly offers a key to many aspects of *Lessico famigliare.* Proust is specifically mentioned in the text as a much-loved author in the Levi family, though sometimes for eccentric and unliterary reasons: Lidia Levi admires Proust because 'era, questo Proust, uno che voleva tanto bene alla sua mamma e alla sua nonna; e aveva l'asma, e non poteva dormire; e siccome non sopportava i rumori, aveva foderato di sughero le pareti della sua stanza' (*LF* 57). His great work deliberately conflates autobiography and fiction and centres on memory and the retrieval of experience through memory, while his use of his own and others' 'family lexicon' bears striking similarities to Ginzburg's.

Borrelli and Woolf suggest there is a fundamental difference in approach in this act of memory: 'il rammemorare della Ginzburg è cosa diversa dalla memoria proustiana: questa dalla ricerca del tempo perduto perviene al tempo ritrovato, mentre il lessico familiare [...] mira a salvare un passato irrimediabilmente passato sul quale è come se non decenni, ma secoli si fossero chiusi'; 'The lexicon, superficially a means of preserving the past, is really a means of leaving it behind.'[21]

I see a very direct link, not just in the idea of a memoir, but in Ginzburg's borrowing of a literary method. Both books have a circular, concealed structure: Sheila Stern points out that there is 'prelude' and a 'coda' in *Combray,* to which Proust was referring when he said in an article in 1921 that '[this musical structure] had been unrecognised even by some very careful readers'.[22] However, more significantly, there are connections that suggest that the curious *lessico* itself derives from Proustian methods. Adam Piette in a recent study has pointed out the links between specific sounds and memory. He writes of 'a kind of literary practice, a mimesis that hears as well as sees the murmurs of the mind, a difficult music of remembered connotations and selves fugitively united'.[23]

In Proust 'la petite phrase' refers to the few notes of Vinteuil's sonata that incarnate Odette for Swann. In French and English the word 'phrase' of course can refer to words as well as music. Ginzburg used this model and used the musical idiom in a literary context. The teasing reference to 'la petite phrase', one of Lidia's own trivial 'phrases', offers a clue. In this way, the writer integrated into the Type-A *lessico* a reference to her use of 'musical' stimuli, as inspired by Proust.

Equally interesting is Piette's observation that Proust alters his style to suit the kind of events narrated. He reserves a lyrical style for events which are largely connected with his own pleasure at memory, a kind of introverted, self-exploratory reminiscing. However, when describing events that are someone else's story and particularly poignant events, such as his grandmother's death, he hones his style down and tends to remove internal references, using what Piette describes as 'the movingly unadorned style',[24] surely a phrase we could readily apply to Ginzburg's lapidary passages, such as those on the fate of the Jews. This technique is even more in evidence in *Albertine disparue*, where there is proportionately less figurative language than in other volumes. In a radio broadcast about Proust given in the 1950s, Ginzburg has made it abundantly clear that she was aware of this variation in Proust's style: 'le frasi si snodavano come serpenti; una sola serata durava centinaia di pagine, e una catastrofe era raccontata nel giro di due parole'.[25]

Piette continues:

> The leitmotif theory the narrator develops on listening to Vinteuil is related to his discovery of 'phrase-types' in literature which adumbrate a 'Passé', 'une même sensation d'anxiété' [...] The phrase-motifs, in both music and literature, gather up a listener's and reader's own past sensations to concentrate them into a complex of feelings 'si organique et viscérale' [...] that they resemble neuralgic symptoms rather than technical narrative signals.[26]

Again, this would be an accurate analysis of Ginzburg's method in *Lessico famigliare*, with its play on 'phrase-motifs' that are no longer 'technical narrative signals'.

The dissecting of Bergotte's literary style later on in *A la recherche du temps perdu* (i. 544) is also very significant: the narrator analyses the speaking and writing style of Bergotte, relates it to the speaking style of Bergotte's family and finds a musical analogy to define it:

> Il y a dans ses livres telles terminaisons de phrases où l'accumulation des sonorités qui se prolongent, comme aux derniers accords d'une ouverture d'opéra qui ne peut pas finir et redit plusieurs fois sa suprême cadence avant que le chef d'orchestre pose son bâton, dans lesquelles je retrouvai plus tard un équivalent musical de ces cuivres phonétiques de la famille Bergotte.

Proust is very interested in speakers' and families' own 'lexicons' and devotes attention to illustrating and commenting on these. There is no doubt that Ginzburg had made a very thorough study of Proust: she had immersed herself in his his work from the age of twenty; in her article 'Come ho tradotto Proust' in *La Stampa* (11 Dec. 1963), she says that once she started reading *A la recherche*, 'mi sprofondai in quella lettura e non lessi, per anni, praticamente null'altro'. In Proust, memory, music and reminiscence (or regaining of the past) are intimately linked. It seems that Ginzburg has combined this musical aspect of the evoking of memory, so fundamental in Proust, with the idea of a family's way of speaking affecting a writer's style, and from the two derived her own unique *lessico*.

To summarize my view of the 'music' of *Lessico famigliare,* then, there are two kinds of style, but they are linked in terms of musical idiom: what has been called the 'cantilenato gemito ininterrotto', 'cicaleccio', or background music,[27] is in fact a melody consisting of the *lessico*, whilst the 'realistic' prose narrative is a kind of silence; Ginzburg seeks silence at the most poignant moments, since she dreads the wrong or inadequate expression. Her references to Proust signal the use of musical memory-prompts, but also clarify her technique of shutting out the personal voices of memory when dealing with the tragedies of other people, however closely they touch her and indeed particularly when they touch her closely.

I would suggest that the issue of silence is not only central to Ginzburg's writing but is a 'problem' for her and a theme of *Lessico famigliare*, expressed, naturally, by absence of expression. An article Ginzburg wrote about ten years before *Lessico famigliare*, 'Il silenzio' (1951), is very interesting in this context (*Opere*, i. 855–9). She opens with a reference to music, and, despite her usual assertion, 'Di musica non ne capisco niente', uses the example of *Pelléas et Mélisande* to introduce her piece about silence. This implies a link in her mind between silence and music, which is not here made explicit, but which to me seems unavoidable. She goes on to write poignantly of her generation's rejection of the language of their parents, their 'disgusto per le parole grosse e sanguinose', saying that 'quelle vecchie parole sanguinose e pesanti [...] quelle loro grosse parole non ci servivano più' (i. 856). However, the new generation finds nothing to replace those words and is reduced to silence: 'tra i vizi più strani e più gravi della nostra epoca, va menzionato il silenzio'. She links this silence with other emotions: 'Del senso di colpa, del senso di panico, del silenzio, ciascuno cerca a modo suo di guarire'; refers to 'il silenzio con se stessi e il silenzio con gli altri'; and discusses psychoanalysis as a fragile, temporary refuge from silence.

The article is a frightening description of the condition of speechlessness ('Il silenzio può raggiungere una forma d'infelicità chiusa, mostruosa, *diabolica*'), ending with a plea for it to be taken seriously as 'il frutto amaro della nostra epoca malsana' (*Opere*, i. 859). I have already discussed the silence in *Lessico famigliare* surrounding the pain concerning the narrator's husband's death, but there is also a great silence surrounding the *io-narrante* too. In the light of the author's writings on silence and her recourse to psychoanalysis, I would suggest that this absence at the centre of an ostensibly autobiographical work implies an unhealthy self-effacement, concealing painful emotions of many kinds, a deliberate self-effacement belied by the apparently detached tone of the narrative.

I referred above to the difficulty of pinpointing parts of the narrative for reference owing to its meandering structure. The workings of memory give us the key to how the narrative proceeds. Memory is not linear but is spurred by almost arbitrary stimuli. This is how Ginzburg's text moves forward (and indeed how Proust's proceeds too). She maintains a loosely chronological structure, dealing first with the family history and her childhood, then the years of Fascism and war, then post-war Italy. However, the narrative imitates the itinerary of memory, fastening on an object in the outside world and calling up the recollection linked with it, deviating from a strictly chronological order. (A prime example, of course, is the portrait of Leone in the post-war Einaudi office, which prompts the belated, retrospective narration of what had happened to him; *LF* 144.) If we understand the texture of the book, we should not expect linearity. Similarly, just as the memory tends to suppress the most traumatic episodes, her text does so also, veering away from them, skirting round them and fastening on elements peripheral to the feared episode. When she tackles this kind of event head-on, when the text is no longer an evocation but becomes a chronicle, the narrator is a different one: she is not the girl in the pre-war family, nor is she the adult with her internalized nostalgia any more, but she becomes an external narrator, and in that sense, detached, though not indifferent or ironic.

All these aspects, the musical device, the shifts in narrative perspective, the Proustian echoes, indeed the way Proust informs the whole work, are all of course elements which suggest the ways in which the book is to be considered *romanzo* rather than *autobiografia*. I suspect also that they contradict the author's assertions that the book was written artlessly, 'del tutto come parlare', 'pura, nuda, scoperta e dichiarata memoria' (preface to *Cinque romanzi brevi*, 17), 'soltanto quello che ricordavo'(*LF*, 'Avvertenza', 3). *Lessico famigliare* is a highly crafted and literary artefact with the literary and musical idioms carefully intertwined. Lidia Levi's banal interpretations of Proust and the narrator's denial of musical sensitivity are part of a subtle joke played on the reader.

Covert Feminism in *Lessico famigliare*

Natalia Ginzburg did not see herself as a feminist. The question of gender as it relates to the creative process was of recurring interest to Ginzburg, as we have seen from earlier statements, already noted in this study, saying she wished to write like a man, and also, for instance, from the essay 'Il mio mestiere', written in 1961 and collected in *Le piccole virtù* (*Opere*, i. 781–896 at 839–54), where she states, however self-deprecating her tone, that eventually, after she had borne children, she realized that women could perhaps write better than men about certain things (i. 851):

Adesso non desideravo piú tanto di scrivere come un uomo, perché avevo avuto i bambini, e mi pareva di sapere tante cose riguardo al sugo di pomodoro e anche se non le mettevo nel racconto pure serviva al mio mestiere che io le sapessi: in un modo misterioso e remoto anche questo serviva al mio mestiere. Mi pareva che le donne sapessero sui loro figli delle cose che un uomo non può mai sapere.

Notwithstanding this mild artistic claim for women, her rejection of feminism as an active political stance is plain from her article 'La condizione femminile', written in 1973 and published in the collection *Vita immaginaria* (*Opere*, ii. 497–685 at 647–53), in which she states unambiguously in the opening paragraph, 'Non amo il femminismo'. However, she quickly modifies this statement by adding that though she dislikes the idea of women being categorized by virtue of their gender alone, she nevertheless supports fully the majority of their aims, 'tutte le loro richieste pratiche'.

She rejects the notion that women constitute a social class of their own, distinguishing between those women in privileged positions and the poor. She admits that 'le donne sono state adoperate e umiliate per secoli', but points out that this is only a small part of the complex relationship between men and women in the modern era. She rejects 'l'antagonismo fra donna e uomo', saying that aggressive feminism arises from an inferiority complex in women as a result of their history of humiliation, but that this is no basis upon which to construct a philosophy. She admits that men sometimes despise women, but says this is 'occasionale e irrelevante' amongst the privileged classes. Amongst the poor, she concedes that men's disdain for women leads to hardship, but links this not to 'la condizione femminile' but to 'la condizione umana'. Traditionally 'feminine' activities, those linked with the home and children, are not in themselves humiliating or servile and, in any case, she adds, if women don't do these things, 'generare figli, e accudire e tener pulite le case dove essi crescono', who will?

She feels that feminism is an idea that has come from the privileged classes, an abstraction that has created havoc and is largely the result of an uneasy conscience amongst privileged women, who, by assuming the mantle of the oppressed, thereby hope to acquire the borrowed false glamour of servitude in the midst of their privileges. She feels there are more appropriate targets for rebellion than 'la specie virile'. Now she returns to the issue of household tasks and accepts that a fair division of this kind of work amongst men and women would be a good thing, but goes on to insist that as women bear children, they are more likely to have a larger share of bringing them up and that there is a special relationship between mothers and children. This bond can become a trap and the woman feels frustrated, but, according to Ginzburg, this is not something that can blamed on society or solved by it, but is part of the human condition.

She derides the notion of women needing to 'realizzarsi' and their blaming society for any feelings of not being fulfilled. She states that there is no 'differenza qualitativa' between men and women, and that feminism insists wrongly that women are better than men. She says they are different, but that the difference 'è la stessa differenza che c'è fra il sole e la luna, o fra il giorno e la notte'. Finally, she says: 'Nei nostri momenti migliori, il nostro pensiero non è né di donna, né di uomo', though it is inevitable that our gender affects what we do, 'i segni femminili del nostro temperamento si stampano sulle nostre azioni e parole'. Ultimately, the ideal condition is where men and women relate to one another and identify with one another without regard to gender.

The article is somewhat naïve, even in the context of the times when it was written. It is interesting that Ginzburg's final celebration of the differences between women and men acquiesces, presumably unconsciously, in an inevitably subordinate role for women, by drawing on the type of binary language whose underlying diminution of women has been pointed out by Hélène Cixous: when male and female is equated with night and day and moon and sun, the woman is automatically placed in a negative or passive position vis-à-vis the male.[28] On a straightforward, practical level however, Ginzburg does not, for instance, consider the fact that when women work outside the home they earn considerably less than men, either because the jobs they do are considered traditionally 'women's work' and the salaries payable are therefore pegged at lower levels than jobs perceived as 'men's work'; or they are simply paid less for doing what men do, despite legislation to curb this; or they are constrained by the household and family responsibilities, of which Ginzburg makes so light, to take part-time work, which inevitably means they are poorly paid and do not acquire employment rights or status at work. These are genuine economic problems faced by women, which are still being addressed in the early twenty-first century and certainly were even more prevalent in the 1970s when this article was written.

Ginzburg's foray into the political feminist debate outlined in 'La condizione femminile' would be merely an interesting curiosity, were it not for the fact that *Lessico famigliare*, written almost ten years before it, in my view, demonstrates feminist attitudes and is therefore in tension with the declared attitudes in the later article. The briefest analysis of the women in the book and the trajectory of their lives, including the narrator herself, reveals dissatisfaction and unease with the position of women in Italian society, even women of a privileged and educated class. Consideration of sociological and historical evidence regarding the situation of women between the wars, during the Second World War and post-war, suggests a context of proto-feminism that is difficult to ignore, particularly taken in tandem with the depictions of women in *Lessico famigliare*.

Lessico famigliare centres on the home, the traditional arena of women's experience and women's writing. The figure of the mother, often a significant and iconic figure in women's writing, has a prominent role in the narrative. She is frequently the source of the *lessico*, the repository of family stories, thus fulfilling a traditionally female role as the purveyor of oral culture, and, as a mother, is the central figure in the family. However, the portrait of this woman is ambiguous. She is clearly an intelligent woman, having studied medicine and with an interest in languages, culture and the arts, but her early studies have come to nothing; her analysis of culture is trivial (she judges the painter Casorati by what he looks like rather than by his work, and Proust by his admirable attitude to the family); and her pursuit of further study is dilettantish (she begins to learn Russian, but does not persevere and the book on entomology is abandoned halfway through).

Ginzburg says 'la sua curiosità non respingeva mai nulla', but at the same time, she is 'pigra'. She fulfils the traditional role of the mother as nurturer, supplying meals for the family, taking provisions to her husband in prison, but in some ways she is unsatisfactory as a parent, for instance in the overly possessive relationship she has with Paola and the way that she favours Paola over Natalia. She is politically committed, in that she encourages her children, husband and friends in the anti-Fascist struggle, but her grasp of political events is always depicted in the most trivial of terms: she is portrayed as enjoying the excitement of the turbulent years of Fascism, she leaves the house regularly on daily errands, cheerily wondering whether 'hanno buttato giù Mussolini' and casually predicting that people will get rid of him imminently, to her husband's evident irritation (*LF* 83–4). Her son Mario's narrow escape from the Fascist police across the river, which was part of a notorious episode followed by mass arrests and antisemitic propaganda, eventually known by the Italian public as the Ponte Tresa affair, for her is represented as most notable for the fact that his outdoor clothes got wet: 'In acqua, col paltò!' (*LF* 90).

Her life, though relatively comfortable, is primarily characterised by boredom: one of the phrases associated with her is 'per non stufarsi' (*LF* 86) as well as other variants on 'stufo' and 'stufarsi'. At one point, she even wishes for sickness, to alleviate the boredom: 'se almeno mi venisse qualche bella malattia' (*LF* 111). Paola complains that she would like a more settled, tranquil mother, 'la nostra mamma è troppo giovane' (ibid.). It is surely not anachronistic to derive from this portrait of an intelligent, lively woman, languishing frustrated in a morass of boredom and trivia, some of which is of her own creation, a more generally applicable image of the position of many women at that time.

Lidia Levi was an educated middle-class woman, brought up in an era when women's rights were an issue on the political agenda. There had already been some gains, championed by Anna Kuliscioff, a writer and militant activist, who is noted in *Lessico famigliare* as someone well known to the family, but Fascist ideology was not favourable to women. In his excellent study on the role of women in Fascist Italy, Giovanni De Luna reveals some startling statistics:

il lavoro, la politica con l'infrangersi delle grandi speranze collettive del femminismo dell'immediato dopoguerra (gli anni 1924, 1926 e 1928 fecero registrare il più alto numero di suicidi femminili dell'Italia contemporanea), la cultura (una donna su cinque nel 1930 non sapeva leggere), la scuola e le facoltà 'ghetto' (nel 1938 i quattro quinti delle laureate uscivano da Lettere, Magistero, Farmacia, Matematica e Scienze), i rapporti sessuali segnati da un capillare e asfissiante controllo sociale, i canoni della bellezza e della moda e, soprattutto, la famiglia, un terreno strategico scelto come prioritario anzitutto dal Fascismo che al nucleo familiare attribuiva il ruolo di estrema propaggine, verso il basso, dello Stato totalitario.[29]

The Fascist Party assimilated the familiarly repressive elements of Catholicism, separating male and female, creating an image of the ideal female, confined to the home, a model of fecundity and passivity. This model did not take into account the growing number of working women, particularly in the cities, nor, paradoxically, was it able to incorporate without embarrassment the phenomenon of the 'Fasci femminili', though the auxiliary role of these women made their 'messaggio di devianza da un modello di normalità femminile' more acceptable.[30] Fascist organizations for women such as 'Gioventù femminile' were similarly instrumental in politicizing the female working classes, particularly the groups most vulnerable to exploitation, including servants, home workers, farm labourers and the new army of office and factory workers. Nevertheless, Fascist ideology strained towards a system in which women returned to the home. As De Luna says:

L'attuazione delle leggi del 1938, tese a espellere definitivamente le donne dal mercato del lavoro rappresentò [...] l'epilogo istituzionale e legislativo di un trend di fondo protrattosi in tutti gli anni del Fascismo.[31]

On the same matter, Alexander De Grand writes:

The Mussolini government was especially hard on white-collar and professional women. The first minister of public instruction, Gentile, restricted the rights of women to teach in certain predominately male upper-level schools and in certain subject matters, like philosophy. The Fascist government made no effort to repeal restrictions on women in the legal profession, and [...] hedged on commitments to bring a women's suffrage bill to parliament. Mussolini finally did allow women to vote in local elections, but, almost simultaneously, in 1926, the government abandoned democratic local administration.

The depression brought a spate of laws further curbing work for women. Preference was given to men in public employment, and in 1933 new regulations limited the rights of women to compete in state examinations. [...] A law passed in 1938 restricted females to no more than 10 per cent of the work force in private and state enterprises, and a 1939 decree defined certain areas of 'female' labour where percentages might rise higher— typists, clerks, telephone operators, and the like. Timid attempts by university-educated women to defend professional career choices were halted around 1934. Instead procreation and child-rearing were set forth as the exclusive functions of all women.[32]

The influence of Fascism on relationships between the sexes in private was no less pernicious. The age-old division, 'madre/amante' persisted, endorsed by Church and State, Mussolini himself offering a model of male sexual behaviour, with his wife and several children, but a succession of casual sexual encounters and one long-term lover (Clara Petacci). Even fashion did not escape politicization, with the frivolity of fashion considered acceptable for the upper classes but '"inverecondo" e "goffo" per le "povere donne" che volevano imitare i costumi dei ricchi'.[33] There was also a feminine ideal in looks, with the voluptuous woman perceived as 'feminine', positive and good for the State, and the skinny, neurotic, 'masculine' woman lampooned as asexual and socially useless. But, as De Luna points out, it was unclear how it was possible to be the ideal woman physically and yet remain 'respectable' in ideological terms:

Ma le forme procaci della 'donna autentica' erano quelle della 'madre italiana' fertile e prosperosa o ammiccavano alla calda sensualità dell' amante'?[34]

This, then, is the background against which the female lives in *Lessico famigliare* unfold. Already, even the apparently trivial emphasis on clothing and fashion assumes a different significance when it is taken into account that a woman's looks and the image she projected through her clothing were monitored by the authorities and a matter for the attention of the producers of propaganda.

However, it is specifically the socialist, feminist context that is most striking. Anna Kuliscioff is described as a close family friend (*LF* 40): 'l'Andreina, amica d'infanzia di mia madre e figlia della Kuliscioff [...] Turati e la Kuliscioff, nei ricordi di mia madre, erano sempre presenti.' It is difficult to believe that Ginzburg can mention her in *Lessico famigliare* without expecting the reader to make the connection of her role in the struggle for women's rights within the Socialist Party, so that, rather as she does in her playful references to Proust, she is alerting the reader to a kind of feminist subtext. For it is undeniable that women as mothers, in the work-place, in the political context and as ideals of 'femininity' are all images that are posited in *Lessico famigliare*, as if for discussion, though without that discussion ever taking place overtly, as I will show in what follows.

Apart from Natalia's mother, there are, of course, several other women in the narrative, and they too have a significance that reaches far beyond their own identities. Most notable, in the context of this examination of covert feminism in *Lessico famigliare*, is the depiction of Natalia's female friends. These women, Lisetta, Lola and 'le squinzie', have all been considerably 'fleshed out' compared to the original manuscript, as outlined in Valeria Barani's article analysing the manuscript of *Lessico famigliare*. This suggests a conscious decision on the part of the writer to give particular weight to their role in the book.[35] The importance of the experience of these women cannot be overemphasized: Lola Balbo and Lisetta Giua are both intelligent, restless women. Both were politically active during the war and were arrested and interrogated and had to flee. Both became mothers at a young age and are described as having needed to become adults too quickly. Both are frustrated in their post-war lives, having been obliged to return to traditional female roles, in which they feel inadequate: they, like Natalia, worry that they are not good mothers.

Lisetta, in fact, does not look after her daughter, but passes her on to her mother-in-law. Nevertheless, in later years, she discovers that she can combine work and being a good mother, though she is almost ashamed of the fact (*LF* 181): 'essendo diventata, senza accorgersene e senza confessarlo né a sé né a nessuno, una madre tenera, scrupolosa e apprensiva'. Lola Balbo was also politically active during the war and arrested and imprisoned. She, like Lisetta, is not a natural mother; 'si occupava del suo bambino con una mescolanza di apprensione e fastidio' (*LF* 178). The Balbo household is not presented as a happy place: Lola's relationship with her husband is restless and changeable; everything, however trivial, is a source of argument. She has great difficulty settling into post-war life: she worked briefly at Einaudi but was not good at it, but she feels the need to work and thinks nostalgically of the war years, when there was a focus for her energies. These details concerning the problems of adapting to marriage, motherhood and to the loss of an active political role in post-war Italy have all been added to the manuscript for the published version of the book:

Il ms. non parla neppure della maternità di Lola [...], né della ricerca di un lavoro adatto a lei, né della sua esperienza in carcere, momento di massima espressione della sua indole di capopopolo [...]. Nell'edizione la Ginzburg traccia parallelamente il ritratto di Lisetta e passa perciò a trattare del suo impiego presso l'associazione Italia-Urss e dei suoi rapporti con i figli e il marito, motivi sconosciuti al ms. [...].[36]

Lisetta had been interrogated by the notorious torturer Ferida and escaped with the help of friends disguised as nurses. In her post-war life, she sees worrying remnants of the Partito d'Azione in the attitudes of those around her, and when she remonstrates, Natalia says her husband 'la guardava come si guarda un gatto giovane giocare con un rotolo di spago' (*LF* 169). This may be an affectionate simile, but it nonetheless implies a somewhat patronizing attitude on the part of the husband, given Lisetta's courageous history. This clash of attitudes, whereby women were accepted as political activists and yet not respected as equals with their male 'compagni', is clearly documented in other accounts and will be discussed more fully in a later chapter of this book, in connection with the autobiography of Tina Pizzardo, the woman known to readers for many years as Pavese's 'donna dalla voce rauca'.

'Le squinzie' are also politically significant women. Ginzburg stresses their rejection of contemporary social values (*LF* 124): 'vivevano in aperto dissidio con la società'. They hate the restrictions imposed on respectable, bourgeois women, however 'easy' the life. All three of the 'squinzie' are Jewish and help German Jewish refugees that have arrived in Italy, and, after the war, one eventually moves to Africa and another becomes a lawyer in Rome. The other 'squinzia', Marisa, is a partisan during the German occupation 'e mostrò un coraggio straordinario', then becomes 'una funzionaria del partito comunista, e votò la propria vita al partito, ma restando nell'ombra, perchè era priva d'ogni ambizione e modesta, umile e generosa' (*LF* 127). Once more, Ginzburg depicts a woman whose public, practical skills go unsung, notwithstanding incontrovertible proof of her worth in a man's world.

The narrator says very little about herself throughout the book, despite its autobiographical nature, but one of the few areas when she does speak of herself is when she focuses on herself as a wife, pointing out her own ignorance of the role and her inefficiency at running the household, which includes a servant Martina. Her discomfort at having a servant is plain (*LF* 123):

Non trovavo mai il momento giusto di dare ordini alla Martina [...]. Non osavo d'altronde darle alcun ordine, io che da ragazza, in casa di mia madre, davo ordini con indifferenza [...]. Alla Martina, non avrei osato ordinare di portarmi nemmeno un bicchier d'acqua.

It seems to me that this marks the dawning of a political and social sensibility in the narrator, centring on the role of working-class women. The newly-married Natalia realizes that she took for granted the work of the family servant Natalina. The post-war years eventually bring new freedoms for everyone, including women, and Natalina is one of the first women depicted in the book as taking advantage of them. In a passage which describes the immediate post-war years (*LF* 160), we are told that Giuseppe and Lidia Levi go back to live in via Pallamaglio, but its name has changed to via Morgari. This apparently trivial detail signals that, for all its apparent return to normality, life will never be the same again. Natalina announces, at this point of transition, that she is going to live independently and charge out her services by the hour. 'Non voglio più essere schiava,' she says, 'voglio la libertà.'

Lidia Levi is baffled at the idea that she personally restricted anyone's freedom, but Natalina's action, moving from 'tied' accommodation to an independence which, we are told in a touching aside, permits her to choose to invite her own friends to her own home ('invitava, la sera, la Tersilla e suo marito a prendere il caffè'), indicates the beginnings of a shift in barriers of class and gender. Any reader tempted to consider this a minor development should bear in mind that Natalina was brought up an orphan in extremely cruel conditions and had been beaten by her first employers, yet nevertheless continued to feel obscurely respectful towards them (*LF* 34), so that the trajectory of her post-war life represents significant social and psychological progress. It is to be expected that Lidia will have difficulty with this concept, because she remains locked into the old archetype, with all its limitations and frustrations, a stance which, as we have seen, is reflected in her adherence to the old *lessico*.

The humorous nature of the portrait of Natalina throughout the book softens the tragedy of her situation. Ginzburg regularly uses humour in *Lessico famigliare* to offset darker aspects of the texts and, to some extent, disguise them, as if she were ashamed of expressing strong feelings or troubling the reader. This is in complete accordance with the traditionally approved role of the female to please and could be read as one of the 'feminine' (definitely not 'feminist') aspects of Ginzburg's best-loved text and possibly a reason for the affection it inspired in the Italian reading public, readers who up until relatively recently, may not have wished their stereotypical impressions to be challenged. The portrait of Giuseppe Levi is interesting in the context of Ginzburg's use of humour, and also because as a father figure he is diametrically opposed to that of the mother: he too represents an archetype, but a male one, with his 'masculine' drive, aggression and dominance. The mother is afraid of his rages, 'aveva una tal paura delle collere di mio padre' (*LF* 61); he regularly calls her 'asina' (and, indeed, when she was young, her brother Silvio called her 'stupida', *LF* 38). Masculine responses in the Levi household are habitually violent (*LF* 35):

Vivevamo sempre, in casa, nell'incubo delle sfuriate di mio padre, che esplodevano improvvise, sovente per motivi minimi [...]. Vivevamo tuttavia anche nell'incubo delle litigate tra i miei fratelli Alberto e Mario, che anche quelle esplodevano improvvise [...].

L'intervento di mio padre era, come ogni sua azione, violento. Si buttava in mezzo a quei due avvinghiati a picchiarsi, e li copriva di schiaffi. Io ero piccola; e ricordo con terrore quei tre uomini che lottavano selvaggiamente.

It seems to me a wilful misreading to interpret the depiction of these episodes and the atmosphere they generate as comic in themselves. What Ginzburg does do, however, is soften the picture of the father with humour. His extreme judgments and reactions are often the source of humour in the book. The idea that this strongly humorous element in the portrayal of her father is a deliberate elaboration on Ginzburg's part, rather than a straightforward, 'true-to-life' description of him, is supported by an interesting variant between the manuscript and the published version:

Si sceglie come esempio più significativo una battuta del professor Levi, indirizzata a sorpresa al figlio Alberto nell'aula dell'Università, la quale, passando da 'Chi è quel maleducato che s'è messo a fumare?' [...] a 'Chi è quel figlio d'un cane che s'è messo a fumare?' [...], viene caricata di una nota di comicità ai danni del padre, beffato dalle sue stesse parole.[37]

Professor Levi does have many good points, ranging from his courageous political commitment to his evident concern for the family's welfare, including caring for them when they are sick, a nurturing 'feminine' trait. Indeed, one could argue that both parents are trapped by contemporary society's expectations within archetypes of male and female, without which they would both have been more comfortable. However, Professor Levi's gentler moments do not cancel out the effects of his dominance and violence within the family. I would argue that the self-effacement of both the narrated Natalia in *Lessico famigliare* and of the adult writer, Ginzburg, are linked to these childhood patterns of male dominance and female submission within the family, which are then played out later on the larger stage of a patriarchal publishing establishment.

In her article 'La mia psicanalisi' (1969; *Opere*, ii. 43–9), Ginzburg writes that she felt a need for the help of a psychoanalyst in the post-war years, because she felt 'piena di colpe oscure e di confusione'. This depression and unease clearly could well have been the result of the traumas of the war years, but she specifically mentions that she felt her parents would have been dismayed and disapproving had they known of her visits to the psychoanalyst. She adds (ii. 44): 'Il pensiero che stavo facendo una cosa che avrebbe spaventato i miei genitori, mi rendeva l'analisi affascinante e ripugnante insieme.' This article has the gently humorous, self-deprecating tone that is very familiar and attractive in Ginzburg's journalism, and she admits that her fears regarding her parents' likely response were probably wrong; nevertheless, the picture that emerges behind her reluctance to 'make a fuss' is of an unhappy adult woman still dominated by her parents. The determinedly humorous portrait of Professor Levi in *Lessico famigliare*, despite evidence of the unhappiness his behaviour causes, and to some extent disguising it, chimes with Ginzburg's tendency generally to shy away from talking about her own problems and her own distress, preferring to leave a gap, or clothe pain in humour.

The condition of women was clearly of interest to the writer. Ginzburg's habitual reluctance to speak about herself extends to a reluctance to talk overtly about the condition of all women. The reader can infer feminist aspects from *Lessico famigliare*, but the book is non-polemical in style in all the areas it touches upon, and in that sense it accords with the article 'La condizione femminile'. The female lives described in the book, however, offer ample material for feminist debate.

In the 1974 edition of *Lessico famigliare* that I have used for this study, there is an introduction by Cesare Garboli, a very close friend of Ginzburg as well as a critic of some note, and in it he draws attention to Ginzburg's reluctance to talk about broad historical events. He calls this restraint 'un pudore infallibile', and he adds (*LF*, p. vii):

> È l'estrema confidenza interiore con la quale un animo infantile, o femminile — che è lo stesso — è solito intrattenersi per conto suo coi fatti degli altri, degli adulti, allineando le pubbliche messinscene della storia sullo stesso livello delle minime occasioni [...].

This introduction was first published in 1971 and was still being reprinted several years later: the fact that in a serious piece of writing a critic could assure readers that the female point of view could be said to be the same as a child's tells us a great deal about public attitudes to women in Italy, even in the 1970s. Ginzburg was still saying in 1990, 'È difficile parlare di sé.' It is hardly surprising that after the repressions of her upbringing, both in society at large and within the home, she should deny militancy in 'La condizione femminile' but choose a subtle form of expression of that same condition in *Lessico famigliare*.

Notes to Chapter 4

1. All references to *LF* are to the Mondadori edition (Milan, 1974); references to other works refer to Natalia Ginzburg, *Opere*, 2 vols. (Milan: Mondadori, 1986–7), unless otherwise indicated. For critical comments, see Clotilde Soave Bowe, 'The Narrative Strategy of Natalia Ginzburg', *Modern Language Review* 68 (1973), 788–95; Alan Bullock, *Natalia Ginzburg* (New York and Oxford: Berg, 1991). See also Cesare Garboli, 'Fortuna critica', Ginzburg, *Opere*, ii. 1577–91, esp. 1580, who discusses negative views of the book as well as positive and sees *LF* as a turning point in the writer's career.

2. Clara Borrelli, 'Lirismo narrativo di Natalia Ginzburg', *Annali dell'Istituto Universitario Orientale di Napoli* 29 (1987), 289–310 at 304–5.

3. Giuliana Minghelli, 'Ricordando il quotidiano: *Lessico famigliare* o L'arte del cantastorie', *Italica* 72 (1995) 155–73.

4. Natalia Ginzburg, *The Things We Used to Say*, trans. Judith Woolf (Manchester: Carcanet, 1997). Cf. Marcel Proust, *A la recherche du temps perdu*, ed. Jean-Yves Tadié et al., 4 vols. (Paris: Gallimard, 1987–9).

5. Natalia Ginzburg, preface to *Cinque romanzi brevi* (Turin: Einaudi, 1964), 17.

6. For an excellent essay covering many aspects of the novel, including a study of the divisions of the text, explaining the varying number between different editions and analysing the links between the sections, see Claudio Magrini, '*Lessico famigliare* di Natalia Ginzburg', *Letteratura italiana*, dir. Alberto Asor Rosa, viii: *Le opere*, iv/2: *Novecento: Ricerca letteraria* (Turin: Einaudi, 1996), 771–810.

7. Borrelli, 'Lirismo narrativo'; Minghelli, 'Ricordando il quotidiano'; but cf. M. Bonfantini, 'Il muto segreto di molte esistenze', *Corriere della sera* (14 Feb, 1965), 3: 'una musica troppo brillante e martellata', and others, quoted by Borrelli, 294.

8. Borrelli, 'Lirismo narrativo', 307.

9. Minghelli, 'Ricordando il quotidiano', 172 n. 17.

10. For a very useful detailed analysis of the components of the *lessico* and other aspects of the style of the book, see Maria Antonietta Grignani, 'Un concerto di voci', *Natalia Ginzburg: La narratrice e i suoi testi*, ed. Maria Antonietta Grignani (Rome: La Nuova Italia, 1986), 48–54.

11. As phrases intended to characterize Pavese, these are thought-provoking, particularly as Ginzburg knew him well and at the time of writing *Lessico famigliare* had seen his private papers after his death and helped edit them with Calvino for the first edn of *Il mestiere di vivere* (see Chap. 3 above).

12. Italo Calvino, *Il sentiero dei nidi di ragno* (Milan: Mondadori, 1993), p. vii.

13. Elio Vittorini, *Il garofano rosso*, idem, *Le opere narrative*, ed. Maria Corti, 2 vols. (Milan: Mondadori, 1979), i, p. i.

14. See Robert Gordon, 'Pasolini contro Calvino: Culture, the Canon and the Millennium', *Modern Italy* 3 (1998), 87–99; McLaughlin, *Italo Calvino* 'Words and Silence: The Strange Genesis of Mr Palomar', 129–44.

15. Italo Calvino, *Lettere 1940–1985*, ed. Luca Baranelli (Milan: Mondadori, 2000), 717 (Oct. 1962).

16. For references to critics who have interpreted the narrative as cold or even cruel, see Borrelli, 'Lirismo narrativo', 290–1.

17. Ibid., 291.

18. Minghelli, 'Ricordando il quotidiano', 159.

19. Garboli, 'Fortuna critica', 1579, 1590.

20. Calvino, preface to *Il sentiero dei nidi di ragno*, p. viii.

21. Borrelli, 'Lirismo narrativo', 309; Woolf, preface to Ginzburg, *The Things We Used to Say*, p. xiii.

22. Sheila Stern, *Swann's Way* (Cambridge: Cambridge University Press, 1989), 8.

23. Adam Piette, *Remembering and the Sounds of Words* (Oxford: Clarendon Press, 1996), 81–141, 45.

24. Ibid., 96.

25. Natalia Ginzburg, 'Marcel Proust, poeta della memoria', Giansiro Ferrata and Natalia Ginzburg, *Romanzi del 900* (Turin: ERI, 1956), 57–79 at 59.

26. Piette, *Remembering and the Sounds of Words*, 82.
27. Borrelli, 'Lirismo narrativo', 292, 309.
28. Hélène Cixous and Catherine Clément, *La jeune née* (Paris, 1975).
29. Giovanni De Luna, *Donne in oggetto: L'antifascismo nella società italiana, 1922–1939* (Turin: Bollati Boringhieri, 1995), 30.
30. Ibid., 46.
31. Ibid., 49.
32. Alexander De Grand, *Italian Fascism: Its Origins and Development*, 2nd edn (Lincoln: University of Nebraska Press, 1989), 112–13.
33. De Luna, *Donne in oggetto*, 48.
34. Ibid., 204.
35. Valeria Barani, 'Il fondo Natalia Ginzburg', *Autografo* 3/23 (June 1991), 71–7 at 73–6.
36. Ibid., 74.
37. Ibid., 71.

CHAPTER 5

Silence and Women's Writing

Women's silence is particularly relevant when considering modern Italian literature, since women are hardly represented in the canon at all, but the culture of female silence affects all women writers and has been fundamental in feminist criticism.[1] The main arguments are summarized by Julie Rivkin and Michael Ryan in *Literary Theory*.[2] Rivkin and Ryan make many salient points about the nature of women's writing, first about the genres favoured by women: banished from education and from public life, women writers had found refuge in literary forms despised by men, in diaries and letters and in sentimental fiction. They add that women have been denied a language with which to speak: as the available language has been the language of patriarchy, they have been silenced over the centuries, and even now, the language in which to express themselves is problematic. They stress the importance of feminist literary criticism in its role to help bring about 'the emergence from silence into language—to undo the silence of those who still do not speak'. Elaine Hedges and Shelley Fisher Fishkin's book offers a selection of interesting essays centring on Tillie Olsen's seminal text, *Silences*, including postmodernist critical approaches to silences.[3] Patricia Laurence's essay in this collection contains many significant points. The following extracts outline the importance of taking into account the issue of women's silence in studying literature and are the point of departure for this part of my study:

Depending upon one's definition of reality, silences woven into the fabric of a woman's text can be an absence or a presence. If reality is perceived according to patriarchal values, then women's silence, viewed from the outside, is a mark of absence and powerlessness, given women's modest expression in the public sphere until the twentieth century. If, however, the same silence is viewed from the inside, and women's experience and disposition of mind inform the standard of what is real, then women's silence can be viewed as a presence, and as a text, waiting to be read. [...]

Silence is the space in narration where culture and feminine consciousness do sometimes reveal themselves, if only we can learn to decipher the psychological and cultural meanings. Ideologically, we are trapped as critics if we cannot shift the reading of silence in women from one of essence to one of position or even, at times, choice.[4]

Women's autobiography has been a particularly problematic form owing to the clear tension between the requirements of writing about the self and the repressive effects of culturally-imposed silence. Bella Brodzki and Celeste Schenck have spoken of the 'strategy of impersonation' in women's autobiography, which takes the form of either excessive modesty about a woman's own achievements, or the taking of a different name, or even 'writing of herself in another woman's voice'.[5] Their introductory chapter to *Life/Lines* is an excellent summary of the field of research into women's autobiography.

Ursula Fanning's article on Aleramo also offers a good précis of the issues involved. In brief, she states that modern criticism has stressed that all autobiography is a kind of fiction, with the distinction between the two being an 'undecidable', as Paul de Man has it.[6] Both autobiography and autobiographical fiction are concerned with self-definition, but it has become clear to critics that whilst men are expected and able to present the reader with a coherent and unified self-image, the picture women create of themselves is more fragmentary. Men find autobiography problematic because they are not used to seeing themselves objectified, whereas for women this is the 'norm' and therefore the autobiographical form is more natural for them. Nevertheless, Fanning sees a difficulty for the woman writer: 'having located herself as object, how does she then present herself as subject, and literally as speaking subject in the case of first-person narrative?'

I would add that the situation is further complicated by the implications of 'the gaze' and the voyeuristic overtones it brings with it, as outlined later in this chapter. It may not still be true to say that women's autobiography has 'a legacy of secrecy, repression and displacement' or that women's lives have a different rhythm.[7] However, it will always be an interesting question whether the restraints and complexities of women's special relationship with the texts they write is necessarily a disadvantage, or whether instead it has given rise to particularly rich and interesting texts. In this context, I intend to focus here on the work on Francesca Sanvitale, who, still writing, has earned a place in the Italian literary canon of the twentieth century. Her work has been the subject of a growing amount of research published in English and Italian, and she is a formidable literary critic in her own right, including commentary on her own writing.[8]

The motif of women's silence is deeply embedded in our culture. Silence, loss or deprivation of speech, dumbness, tongues: all are motifs that feature regularly in folk-tales, in similar guises across different cultures and across the centuries. The importance of folk-tales and fairy-tales in our culture has not gone unheeded by scholars: Bruno Bettelheim's study of the psychological importance of fairy-tales is well known, and Jack Zipes has written authoritatively on the political importance of folk- and fairy-tales.[9] Stith Thompson's great motif-index lists hundreds of tales featuring speech or the absence of speech as a central aspect of a story.[10] A person might refuse to speak out of grief (Thompson F1041.21.3.1), a silent person is made to speak (H1194.0.1) or magic results from speech (D1774). The logical connections between silence, secrecy and furtive behaviour lead to some bawdy tales, such as the stories of speaking genitalia (K1569.7 and H451). In another tale, witnesses are discredited by being tricked into talking nonsense, thus invalidating their earlier evidence by association (J115.1).

These stories apply to both men and women, but there is no doubt that male and female silence is presented differently. It is striking how often female speech is depicted as worthless nonsense, and, conversely, female silence is prized as virtuous or actually redeeming. Examples of this type include the tale of the minstrel's wife whose tongue is discovered to be the heaviest thing on board, and she is thrown out of an endangered boat into the sea (Thompson T251.1.5); or conversely, the princess who breaks her own virtuous silence, but only does so because she is obliged to in order to avoid calumny (K1271.1.2).

This devaluation of female speech is also commonplace in Christian tradition. The following is quoted by C. Grant Loomis in his study of the blending of folk-tales and Christian legend:

When a talkative and abusive hostess stormed at Dominic and his fellows for refusing to eat the meat which she had cooked for them, Dominic imposed silence upon her by a word, and the woman's tongue did not wag again for eight months. Upon the return journey Dominic was moved by the woman's quiet appeal and, to the despair of her husband, freed the paralysed tongue.[11]

In this brief summary of the tale, the contrast between the 'word' of the male representative of Christianity, with its connotations of wisdom and godliness (*logos*), and the negative portrayal of the woman's speech, 'talkative and abusive', 'stormed', and her wagging tongue, implying noise without sense, could not be more unequivocal. The woman is freed from her misery by her 'quiet appeal', so that it is implied that it is her silence which is rewarded, and though there is enough humanity in her gaze to move the saint, the tale nevertheless ends with the 'humorous' aside, 'to the despair of her husband', suggesting that, even after this punishment, the lesson is unlikely to have been learnt, and the woman's voice will still be better unheard. The tone of this passage, of course, almost certainly reflects the attitudes of the time of its transcription (mid nineteenth century), as much as the episode described reflects attitudes in earlier centuries. In each case, society's stance has clearly been that the ideal role of the woman is a silent one.

Marina Warner, in *From the Beast to the Blonde*, has collated a wealth of information about this extremely powerful motif of women's silence in folk tradition, and gives ample evidence of the value placed on women's silence and the corresponding hatred inspired by a woman with a voice. Fairy-tales, passed on orally by women to children and to other women, were a means of exchange of views and information between women denied a public voice. The path to recognition of the female voice was not an easy one (*BB* 29):

> The last decades of the seventeenth century saw an early outbreak of feminist argument, and the right of women to voice their opinions was at the centre of the struggle. Christian tradition held the virtues of silence, obedience and discretion as especially, even essentially, feminine, but this view spread far wider than the circle of the devout. The Silent Woman was an accepted ideal. That cliché about the sex, 'Silence is golden', can be found foreshadowed in the pages of Aristotle: 'silence is a woman's glory', he writes in the *Politics*, adding, 'but this is not equally the glory of man'.

As I have noted in the Introduction to this book, the naming of the wicked in fairy-tales undoes their power, leaving only omnipotent God as the 'Unnameable'. Silence and its undoing is also part of the political power of fairy-tales (*BB* 150):

> The silent princess embodies the audience of fairytale as well as taking part in the story itself, because the tale itself exists to excite responses, to bring life, to assert vulgar rude health against pale misery and defeat, to stir laughter or wonder or tears or hope. Fairytales put an end to mutism; even when they are about dumbness and dumblings, they break the silence.

Warner reminds us (*BB* 148) that Italian literature boasts the 'foundation stone of the modern literary fairytale' in the cycle of fifty tales by the Neapolitan Giambattista Basile, published in 1634–6.[12] This contains some of the earliest written versions of stories that are now very familiar, such as 'Cinderella' and 'Sleeping Beauty'. Basile's work consists of a frame story of a princess who cannot laugh. Eventually she is moved to uproarious laughter by the sight of an old woman slipping and revealing her genitalia. The old woman then curses the princess for her laughter, and this sets in train a long series of events, including the usurping of the princess's place by a false bride and a cycle of fifty stories, ending with the restoration of the rightful princess to her place at her princely husband's side. This traditional sequence of events is told via a series of varied and exuberant tales, often bawdy and grotesque, clearly intended for an adult audience only and a long way from our modern perception of the function of a fairy-tale. Once fairy-tales moved out of the oral sphere and were written down and therefore came under the influence of publishers, with an eye to what the public would accept, fairy-tales have been adapted to suit the prevailing morality, usually leading to an increasingly submissive role for the female protagonists, until the late twentieth century, when attitudes towards women in the Western world start to change. As Warner points out (*BB* 281):

Notions of decorum for young women affected the selections of editors, too: the process by which the Grimms gradually made their heroines more polite, well-spoken, or even silent, from one edition to the next, while their wicked female characters became more and more vituperative and articulate, was replicated in mass children's publishing of the nineteenth century, and tales of plucky or disaffected young women who baulk their suitors, defy their parents or guardians and generally offer opposition to their lot often had to wait until, in the renewed feminist mood of the 1970s and 1980s, they were reclaimed by pedagogues with other views of appropriate female conduct.

The wronged daughter in fairy-tales is often the victim of incest. In early versions of stories, this is made clear: the father has incestuous desires for his daughter; but in later, more decorous versions, the unnatural behaviour is transferred, and wicked stepmothers tend to take over the role of tormentor.[13] In this context Warner refers to 'fairytale's power to speak of the unspeakable through its dreamlike distancing of the story with fantastic strokes of magic, articulate beasts and fantastic settings' (*BB* 351–2). This is of course also the case with the modern female writer's attraction for the fantastic as a story-telling mode, except that here, one suspects the 'unspeakable' is also the notion that women might have more to say than what relates entirely to the domestic, which has been their field of enquiry traditionally.

The psychological influence of fairy stories on readers and writers cannot be underestimated. Archetypal plot-lines, seen in fairy-tales, underpin many narratives in different genres and eras. Some of the most striking of these plots centre on motifs of silence, often women's silence.[14] One type depicts the daughter as a wise sybil who reveals a truth cryptically and then waits in silence for those around her to unravel it. This, for instance, happens in the tale 'Love like Salt', familiar in many cultures, in which the King asks his three daughters how much they love him. Two offer extravagant similes, but the third suggests, 'as meat loves salt'. The king casts her from him, offended, not realizing that her reticence conceals a deeper emotion than she is able to articulate. Only many years later, when the other two, shallower, daughters have betrayed him, does he chance upon the third daughter's wedding feast. Recognizing her father, the daughter orders the whole feast to be served without salt. The guests are unable to eat, and finally the father realizes what his daughter meant and weeps. Elements of this story are, of course, echoed in Shakespeare's *King Lear*.

Griselda, a character who appears in many literatures, including Boccaccio's *Decamerone* in Italian, is an example of the patient female who endures hardship and injustice without voicing complaint and is therefore considered the epitome of virtue. Notable examples of female silence occur in two of the Grimm brothers' tales, 'The Twelve Brothers' and 'The Six Swans'. The central motif of this story-type is that the sister can only save her brothers from the curse of her own birth (as she is guilty of being the only female sibling) by enduring various trials in silence until her brothers are released from the curse. When all tasks are complete and the brothers are saved, she regains her speech, can laugh, cry and proclaim her innocence. In Classical mythology, Tereus rapes Philomela and then cuts out her tongue to prevent her telling of his crime, but she weaves her account into a tapestry. This is an early example of a version of this story-type, where silence is imposed on a woman in order to conceal an injustice; and it is particularly interesting in the context of women's writing in that it depicts a means of expression that is specifically feminine, the craft of weaving, and is not speech, the traditional province of the male.[15]

'The Little Mermaid' is a relatively modern story, written by Hans Christian Andersen in 1836–7, but derived from traditional oral tales from Eastern and Western culture. With its depiction of the mutilation and silencing of a girl on the brink of womanhood, it is a particularly frightening and disturbing tale, and yet was considered suitable fare for children and enjoyed enormous popularity.[16] This story has potent psychological undertones, concerned with burgeoning female sexuality and the need to curb it or contain it by a suitable sexual match authorised by society. In traditional tales, often the female is released from her silence and suffering by sexual initiation, in versions for children presented as the rescue of the princess by a prince, the prince's kiss in 'Sleeping Beauty' being a simple and clear example of this. In this apparently harmless and well-loved tale, the princess, on reaching sexual maturity, is denied not only speech but life itself as she lies as if dead, until she is authorized, by the arrival of a sexual partner, to live and speak.

Ruth Bottigheimer has pointed out the socio-cultural implications of female silence in the Grimms' influential stories.[17] She has analysed the difference in the kind of silence or silencing experienced by male protagonists and comes to chilling conclusions:

Male silence exists, too, but it is far briefer and much less restrictive. [...]

Female and male silences differ markedly from one another [...] The redemptive female silences [...] last for years, but redemptive male silence is both brief and attenuated. [...] In social terms, women and girls at every level from peasant to princess may be deprived of speech, whereas the two men on whom silence is imposed as a redemptive precondition both emerge from lower social orders (artisan and merchant families).

[...] depriving a girl of speech is particularly effective in breaking her will. This completes the equation of speech with individual power and autonomy.

[...] Sexual vulnerability also permeates tales of muteness.[18]

In the very act of telling stories, even if they were stories about the virtue of silence, women were breaking silence and were therefore transgressing. Silence was seen as desirable by society, a means of legitimate oppression, but in fairy-tales women have had the ability to turn this around and use their silence as a form of strength, a magic spell launched against the curse upon them. In real life however, this has taken the form of secrecy, subversion or submission, and real emancipation has only come when a voice has been granted to women.

These cultural influences inevitably are reflected in some way in women's writing. Women are the natural heirs to the tradition of the telling of folk-tales, as tales used to be exchanged orally between women in domestic settings; they are also often at the centre of those tales' subject matter. The dilemma for women is how to write about themselves, but depicting themselves differently to how they have been portrayed in the past. Any discussion of the nature of women's writing entails engaging with many issues: these include female self-image, the emphasis in female writing on the physical and on familial relationships, sadism/masochism and voyeurism/fetishism, the flight into the fantastic, images of mutism and oppression, debates about language and communication.

Theoretical analysis of 'the gaze' is extremely relevant to any study of women's self-representation in literature. Vision has always been accorded special importance in the hierarchy of the senses. In classical culture, the possibility of sight was equated with being alive; Maurizio Bettini describes the myth of the statues sculpted by Daedalus, which had open eyes, endowed with a gaze, and therefore had to be tied up, otherwise they ran away: the possibility of looking (*blepein*) gave them life.

If the statue can see, it is no longer a statue. If something can move, it is somehow alive; the same apparently is true of anything that can see.[19]

In 'The Empire of the Gaze', Martin Jay summarizes the importance of vision in Western culture and how sight has been particularly privileged and often equated with understanding and the intellect. The importance given to sight has had repercussions in discussions on psychology, sexuality and politics, and it is only relatively recently that modern literary theory has seen a shift in emphasis from sight to the word.[20]

However, some of the most interesting observations on 'the gaze' have been generated by film criticism. E. Ann Kaplan draws attention to how theoretical developments in the literary field have been used by feminists to analyse the representation of women in film.[21] Women, it is suggested, have been depicted in mainstream films not as signifiers for a signified (a real woman), but rather have become an elision of the two, becoming a sign that represents something in the male unconscious. Freudian theory indicates that the male spectator's unconscious instincts lead him to represent the female in either fetishistic or voyeuristic terms (and that the male-dominant film

industry has created female figures that encourage the male spectator
to draw on these elements in his unconscious). The male gaze is
problematic, not only owing to the way it objectifies the female, but
in the domination and possession it implies (the female receives and
returns the gaze but cannot act on it). Voyeurism is linked to
dominance and control; fetishism apparently builds up the woman
into a object of beauty, phallus-like and therefore unthreatening and
satisfying as an object. Neither mechanism represents woman as
woman, but rather as non-male.

Kaplan takes all these arguments and offers the question whether
they need to be true, whether women can appropriate the gaze. She
quotes feminist critics who have refused to accept the roles suggested
for them by male and female theorists and have found 'many examples
of pleasurable identification' in Hollywood films. The double bind
comes in the realization that women have been most pleased by films
that portray them as objects of the male gaze; in other words, 'the
pleasure comes from identifying with our own objectification. Our
positioning as "to-be-looked-at", as object of the gaze, has, through
our positioning, come to be sexually pleasurable'.[22] There is no doubt
that women's fashions and female behaviour during the years of sexual
maturity (and sometimes before) show strong evidence of the female
desire to display herself as a sexual object. This is particularly true in
affluent, urban Italy, where great store is set by physical appearance
and sexual display is commonplace. Kaplan examines the
psychoanalytical reasons that may explain women's pleasure in
'objectification' and cites evidence to suggest that women's sexual
fantasies often involve her being 'the object of men's lascivious gaze'.
She notes in connection with male and female psychological
responses to film:

our culture is deeply committed to clearly demarcated sex difference, called
masculine and feminine, that revolve on, first, a complex gaze-apparatus;
and, second, dominance-submission patterns. This positioning of the two sex
genders clearly privileges the male through the mechanisms of voyeurism and
fetishism, which are male operations [...].[23]

She goes on to discuss the centrality of the significance of
motherhood and the way it is defined in our society, the importance
of the mother–daughter relationship, and the position of motherhood
in psychoanalysis. She sees motherhood as 'a place to start rethinking
sex-difference'.[24] Her conclusion is that whilst society (patriarchy) has

manipulated the gaze 'to prevent the eruption of a (mythically) feared return of the matriarchy that might take place were the close mother–child bonding returned to dominance', the origin of the gaze is 'a *mutual* gazing, rather than the subject–object kind that reduces one of the parties to the place of submission'.[25] This kind of gaze is first set in motion in the early bond between mother and child and is distorted by later conditioning. She concludes with a plea to return to this mutual relationship between the sexes, rather than the pattern of polarities, male/female, dominant/submissive, active/passive and so on. Such a conclusion validates the decision of so many women writers to scrutinize this important relationship in their work.

It is clear to me that connivance in their own objectification in an era when women have been encouraged to rethink their position in society with regard to men is bound to lead to confusion of response in all women. Women writers, hoping to create works of art that have some significance as depictions of the way life can be, and aiming to deepen our understanding of human experience, therefore find themselves in a curious situation. On the one hand they wish to show their readers what women are like and what women's lives are like, and therefore by implication what they themselves may be like; but on the other, this is bound to feel similar to self-exposure and uncomfortably close to that deliberate display familiar to the female for the purpose of awakening sexual interest in the male. In women, the desire to narrate and communicate is in conflict with a fear of speaking out, which, in the female, as we have seen, is culturally frowned upon, and also affected by a reluctance to take part in the voyeuristic/fetishistic power-play that underpins many of our relationships. This is a dilemma that does not affect men in the same way.

Italian Women Writers and Silence

We have seen how women's silence is a motif in folk- and fairy-tales, but also a political, social and psychological influence in women's lives. In Italy, this abstract imposition of silence has been mirrored by the concrete phenomenon of the absence of women writers in the canon. A movement towards the rehabilitation of women's writing has been active, but it has had an almost archaeological flavour, since women's expression has been so effectively repressed by the literary establishment in Italy. However, the twentieth century saw a burgeoning of women's writing, beginning with certain key texts and authors, notably including Sibilla Aleramo's *Una donna* (1906), Anna Banti's *Artemisia* (1947) and Natalia Ginzburg's and Elsa Morante's fiction. Silence or secrecy has often been at the heart of novels written by women, depicting lives led in obscurity and concealment, with fundamental episodes in a woman's life sources of shame rather than celebration.

The motif of silence is central to Dacia Maraini's *La lunga vita di Marianna Ucría*. Her silent duchess, a victim of incestuous abuse struck dumb by shock, is an excellent example of a direct descendant of the wronged mute girl in a fairy-tale. Maraini depicts a woman, however, who succeeds in turning her muteness to her advantage: she exploits her practical need to write as a means of basic communication, in order to acquire education, culture and eventually independence.[26] As Sharon Wood puts its (*IWW* 229): 'A number of readers in Italy understood this work as a classically feminist novel which vindicates the historic silence of women, their absence from discourse and culture, and restores them to their rightful place as subjects rather than objects of the cultural order.' The book, which also examines the mother–daughter relationship and depicts the protagonist's gradual rediscovery of her own sexuality and sense of identity, contains many of the elements central to feminist argument. These same fundamental issues are approached in Sanvitale's *Madre e figlia* (1980).

The pressures of silence on female writers, however, have affected not only the content of what they write, but also the style. Firstly, there is a strong tendency for the narrative voice to be disguised in some way. Women writers are psychologically hampered from assuming the third-person omniscient voice, which we associate with God, with maleness, with justice and truth, but also with cruelty and control. This leaves them with the first-person voice, but the female writer then runs the risk of being accused of writing thinly-veiled autobiography. The woman author is unable to write openly and authentically as a woman without shouldering a baggage of associations, so she is driven towards strategies to conceal her 'self', devising complex narrative structures and assuming disguised narrative voices. Secondly, many twentieth-century women writers in Italy have tended towards fantasy as a setting for their work. Here I am not referring to writers such as Grazia Deledda and Elsa Morante, for instance, who create fantastic or mythic worlds, but which are based closely on the familiar and domestic or on traditional social patterns.

I draw the reader's attention rather to authors such as Paola Capriolo and Francesca Duranti, in whose work the fantastic world depicted offers an alternative, though parallel, universe to modern society.[27]

Angela Carter's fiction, an area of study far too vast to approach here in any detail, has undoubtedly been influential in this area of women's writing. Carter's brilliant fictional universes are, rightly, the subject of a great deal of scholarly attention. Here I note only one striking connection, which will be of interest to students of Italian literature and is relevant to our discussions of the power of the gaze: the parallels between Carter's women's prison in *Nights at the Circus* and Capriolo's prison in two of the stories in *La grande Eulalia*,[28] and the link between both of these and Foucault's prison in *Surveiller et punir*.[29] All three writers depict a lone jailer who sees all. The dominant and punishing nature of 'the gaze' is evident, but it seems to me there is another, even more insidious aspect that affects how women write. The prison governor in these created environments is an omniscient, Godlike figure. His gaze is ambiguous: it is both just and oppressive. (Carter's jailer is a woman and an unpunished murderess herself, and is therefore an ambiguous figure in all senses, typical in this writer's fiction, underlining and parodying the accepted 'norms' in society.) At the same time, as Foucault points out, if we are forced to gaze upon something detestable (he gives the example of a public execution), our own gaze can become an instrument of others' power over us, by enabling them to instil fear into us. The *auto da fé*, in fact, in Maraini's *La lunga vita di Marianna Ucría* has precisely this function, intended to impress upon the child the supposedly God-given authority and respectability of the oppressive, terrifying and cruel ruling élite.

I would argue, then, that the movement away from the 'real' and the everyday in some modern women's writing is part of a strategy aimed at deflecting the reader's attention from the writer as female. If a female writer describes the everyday world, there is a tendency to pigeonhole her work as 'trivial' or loosely autobiographical. Indeed, women writers have themselves traditionally been drawn to this kind of writing, for the reason that inevitably their experience was circumscribed by the domestic.[30] A twentieth-century woman writer, by deliberately setting her story beyond the boundaries of the everyday, side-steps these criticisms and avoids the temptation to slip into autobiography.

Natalia Ginzburg is an example of a female writer who has been at pains to avoid the pitfalls (as she assesses them) of autobiography. Her fictional protagonists have therefore been as far from her real 'self' as possible, distanced by her famously laconic style as well as by the background and experience she attributes to them. However, as we have noted in the previous chapter, and as has exercised critics, curiously, even her autobiography lacks the personal details about the autobiographer that one would expect from an author of either gender. Her journalism is far more 'personal' than her autobiography, and a stronger individual voice emerges. This is a different kind of displacement of the female protagonist, in a process whereby the figure normally central to the autobiographical genre disappears altogether. In *Lessico famigliare* she is present only through the vision of the world she conveys and through occasional references to her by other characters, often somewhat negative in tone ('non da spago', for instance, as Natalia's mother likes to say). The title of the collection of Ginzburg's radio conversations, *È difficile parlare di sé*, is highly significant. Her granddaughter notes Ginzburg's reactions to the experience of taking part in these conversations in the preface to the book:

Era stanca, diceva, ma anche contenta. 'È difficile parlare di sé, ma bello' m'aveva raccontato. Della seconda telefonata, ricordo una nota particolarmente triste nella voce. Si sentiva un po' messa a nudo, e me lo fece capire.

Later, she adds:

C'era in lei un silenzio, un silenzio intimo e profondo. [...] Ma era il suo un silenzio per nulla ozioso, anzi galoppante, arioso e meditabondo. Un silenzio dove lei riusciva sempre a trovare una voce, cosí da poter scrivere e commentare i fatti del mondo [...].[31]

I suspect this positive interpretation of the mood of her grandmother's silence may be wishful thinking on the part of Lisa Ginzburg and that Natalia's silence was more painful than this description suggests. Nevertheless, the point remains that Ginzburg found it difficult to speak of herself and felt exposed when tempted into doing so. This is a kind of template for the experience of many women writers attempting to express themselves in a world of words that is not favourable to the female voice or familiar with it.

Francesca Sanvitale's 'messaggio senza suoni' in *Madre e figlia*

Sanvitale's best-known and probably most admired work is *Madre e figlia*. The novel centres on the intense relationship between mother (Marianna) and daughter (Sonia). In the early part of the account we learn of Marianna's life as a child and young woman, adored and pampered by her well-educated, rich parents, in aristocratic society in the late nineteenth and early twentieth centuries. Through descriptions of her family background, we experience the glamour of the Austro-Hungarian empire. Disappointment in love and the death of her beloved father combine to drive Marianna into a disastrous liaison with a handsome, married officer, by whom she has one daughter, Sonia. The officer, deceitful, neglectful, resentful of his sudden responsibility, keeps a chilly distance, visiting just often enough to become a frightening and inhibiting figure for both mother and daughter. Reduced to a life of subterfuge and loneliness, isolated with her illegitimate child in a hostile environment, Marianna retreats into a psychological blankness, which forces an unbearable emotional burden onto her daughter, through whose eyes the story is told. Sonia's account creates an evocative picture: Milan in the Fascist years, her education as a social outcast amongst nuns, a life moving from one dismal rented room to another in an attempt to escape the wrath of her father's vengeful wife, in short, two vulnerable people attempting to live a discreet and 'respectable' life in a prejudiced, increasingly violent and morally confused society.

Sonia's adolescence and sexual awakening are marked by experiences with male relatives and friends that the modern reader might describe as abusive, but which the narrator, emotionally numb, presents as merely strange, further examples of an inexplicable world. She seems to experience them in neutral mode, and it is left to the reader to decided what damage has been done. Later, she drifts into sexual encounters and marriage, still with the sense of dislocation that has marked her life. Sonia desperately shoulders responsibility for her mother from an early age, and it is clear that this pattern of duty coupled with guilt and resentment has been set from the very beginning. The result is an oscillation between the two women of love, hate and exasperation. Women's bodies are portrayed not as objects of desire or instruments of power, but rather as their destiny; abortion, miscarriage, childbirth and breast cancer are described with brutal frankness. Even at the lowest point of Sonia's mother's physical decay however, the two women engage in rivalry over the young doctor treating her cancer. Women's dependence on men, financially and emotionally, and their correspondingly ambiguous attitude to one another are examined pitilessly. Theirs is to a great extent a willed dependency: by the end of the novel we discover that the officer's wife was never in pursuit of her husband's illegitimate family, and we are obliged to conclude that the women preferred to believe in the almost fairy-tale wickedness of another woman rather than in the banal fact of the officer's neglect. The book ends with Marianna's death, but Sonia is still attached to her mother by a bond of passionate love that has barely loosened.

Madre e figlia is particularly significant in the field of women's writing in straddling fiction and autobiography in a manner that chimes with the modern preoccupation with differences and similarities between the two genres. It is important not to concentrate too much on the figure of the author, and I fully concur with Ann Jefferson's warning against 'the presumption that authors never talk of anything except themselves'.[32] I do not propose to return to this method of criticism, and all the books I discuss in this study are literary artefacts, even those that might normally be defined as chronicles or as documentary in intention, such as Ginzburg's autobiography or Levi's account. However, it is clear that, just as both these texts, by their very nature, inevitably invite comparison with the author's life, so *Madre e figlia* also invites this kind of comparison, being both autobiography and novel.

In her collection of essays, *Camera ottica*, Sanvitale offers a kind of 'factual' gloss on her novelized version of the relationship between mother and daughter.[33] 'Il mito e la persona', in the section called 'Mia madre'(*CO* 183–7), reads like a summary of the components of the novel: the author describes the love between mother and daughter, a glorious, abandoned love more familiar in descriptions of sexual passion; she describes their happiness, but also delineates the uncertainty and difficulty of the situation of mother and daughter, in the absence of the father husband, two women living without the social and financial protection of a male figure in the Italy of the 1930s. The tone, however, is ultimately positive, with Sanvitale's perspective as a wise, lucid, now mature observer, clear and overt. Here the voice of the essayist and the subject of her narrative (herself when younger) are as one; this essay is a lyrical and moving account, presented as fact.

Many of the same details, the same stimuli, are at the heart of *Madre e figlia*, but in this work, the tone is different, some other aspects of femaleness and darker sides of this seminal relationship, emerge as a result of this being a creative work. I do not seek to establish which account is more 'true' in terms of Sanvitale's biography, as this is a literary study, not a biography of any of the authors whose work I examine. However, the work of art conveys nuances of female experience that are not apparent in the essay, and I would argue that the method of conveying them is related to the instinct of the female to conceal herself and therefore consists of a type of writing that I suggest is specifically or typically feminine.

In 'Autobiografia e no', Sanvitale begins with the observation that writing often seems to have occurred independently of its author: the author, rereading her own work after some time has passed, wonders whether and how she could have produced this material (*CO* 188):

> Dunque il sospetto di uno sdoppiamento, il dubbio sgradevole di trovarsi davanti ad un prodotto estraneo. Prevalgono stupore e qualche volta persino ammirazione per pagine che sembrano inedite perché dimenticate. O, al contrario, vergogna e ancora stupore per un uso dell'espressività che non si condivide piú, che di sicuro non ci appartiene, *non è nostra*. In tutti i casi, negativi e positivi, la scrittura è diventata 'altro' che non si potrà ripetere né imitare. Ciò che ci ha preso anni di lavoro e vita, si è allontanato per sempre.

This statement is interesting taken in connection with psychoanalytical observations regarding the unconscious: creative writing seems to stem from a source in the mind that is at least partially ruled by the unconscious.[34] This suggests that psychological influences and pressures affect all writers far more than they are consciously aware of, in turn implying that women's experience as females sets them apart from males and may make them write differently. This is not, as Sharon Wood warns, allowing oneself to fall into the 'trap of biologism, whereby anatomy rather than literary or political effect effect is seen to be the repository of value',[35] but acknowledging that a woman's psychological conditioning is different on account of important cultural factors.

In fact, Sanvitale now addresses this question of the difference between male and female writers in an important discussion of the nature of literary creativity, in which the image of the silent woman is significant. She says that all writers are affected by the times in which they live, so there is both a cultural and a subjective process at work.

Psychological pressures on a woman writer are enormous, she says, because women are far more bound than men by what is expected of them in society. Men have a psychological mandate to use words, bestowed by society, whereas women labour under a parallel psychological restraint. Men have an entire literary history behind them to validate their endeavours; women start from a different standpoint (CO 192–3):

La singolarità, ovvero unicità di chi scrive, è innegabile, tuttavia, lo scrittore, anche se inconsciamente, è un minuscolo anello, un esempio di un ondivago percorso storico dal quale è impossibile dissociarsi o sfuggire. [...] Non c'è discrezione od opposizione che resista allo spirito del tempo, la colla che lega inesorabilmente l'orizzonte storico agli scrittori e alla loro formazione.

E cerchiamo di capire almeno la sovrastruttura di questa 'unicità'. Per chiarezza espositiva parlerò di un processo culturale e un processo soggettivo di individuazione, quindi psicologico. Può valere nello stesso modo per ambedue i sessi? Non ne sono sicura. Sono sicura che, nel caso di una donna, ancora oggi e forse per molti altri anni, il secondo punto rappresenta, in modo piú essenziale e fondante, il fulcro della questione, senza il quale non si dà scrittura ed è quello che richiede piú tempo e piú forza morale, la forza che occorre a imporre libertà al proprio mondo poetico.

Credete che sia poco? È moltissimo. Per una donna è una fatica particolarmente dolorosa, silenziosa, inafferrabile spesso, che ha nascosto in passato (e forse nasconderà in futuro) rese sconosciute, talenti sprecati, silenzi. [...] Il primo punto era ed è arrivare al rifiuto interiore dei padri e delle madri, che non sono solo famiglia di partenza e di arrivo, ma gruppo sociale, stato sociale, resa dei conti a pressioni indistinte che pure negano la libertà del cuore e si configurano come larve intorno al tavolo di lavoro [...].

Le donne, a differenza degli uomini, sono piegate da una speciale paura, hanno sempre vissuto cercando di corrispondere a ciò che si voleva da loro, immerse nel silenzioso corteo che le accompagna dall'infanzia alla morte. Spesso sono riuscite e riescono con apparente indipendenza a mimetizzarlo, nasconderlo, lasciare che esista solo nel profondo della loro vita inconscia. Ma il risultato si ritrova proprio nel 'taglio' del mondo poetico.

[...]

Ma sorge spontanea una domanda: perché una tale difficoltà di individuazione dovrebbe essere diversa per gli uomini e per le donne? Perché è la storia che ci dà un mandato, anche interiore, o ce la nega. Il salvacondotto verso la parola che viene dalla libertà della psiche non è stato mai concesso alle donne 'ufficialmente' e siamo arrivate solo allo stato di fatto che di solito precede la legge. Qualsiasi legge non può essere sottintesa ma deve essere chiaramente espressa e condivisa dalla comunità. La libertà interiore dello scrittore maschio ha alle spalle la storia della letteratura. Non è la stessa partenza.

She goes on to speak in more detail of the influence of family and others on the female writer and the sense of needing to justify oneself with these ghostly observers and critics, leading to self-censorship ('la censura su se stessi') and a tendency to select 'tranquille imprese letterarie', 'safe' narrative themes (CO 195). This chimes with the discussions in the extensive writing about women's autobiography and autobiographical fiction, where critics have noted precisely these features in women's writing.[36]

Nevertheless, despite these perceived obstacles, Sanvitale's recurrent concern has been with the problem of representing realtà, a task she considers to be central to the writer's art. She also made the choice to create female figures as part of a personal investigation into the nature of identity (SW 97): 'prima dovevo affrontare personaggi femminili proprio per una ricerca di identità'. Mother–daughter relationships are an important element of this investigation. In Camera ottica, Sanvitale talks of the mirror effect of mother and daughter and its effect on women's writing. The mirror and women's relationship with their own selves reflected have been the subject of detailed study, both in psychoanalytical and cultural terms.[37] Images, self-images and external models of looks and behaviour play an important part in Madre e figlia, where the two female protagonists are constantly aware of their 'reflection', whether in other people's estimation or in photographs or representations of filmstars they feel they should emulate. Sanvitale says that generally women have written from the daughter's point of view, and she defines the daughter's relationship with her mother specifically as seeing the mother as a mirror image of her own self and yet a figure that does not yield her secret, which is no less than the elusive secret of feminine identity (CO 209):

La madre sta di fronte, è la figura al di là dello specchio [...] però il personaggio fino all'ultima pagina sfugge, non si concede alle suppliche, resta inconoscibile come se tanto spreco d'attaccamento, di contrasti e di dolore alla fine non sia servito ad avviciniarsi, a capire la reciproca femminilità. Il segreto che la madre tiene per sé e che la figlia non riuscirà mai a svelare.

This puzzle regarding identity expresses itself in Madre e figlia with the shifts from one voice to another, as has been noted,[38] but all critics assume the author writes ultimately as Sonia because of the autobiographical correspondences. However, Sanvitale has implied that she identifies at least as closely with Marianna (SW 101):

sono affezionata alla figura di Marianna, la contessina protagonista del romanzo *Madre e figlia*, non posso dire che sia completamente altro da me, perché fa parte di un universo femminile a me non estraneo.

In the context of a search for identity, this fluidity reflects confusion, on the part of the narrator, whoever that may be, but also the fundamental confusion of identity of modern woman, torn between traditional images of femininity, the perfect mother and lover, and ideals of freedom, independence and equality in a masculine world. In the Wright interview, Sanvitale talks of the 'malattia' of the protagonist, saying, 'c'è la questione della malattia della protagonista, che ha qualcosa di simbiotico con la malattia di mia madre' (SW 94). Again, the author blends the two identities, making a link between the protagonist daughter in the book, the fictional representation of her own 'self', and the real-life figure of the writer's mother. There is a shifting in and out of the identities of the two women, as pointed out by Ann Caesar in a comment endorsed by Sanvitale herself (*CO* 209): 'narrator and reader, mother and daughter slide in and out of each other, interact in such a way as to create a sense of continuity in and beyond the narrative itself'. The *malattia* consists at least partly in this confusion of identity.

Her declared method of representing reality is by means of detail. This is clear from the essays in *Camera ottica*, and also is notable in her interview with Simona Wright. In *Camera ottica* (*CO* 198), Sanvitale says of Kafka's *Metamorphosis*:

Ma l'irreale astrazione di una metamorfosi impossibile, è resa possibile solo attraverso un senso estremo della realtà, solo attraverso la scelta di particolari ossessivi, significanti e precisi [...]. Questo, infatti, è ciò che chiamo senso della realtà e pregnanza dei particolari. Non certo l'appropriarsi di uno smalto visivo proprio di qualsiasi storia da teleschermo.

[...]

I particolari: mi pare persino che l'arte della scrittura nasca di lí e vi finisca, ed essi siano la gioia sicura di uno scrittore che se ormai crede di aver perso il bandolo della vita, ha trovato alla fine, attraverso questa piccola sapienza, quello della scrittura.

This emphasis on detail can be described in terms of any of the senses, but Sanvitale relies most often on the visual, and consciously privileges the visual, as she suggests in a selection of quotations from Flannery O'Connor, which she gives in Italian at the end of this chapter of *Camera ottica* (*CO* 202). For instance:

'Per lo scrittore di narrativa tutto trova verifica nell'occhio, organo che, alla fin fine, implica l'intera personalità, e quanto piú mondo riesca a contenere. Implica il giudizio. Il giudizio è una cosa che ha origine nell'atto della visione, e quando non parte di lí, o ne è scisso, allora nella mente esiste una confusione che si trasferirà nel racconto.'

'I narratori che non danno importanza a questi particolari concreti peccano di quella che Henry James definiva "specificazione fiacca". L'occhio scivola via sulle parole e l'attenzione si assopisce.'

So, Sanvitale describes the condition of the woman writing, acutely and personally aware of her critical audience and unendorsed by a male-dominated literary history; she lays emphasis on the faculty of sight and visual details as a means of conveying reality, and the piece finishes with a statement that despite the 'singolarità' of the writer, s/he must be aware of 'una fatale cancellazione [...], la cancellazione di un io che deve via via essere superato e dimenticato' (CO 203). Although Sanvitale mentions this in connection with Flannery O'Connor, it is also consistent with the displacement of the female figure, seen regularly in women's writing. The central female character assumes a shadowy nature or is all but invisible; often a narrative is related by someone not at its centre; an omniscient female narrator is extremely rare, though she is disguised sometimes as a male voice.

In the interview with Simona Wright, we are reminded of Sanvitale's early career in television as a scriptwriter. Sanvitale stresses that she perceives a strong link between the two forms of communication, screenplay and writing, but the difference is in 'espressività'. This she feels can only be found 'nella parola poetica o nell'immagine rappresentativa di un romanzo' (SW 89). There is strong emphasis on 'la facoltà visiva' (SW 92). She wants her characters to be psycho-logically coherent and their visible actions to be consistent with their inner selves (SW 91): 'La psicologia è una cosa seria. Se un personaggio fa un certo gesto, questo deve corrispondere ad un suo essere interiore, di pensiero e di azione.' However, 'la narrativa non è l'arte del pensiero [...] è l'arte di visualizzare il pensiero' (SW 92). This is a strikingly clear statement of her poetics, borne out in her fiction, which has strong echoes of Peter Schwenger's textual envisioning. Perhaps this is one of the ways in which words can be more powerful than visual images, as the suggestion of words is infinite whereas pictures tend to be self-limiting.

In this same interview, Sanvitale goes on to discuss the power of words and how reality 'ci arriva attraverso le parole' (SW 94). This goes further than merely stating the obvious, that reality is described or conveyed by writers via words: for Sanvitale and, she suggests, for many poets and writers the world is actually created and made real in the mind of a person by means of words. This is made very clear in *Madre e figlia* when Sonia starts to name objects as a result of learning to read and write, and the naming of the objects gives them reality (*MF* 32). This concept is disturbing in the context of imposed female silence, as it is clear that if a mental landscape is created by words, the imposition of silence is bound to have far-reaching psychological effects. Indeed, the social and emotional vulnerability of the women in Sanvitale's novel is reflected by Marianna's carelessness in naming objects. In this section of the book, the thematics of silence emerges clearly, and secrecy, loneliness, vulnerability and wordlessness are all seen to be connected (*MF* 31):

Un'ombra silenziosa avvolgeva la signora Marianna e Sonia nella casa di via Porpora e sapeva di magia. 'Silenziosa' perché la sensazione di chi entrava in quella casa era che non esistessero oggetti e quelli che si vedevano fossero per disposizione di una cattiva fata fissi al loro posto, inservibili, resi finti. La loro solitudine era completa e cosí nulla di quello che vive in una casa aveva occasione di essere nominato ad alta voce e inoltre la signora Marianna giorno per giorno perdeva l'uso di tante parole.

Verso Paola (1991) places silence versus language at its heart and links it specifically to sexuality. The protagonist's wife has developed a love-making technique based entirely on her skill with words, and it is this which fascinates the protagonist. He revels in the delicious sensuality of his wife's use of words both to signal imminent love-making and during the act itself, so that the words replace the woman herself and acquire the status of a fetish (*VP* 6–7):

Che cosa c'era di meglio che giacere passivo recipiente di un impasto perfetto di parole che oltre alla beatitudine della ragione offrisse la beatitudine delle immagini e diventasse un percorso verso il piacere del corpo?

Without this gift for sexualizing herself via language, Matilde would lose all her sexual or even human appeal: 'Matilde senza le corde vocali sarebbe diventata un inutile fagotto' (*VP* 12). Nevertheless, he seeks out a mistress who is the opposite, who is wordless during sex and cautiously parsimonious with language generally. The mistress, Evelina, 'usava il linguaggio, conscia di servirsi di un mezzo ad alto grado di pericolosità e difficoltà, diventato equivocabile e usurato' (*VP* 13). In this novel, words and silence are made an essential element of the interaction between the sexes. But for the male protagonist, having reached a crisis in his life, he feels drawn to a solution defined by silence. Though he is unable to explain exactly in what way silence plays a part, there is an obvious implication that he seeks escape from the power exercised over him by the words of a woman (*VP* 14–15):

arrivato a un parossismo d'inquietudine, quando niente di ciò che aveva contribuito a costruire, casa rapporti carriera, gli sembrava confacente, avanzavano quietandolo e spingendolo verso la notte due grandi pensieri [...]: un sistema di vita dove predominasse il silenzio (e immaginava di lasciare Matilde e costruire un novo rapporto con Evelina) e ipotesi continue di allontanamento da ciò che conosceva, che in qualche modo sempre con il silenzio avevano a che fare, ma che riguardavano solo lui.

The importance given to words in Sanvitale's fiction imbues them with an almost totemic status and they themselves become objectified. As a writer and an individual, she has stated that she deplores the loss of power of the word (SW 102):

La parola perde ogni giorno di significato, non ha piú quel valore polisemico che era una sua caratteristica peculiare, sembra non voler dire piú niente. Le smentite, ad esempio, in Italia sono all'ordine del giorno, si può dire tutto e smentire tutto [...]. La parola non ha piú valore, e non esistendo piú il valore non esiste neanche la punizione per il delitto di parola, per cui io posso dare di ladro, di assassino, di vigliacco a qualcuno, e mentre cento anni fa c'erano i duelli, gli schiaffi, le denunce, oggi mi sembra che tutti possano dire tutto, e questo è orribile. Questa svalutazione è pericolosissima anche per gli intellettuali e per gli scrittori, perché non dare un significato importante alla parola significa non credere piú che la letteratura abbia un senso profondo, per se stessa, ma che sia un gioco, o peggio una utilizzazione, e questo non può che portare alla morte della letteratura.

This examination of Sanvitale's creative world, then, reveals that words are essential to create objective reality, yet they are themselves objectified; and also she declares a 'rapporto intensissimo con gli oggetti' (SW 95), with emphasis on detail being the means of conveying reality, including psychological states. It seems to me that these are complex relationships and that there are illuminating links between an interest in objects, a fetishization and objectification of language, and the notion of the female writer objectifying and being objectified. I would argue that Sanvitale's very striking stylistic devices are a response stimulated by the intrinsic contradiction of female reluctance to speak, coupled with her desire to tell. These devices are not only a focus on detail, but also recourse to connections with paintings, cinema, photography and framed images; in short, emphasis on the visual filtered through society's cultural and artistic influences. These connections take the form of narrative techniques, but also emerge in the content of the text.

Other critics have noted the book's tendency to use photographic images; for instance, Wood speaks of 'a series of snapshot memories' (*IWW* 241). However, the technique is more accurately defined as cinematographic. The striking opening is a 'sequence' of the different eras of the mother, her image in photograph and memory appearing, then 'fading' as in film into the next image. Alongside this stylistic technique, we also find film culture, theatre or spectacle, depicted as an integral part of the lives described in the text, and actually shaping the attitudes of the protagonists. Mother and daughter go to films. They initially love Shirley Temple, but eventually are sickened by the film sequence representing the father as a drooling baby, because it offends their sense of how the world should be, with the male figures as dominant and responsible. Sonia casts herself and her uncle, in their incestuous entanglement, as stars in an Audrey Hepburn film. There are images of the circus, the opera; Zio Paris promises Sonia that, when she grows up, she will have a stadium full of people at her feet, as witnesses validating her beauty.

The women in the book see themselves in cinematic terms in a world of reflection. The rich and detailed descriptions of fashionable clothing are images imposed on women (and selected and embraced by them); but there is a sinister progression between accepting the apparently harmless roles offered for women by all these visual prompts, and the behaviour of the female in real and important episodes in her life. Even the incestuous encounter with Zio Paris is seen in terms of a 'commedia': it becomes the 'volgare e lasciva caccia tra serva e padrone', and Sonia reacts 'come una puttanella da commedia' (*MF* 108). Her mother's refusal to see what is happening between Zio Paris and her daughter at this point is later interpreted by Sonia as 'una losca omertà' (*MF* 109). The notion of *omertà*, normally associated with discussion of the Mafia, meaning the conspiracy of silence surrounding a crime or injustice inspired by fear and a sense of hopelessness, is only too appropriate as an image of her mother's general attitude to the condition of women.

Or else the 'theatre' of the women's lives takes the form of a set-piece predetermined by custom, so the visits of the absent father are described as 'il rito richiesto' of the 'guerriero nel castello' (*MF* 111).

These roles are not always played out willingly by either party, but rather somewhat wearily. Eventually fantasy and the distance from daily reality that Sonia has cultivated and lived throughout her life becomes preferable to reality. She realizes that she has always fantasized about 'il tema dell'incontro fra uomo e donna, vissuto come in un film o un racconto, quindi irreale' (*MF* 204). However, she asserts that this process confers 'libertà', suggesting a wider and controversial issue that perhaps the much derided subject matter of women's literature through the centuries, the romantic and sentimental ideal love affair, by offering escape from everyday reality, actually confers freedom rather than merely reflecting women's slavery. The fact that Sonia really believes this presents her as a truly helpless victim of these idealized images. At any rate, this frame of mind has become habitual. Sonia does not wish her pleasant fantasy about her mother's young doctor to be disturbed by the intrusion of reality (*MF* 209):

Preferiva portarsi a casa le immagini, la gioia già passata della sigaretta e del silenzio, delle parole scambiate, delle espressioni già diverse e trasferirle nel patrimonio raccolto nella grotta delle fantasticherie.

This idea of role-playing between men and women, even in their most intimate encounters, is a troubling concept for Sanvitale. She has spoken of how sexuality is said to differ for men and women, admitting she cannot imagine the difference (SW 97):

Non ho mai capito quale fondamentale differenza potesse esserci [...] nel valore di un'esperienza sessuale. Mi sfuggivano completamente le distinzioni, che credo derivino da una differente impostazione culturale.

She goes on to speak of her horror at the idea of 'un sesso teatralizzato', in which the two people play a role and therefore waste this opportunity for harmony and remain isolated: 'In questo modo l'atto sessuale, che potrebbe essere un momento di grande comunione e di grande conoscenza, diventa un momento di grande solitudine e falsità.' Her short stories emphasize the impossibility of genuine and natural relationships and the tendency of the female partner to put on a 'show', but usually because the man requires it, so that the woman becomes 'una attrice del sesso, piuttosto che una partecipante attiva'. In such a case, the woman's and the man's role turn in to a form of voyeurism and exhibitionism at the same time.

It is of course logical to relate this way of seeing to Sanvitale's earlier career as a scriptwriter; nevertheless, I feel there is a profounder meaning to this way of representing the world. The depiction of theatre, film and spectacle as central to the women's lives suggests a view of life as something externalized, to be lived for its outward appearance to others, life merely as something to be viewed by others. Zio Paris makes it explicit that self-esteem comes through the filter of other people's gaze: 'nessun specchio ti dirà mai quanto sei bella come i miei occhi' (*MF* 98). The emphasis on objects and on visual techniques both deflects the reader's attention from the inner workings of the characters, whilst at the same time illustrating them highly effectively. In this paradox of style, Sanvitale achieves an aura of privacy around her central characters, but with no loss of immediacy: by concentrating on visual detail, the writer depicts both characters and emotions accurately but also succeeds in maintaining a distance as a narrator. This is surely a means of showing without revealing. Its indirectness is its significant aspect, and goes some way towards solving the tension between the female desire to display and the fear of exposure, the fetish and voyeur relationship.

In countless examples, we see the female objectified, portrayed in terms of an image, often with her happy compliance: a fashion-plate, a photograph, a film star, a brothel photograph. Sonia learns early the power of the female body, however grotesque that body might sometimes be. When her father takes her to see the dancers (another theatrical spectacle), along with a mass of men, including soldiers, 'un muro grigioverde e puzzolente', her response is ambiguous, 'gioia malvagia', a sense that she has been permitted to see something not meant for her. The passage conveys both disgust at what she sees, but also a perverse delight, which is later echoed in her perverse connivance at Zio Paris' incestuous enslavement (*MF* 52):

Le cosce rosa e incipriate delle ballerine che si alzavano, traballanti e molli, avevano una stonata oscena sgradevolezza che la faceva sconfinare nella gioia. Lo sballottio dei grossi seni tra i lustrini, l'ondeggiare dei fianchi, degli ombelichi nudi, i lamentevoli acuti titillanti e le risate sopratono che slargavano bocche fiammeggianti e unte, le comunicavano un tremito che poteva essere voglia di ridere o di piangere, come il solletico puó diventare una tortura.

The use of the idioms of film and the conjuring up of images taken from art, episodes all 'framed' either by an imaginary camera or the edges of a painting, form part of the voyeuristic texture of the book. Within this are many scenes in which someone spies voyeuristically on someone else. The emotive and slightly pejorative word *spiare* is often used: for instance, Sonia's avid gazing on the naked body of the suicide, Iris (*MF* 30), Sonia noting with irritation the cleaner's transformation into honoured guest 'Dalla porta socchiusa della sua stanza, Sonia spiava' (*MF* 129), or her sense of exclusion seeing the caring husband tending to his wife in the hospital, 'Spiava gli sguardi di intesa tra i due (*MF* 175).

The adolescent Sonia connives at the voyeur–exhibitionist relationship with her uncle when she allows him to glimpse her naked through her bedroom door and sees herself in terms of 'una vecchia fotografia da casino', photographs which are themselves examples of voyeurism (*MF* 96–7). Voyeurism is everywhere, is part of the texture of the book and is intrinsic to the women's condition: they feel themselves obliged to observe only, and not act. They are in fact invisible because of their social position. The writer then observes her protagonists, observes herself writing about them, and observes them observing the world. The cumulative effect of these layers of images is a further paradox, because the method acts to deflect the gaze, to protect the female from exposure, ultimately, despite her apparent self-revelation.

Frequent direct comparison with painting throughout *Madre e figlia* intensifies this distancing effect. The overtly conjured portrait 'simile a un quadro di Casorati' is a good example (*MF* 80–1). Likening scenes of real life to paintings introduces a note of artificiality and stasis wholly in keeping with the situation and emotional attitudes of the women depicted, and enhances the sense of distance and emotional detachment between writer/protagonist and reader.

If Sanvitale concentrates on objects, in *Madre e figlia* she objectifies the body too. This takes the form of giving women's bodies and their objectification a central role in the narrative. Women judge themselves by their looks, their bodies and their clothes, so Sonia compares herself with Costanza, and Marianna's threadbare red woollen suit denounces her as poor and lacking respectability. Nevertheless, this same object has power. Sonia knowingly uses the beauty of her adolescent body to torment her uncle Paris (*MF* 96–7). The female body is the site of great suffering, where the physical and emotional are inextricably linked. The book is testimony to the physical and psychological pain associated with the female body: miscarriage, abortion, mastectomy. The sites of the body dedicated to passion in idealized worlds here are mutilated and savaged. A harrowing passage is the account of Sonia's visit to the hospital to give birth to the child that has died *in utero*. Sanvitale uses the effects which have become familiar to us; once more the reality of Sonia's situation, her sense of isolation and loneliness is translated into an artificial, visual scenario imagined by the character (*MF* 176):

In un quadro lei sarebbe stata messa in un angolo e gli altri della saletta, una società intera, di fronte, nello schema del processo, a fissarla con sospetto.

After the operation, she weeps, covering her face with both hands, one hand over her eyes, one over her mouth, ashamed of her feelings, as if covering the visual evidence of her distress will be enough to hide it effectively (*MF* 177). Now her body is 'una tomba scoperchiata'. The people around her refuse to talk about what has happened or the dead child. Words suddenly have no meaning, Sonia can hear herself speak, her own words, but 'non le pensava piú'. Her trauma now expresses itself in fanatical application to crossword puzzles: meaningful words have been denied her, so she concentrates on meaning devoid of context, where there are words without communication. This is a powerful metaphor for the inability of the outside world to understand the traumas connected with women's experience and the necessity for women to find means of using words differently to express their emotions without 'embarrassing' the rest of society.

I have said that the body, particularly the female body, becomes a focus of attention, but the hands of both sexes are often used to express emotion. This in itself has links with techniques in painting, theatre and dance, where gesture replaces facial or verbal expression. By focusing on the hands of both men and women as a means of conveying emotion, Sanvitale transfers reference from the psychological state of the protagonists to their bodies, using the hand as an emblem of response. The examples of this use are too numerous to list exhaustively here, and the significance of the hands will strike the reader also in many of the passages I quote in this chapter, but I select a few instances here to illustrate the point. When Sonia has confronted Marianna with her knowledge that her mother is not married and has shamed her into quivering deference, she grasps her mother's hands in pity. The hands represent the mother's isolation, poverty and social and physical reduction; they also represent the moment of reconciliation between mother and daughter (*MF* 132):

Si inginocchiò vicino alla madre neonata e le prese le mani. Erano gonfie, fredde e ruvide. Le avvicinò alla bocca e le scaldò con il fiato.

In the nightmarish description of the abortion, the doctor's hands are a constant focus (*MF* 148–52): 'disse il ginecologo lavandosi le mani', 'stava infilandosi i guanti di gomma. Vide la mano alzata, le dita spalancate, schifose nella gomma trasparente', 'le mani del carnefice', 'alzò la mano con il guanto insanguinato sulle dite'. The Cimabue Christ, rescued from the mud of the floods in Florence, is raised by 'mani pietose', in a complex, multilayered image of an artistic representation, viewed on a television screen, representing emotion transmitted through the centuries and conveyed in terms that could be used to describe a painting of, for instance, the deposition of Christ, the 'mani pietose' tenderly bearing the body (*MF* 160–2). A final example of extended focus on the hand is the scene in which signor Andrea teaches the child Sonia to dance, and in the process, involves her in sly sexual gratification, mainly for himself, but also, controversially, to some extent for Sonia. Here, the older man's gradual seduction of the child during a dance is a ballet of hand movements, and even the girl's response to his engorged penis is described in its relation to her hand by the word *prensile* (*MF* 60–2):

La mano destra si posava cauta e ferma dietro la chiena di Sonia, la sinistra prendeva dolcemente la sua mano [...]. [...] con la mano alla sua spalla [...]. La mano del signor Andrea premeva sulla schiena [...]. La piccola mano nella mano del signor Andrea stava acquattata come in un nido, il signor Andrea piegava il braccio vicino al petto, portava il nido con la manina vicino al cuore [...]. [...] la mano dietro alla schiena si spostava in una carezza continua [...]. Il suo corpo [...] era cera molle tra le mani del signor Andrea. [...] Teneva la manina nella sua, sotto la vita, vicino al suo corpo. Nel buio del salotto rosso appoggiò la manina che aveva aperto con delicata autorità, dalla sua mano sul suo corpo, in basso, all'inguine, dove Sonia sentí qualcosa di gonfio, solido, un oggetto piacevole e prensile. Il signor Andrea tratteneva la manina coprendola con la sua [...].

This emphasis on the hands in such a scene, adding to the sense of detachment, both psychological and physical, is part of the highly sophisticated exploration in *Madre e figlia* of the nature of sexual experience.

There are many possible examples of this method of depicting the emotional via complex visual montage effects, but detailed analysis of a few scenes will suffice to show how this emotional displacement onto objects functions, and how it is sustained through long passages of narrative, acquiring an inner narrative logic of its own. One instance is the contrast between the social situation of Sonia's cousins,

Aldo and Elisa, and her own position. The cousins are securely
bourgeois, living in comfort in a pleasant home, sanctioned by the
marriage, the legal status, of their parents, Marianna's cousins. This
security is rendered by a visual image. First, there is the description of
the apartment (*MF* 70):

Una fuga serena di stanze, dove in pace riposavano ritratti di sposi e bambini
in cornici d'argento, bomboniere e scatole, un pianoforte con uno scialle
rosso fino a terra.

This is clearly cinematographic and visual in inspiration: the eye (or
camera) follows the succession of rooms, alighting on objects. The first
objects are in themselves visual representations (portraits), framed in
their turn; then there are boxes, containing good and desirable things,
and finally the piano, covered with a shawl. Images are placed within
images: the picture within a picture of the portraits, then our inner eye
sees what is next described then imagines the possible contents of the
boxes or the patina of the hidden wood of the piano. There is a piling
up of visual stimuli, all related to domestic well-being.

Similarly, the comfortable, secure tenor of the cousins' life is conveyed
by the list of their activities, the 'pace di fatti e fatterelli che si svolgevano
lungo la loro giornata'. Aldo's perfection is rendered by minute
description of his appearance on different occasions, one image melting
into the other: his tennis clothes, his racquet, tennis shoes; or his party
clothes, his hands on the piano, his crayons in his hand, his riding clothes.
The image of his hand as it executes a drawing melds with the drawings
themselves, of horsemen, which in turn immediately meld with the
image of him as little horseman: 'matite alla mano, cavalieri e cavalli,
pittore; pronto per la lezione di equitazione' (*MF* 70). Sonia is transfixed
by his shiny leather riding boots, which of course recall the same kind
of boots worn by her father and represent both fear and fascination,
with clear fetishistic significance (having almost textbook status as a
fetish, which stands in for the object of desire) as we recall from this
passage earlier in the book (*MF* 24):

In un tremito intenso la sua mano accarezzava furtivamente gli stivali, sentiva
i segni del cuoio e scivolava sul nero brillante fino all'orlo che serava il
pantalone grigio verde troncato sotto il ginocchio da uno sbuffo laterale. In
un lampo della fantasia, o in un sogno, aveva imaginato che uno stivale lucido
le premese le costole del petto tanto da sentirle scricchiolare, schiacciandole
il cuore con forza fino a un brivido oscuro di colpa per quello spasimo che
la riportava alla realtà.

The moment when Aldo casually reveals to Sonia the scandal of her own illegitimacy is prefaced by his glance at a framed photograph of his own parents on their wedding day. Sonia cannot 'prove' that her parents are married because she is unable to conjure up a picture (a visual 'proof', even if only her mind's eye) of her mother's wedding dress. In this way, this central episode links Sonia's sense of social and financial insecurity, feelings of estrangement from her father, and the revelation that she has been the victim of deceit; all via visual images, often containing other visual images within them or referring to others already lodged in our consciousness. When Sonia confronts her mother with her newly-discovered knowledge, the scene is described in terms of Marianna's hand outstretched to her daughter (and refused), desirous of her compliance in their 'vergogna taciuta'. The matter is never mentioned again. The notions of silence, secrecy and shame are interwoven with a style built upon images replacing overt statements.

Another example of this focus on objects and on visual clues to represent emotion or intellectual response occurs when Sonia's father gives her the fur coat: it is an object that represents many things, subconscious meanings doubtless, but also it is an embodiment of the other woman or women in Sonia's father's life, and Marianna refuses to see this. Sanvitale expresses this actually in visual terms (*MF* 115). The mother evades her daughter's question, 'Di chi è la pelliccia, secondo te, di chi è la pelliccia?', with a physical movement of the eyes: 'La madre sviò lo sguardo e rispose a casaccio — Per me hai la febbre. Non ti agitare cosí.' The fur represents visual evidence of what is really happening, and the mother is determined not to see.

Sonia's reaction takes the form of a feverish dream and the assuming of male heroic roles. The text then moves immediately onto the account of Sonia's first sexual experience. This is a key scene, where the event is narrated entirely in detached terms. First we have emphasis on the hand: 'Se la mano del ragazzo entrava nella sua orbita e arrivava vicino al suo corpo, Sonia non si ritraeva ma la seguiva': it is a negative event, 'un vuoto d'attesa'. Then Sonia 'imitava i gesti dell'altro senza accorgersene e provando un gran piacere nell'ubbidienza'. This is an example of what Sanvitale talks of in the interview, where a sexual encounter becomes a performance, an act. The long build-up to the actual act becomes an examination of masculinity; the boy represents Sonia's admiration for the male figure and yearning to be part of this male world, even while accepting and recognizing her own separateness. This same maleness becomes later the aspect that separates them (*MF* 121):

— Ti voglio dire una cosa che non ho mai detto a nessuno, — mormorò il ragazzo. — Vorrei essere uguale a mio padre e non ci riuscirò mai.

Lí per lí Sonia pensò che ciò che aveva sentito era importante, bellissimo, anche perché tale desiderio non avrebbe mai potuto sfiorarla. Provò quindi una specie di ammirata invidia; una devozione quasi, un riflesso di ringraziamento e di preghiera, come se fosse magico che esistesse una simile volontà dentro al ragazzo che cosí era posseduto da una forza, il riflesso di antichi riti e di antiche stregonerie. Insomma, con una brevissima intuizione, le apparve quasi un essere consacrato. Lo strano fu che molti anni dopo proprio questa frase si rivelò fonte di rancori e diversità; annullava ciò che c'era stato di profondo nel loro reciproco amore e all'incirca suonava per Sonia come una sentenza di morte che il ragazzo aveva dato ai propri impulsi, alla propria vita.

After the love-making, silent for the positive reason of the power of their feelings, the section ends with Sonia's responses (*MF* 123):

Eroe: prode, forte, coraggioso.
   Semidio, paladino, cavaliere, guerriero, grande uomo, campione; modello, esempio.
   Personaggio, protagonista.

The effect of sexual initiation has been to reaffirm the notion of the male figure as hero, both in literature and culture, and also in life. The male figure is to be emulated, and he is always the central personality, the protagonist in life. The scene shifts to the father's attempt to make Sonia marry and his locking her in her room until she changes her mind. In the melodrama of this episode we see the male figure placed centrally in an episode that seems staged and where the male is dominant though not heroic, and contrasts strongly with the heroic images revealed to us in the newly deflowered Sonia's mind. The claustrophobic argument in the room turns to the father's own marriage, and when challenged, he implies that the truth has been distorted by Sonia's mother, to which Marianna responds indignantly (*MF* 127):

— Non ho detto niente, — interloquí con vivacità la signora Marianna, — che cosa c'entro io?
   — La mamma non c'entra, — riaffermò Sonia con voce adirata.

Here the women unintentionally and unanimously succeed in

marginalizing the mother's role, declaring her to have been nothing to do with this relationship, which in fact has shaped the lives of both mother and daughter. The women are complicit in their own effacement. Nevertheless, this collusion involves a kind of satisfaction at the acquiring of power within the female nexus of relationships: the episode ends with Sonia's thought that 'La madre infatti era sempre stata sua, soltanto sua' (*MF* 128). This is part of the continuum of responses that ensures that the women in some way connive at their own enslavement to the lie about their real position in the husband/father's life, opting to believe the melodramatic story about the vengeful wife on their tracks with a revolver, rather than the demeaning, but ultimately less damaging reality of the officer's desire to hide their existence for social convenience.

Linked with the techniques of distancing already examined is the emphasis on landscapes: in paintings, in dreams, in children's literature, in Africa, in the mind's eye (as in Marianna's father's letter), on the island where Sonia experiences her sexual initiation. In contrast, there are also the depressing 'giardini pubblici'. This is an urban tale, and the squalid nature of real human experience, particularly sexual experience, is appropriately set against the squalid topography of the city. These are all presented as 'settings'; there is something artificial, imagined about them, particularly when they are pleasant settings. Nature's role is as a backdrop. and it can be manipulated, as in a film, with the real subject revealed as the human figure within it. This has echoes of the Garden of Eden, which, after all, was the theatre for sexual initiation and the first misunderstanding between men and women, the first 'sesso teatralizzato' (SW 97).

In this way we move through plays, paintings, landscapes and eventually mythology. Life becomes a dream and finally a myth (*MF* 116):

Il confronto con il padre prima si profilò e infine scoppiò in tutta la sua forza. Lei si comparò a Orlando nella sua ira, al pelide Achille nella sua forza, a Ercole che regge le colonne, a Davide e cosí via. Quando la vita s'incaricò di provare che tutto ciò era stato prevalentemente un sogno dovette ammettere che da quel giorno però gli dei moltiplicarono le prove che lei, benché in difficoltà sempre piú notevoli, riuscí a superare. La sua vita dunque si trasformò in un mito.

The prevalence of dreams or imaginary sequences in the book underlines this mythical sense. All these aspects, art and films, dream and myth, landscape as *topos*, focus on detail, distance the reader from the women at the centre of the novel. Although these devices also illustrate and enrich the author's picture of her characters, nevertheless they introduce a note of distance, artificiality, unreality, which 'protects' the female protagonists from too close a scrutiny. If the book is an exploration of reality, often in its most intimate and personal aspects, it nevertheless operates using many distancing devices. It is a paradox of style versus content that nevertheless succeeds in being expressive and evocative.

I will conclude this study of *Madre e figlia* with an analysis of two important passages, which illustrate the aspects of Sanvitale's style and its relationship with the stance of the female writer that I have outlined above. I have referred to *Madre e figlia* as a 'messaggio senza suoni'. The phrase comes from the scene in which Sonia, now adult, driving with her 13-year-old son and his 16-year-old friend, see the body of a suicide hanging from a tree along the road from Siena to Rome. This is a key episode in many respects, illustrating fundamental aspects of the novel in terms of style and content. The book as a whole is a profound study of emotion, describing the emotional intertwining of two women, but it is also an emotional response to history, to the world around the women and to the men in their lives. This response is conveyed through pictures. The pictures are of course made up of words, but still the primary stimulus is visual, not abstract or discursive: we are invited to create pictures in our minds to represent the feelings and thoughts as well as the events. Sanvitale signals this technique in several places by reference to the idioms and processes of film and painting, and the 'messages' in the book are conveyed by a series of pictures.

The passage about the suicide begins with a likening of nature to art: 'la natura è dipinta. Il verde è un fondale lontano.' Now the silence of the landscape is mentioned as a calming element, though there is sound in the car, as the boys are playing the guitar and a flute. Suddenly the travellers see a police car, the boys stop playing, and at the same instant they see the body hanging below the level of the road. The scene is likened to a painting, 'una deposizione', the hanging body and the two policemen reaching up to its feet. The images borrowed from painting continue: 'in rilievo sul fondo', 'una forma nel quadro'. Then, apparently, sound bursts into the scene and yet logically it must in fact be silent (*MF* 84–5):

In rilievo sul fondo di una natura estranea e immobile, l'uomo attaccato alla corda è solo come nessun altro visto prima di lui. È anche una forma nel quadro ma nei nostri occhi arrivano per intero la sua solitudine e la sua disperazione con un grido acutissimo che rimbomba.

Fermo l'automobile e, in contraddizione, esclamo: — Non guardate! — Non potevo dire: — Non ascoltate! — e perciò mi resi conto che il messaggio senza suoni, stampo del terrore, era arrivato a loro. Mi voltai per proteggerli, loro chinarono gli occhi. Erano impalliditi, avevano posto gli strumenti.

Misi in moto. Il silenzio che partiva dall'uomo ora piccolissimo attaccato alla corda in mezzo a una muraglia verticale di verde senza cielo in noi diventava immobilità e ghiaccio.

The episode has particular resonance in the context of any discussion about silence. Sanvitale moves freely between the senses of sight and hearing. The shock of the sight actually becomes 'un grido' in the brain, a shout that expresses the suicide's pain, without articulating it. This is a metaphor, the 'messaggio senza suoni', which holds good for many of the finest moments in the book.

In terms of the narrative, the effect on the boys, for the moment at least, seems to be to provoke a great hunger for life. However, the implication is that the image will acquire further life of its own both for the children and the writer. For the narrator 'l'impiccato fu chiuso nella memoria', but she notes: 'Non so che strada farà nella loro.' Having said the image is shut into her memory, nevertheless she links it with a composite memory of Sonia, by immediately turning to an image of herself as a young girl, an image deliberately and overtly 'coloured' as it assumes fictional form.

She sees Sonia, wearing a blouse she knows was blue, but 'insisto a ridipingerla colore del glicine', in a devastated room. We cannot know whether the devastation is due to poverty and neglect, some act of domestic violence, or bomb damage; any and all are implied and possible. A glance in the mirror by the narrator in the notional present of the novel provides the visual stimulus for a memory of 1945, when, we are told, Marianna's teeth were just the same as the teeth of the narrator reflected in the mirror. By the end of the war, Marianna is exhausted by poverty, the Colonello has lost his house and lands in the bombing, Sonia has grown into a woman. The link between these memories and the memory of the hanged man is not made specific and yet the image of the suicide, a lonely, desperate figure, the iconographic connection with sacrifice, tragedy and renewal, enrich our understanding of the bleakness of the war years and the sense of weary defeat at the end of the conflict. The writer demonstrates how visual images blend with one another and the emotion contained in one 'picture' flows into the next.

There is another key passage where many of the elements I have individuated come together. Towards the end of the book, Sonia's mother is ill and has gone into hospital. Sonia is struck by the silence at home, but it is not just the silence of a lack of voices, but it is as if the body itself generates a noise in the mind (*MF* 191):

La cosa che piú la colpí fu il silenzio: un silenzio interiore grandissimo come se il corpo fosse stato il teatro di una conflagrazione, di un rombo assordante uguale a quello di una bomba atomica.

Now the silence moves from the body to the picture ('quadro') of the scene outside observed through the frame of the window, a scene viewed also as if on a stage, from the wings ('sipario'). Sonia watches as if in a painting now herself (*MF* 192): 'Di solito stava seduta composta, con la testa diritta, le mani congiunte in grembo, immobile ma proiettata verso l'ignoto.' Now two men appear on this stage ('tale scenario'), as if part of a film ('in due sequenze mute brevissime'); one is her father, one her husband. The image of the father is whirled away into the void, 'con un effetto di rimpicciolimento brusco fino a sparire', and we learn that he is now dead. He is gone, but still has his totemic, godlike power: 'emanava la crudele fissità e l'enigma di un totem; e da questo idolo uscivano forze repulsive e ingiuste' (*MF* 193). The father now fades into an image of the husband in the act of leaving home for good. These are not remembered images, but a visually expressed collage of imagined scenes. They are 'l'effetto di momenti che non avevano immagini' (*MF* 194).

In this way they are related to a further technique in *Madre e figlia* whereby what is declared as the remembered and the imagined are conflated in a way that again distances the reader whilst nevertheless gripping the imagination. Often the book steps out of the illusion of a created reality and reminds us that it is an imagined or imperfectly remembered artefact. Examples of this are the narrator's voice telling us that she has created these images right from the first lines of the book, 'Non so perché [...] ho inventato'; or her command 'Ascoltami'; or telling us that she is seated at her desk looking at the piece of 'madrepora'and inspired to write (*MF* 3, 57, 82).

In a striking example of detachment from the creative process, Sanvitale displays what can be read as a virtuoso technical sample of how to create a scene in a novel. The sequence of descriptions concerning the return of Zio Federico from the colonies and his death, fall into the category of the imagined, not remembered, and so all are depictions of possible scenes, based on the few factual details available. Here, Sanvitale imagines three versions of Federico's death, all inspired by a letter from Federico's wife. (*MF* 138–46). The first is exotic melodrama, borrowed from films and Romantic literature, the second more 'natural' but still dramatic and owing much to sentimental and romanticized images, and the third prosaic, though still through ironic interjection indicating that it may be based largely on Marianna's interpretation of events. We are constantly reminded that the work before us is only a version or possible representation of reality, filtered through voices that are not necessarily trustworthy or speaking the 'truth'.

Deceit and silence are at the very heart of this book. The lives depicted in *Madre e figlia* are a tapestry of secrets and deceptions: the women's attempt to pose as respectable, the false story of the vengeful wife with the revolver, the husband's desire to keep their existence secret, the secrets between mother and daughter (for instance, Marianna hides the existence of her brother Giacomo), the public conspiracy of silence about the reality of Fascism as Sonia grows up. These details of plot are consistently interwoven with images of silence, as we have seen. Silence, particularly of the wronged woman, is deeply rooted in our culture, and women's autobiography and autobiographical fiction habitually seek to displace the female voice.

In a parallel displacement, in this text, the thematics and the style rely on visual images. The power of the writing in *Madre e figlia* does indeed lie primarily in the details: this is a book full of feeling, but it is all expressed visually; it is a book of objects objectified. In this complex novel, we have a paradoxical depiction of the woman as object and yet also of the world as observed by her. Objectifying is particularly appropriate, since the theoretics of 'the gaze' and Freudianism suggest fetishism and voyeurism go together and are linked in film images of women. Emphasis in the novel on the idioms of film reinforces this link. The book makes a fetish of objects by its visual descriptions, and depicts the women protagonists as voyeurs of other lives, so turning the whole object–fetish relationship on its head. *Madre e figlia* subtly explores wide-ranging literary and cultural issues vital to an understanding of twentieth-century culture, including the nature of fiction and autobiography, the nature of the creative process, the influence of mass media and the cinema, changing sexual mores, women's place in society; and at the centre of all this lies the fundamental question of the unsaid.

Notes to Chapter 5

1. For an overview of the political and cultural issues concerning women's writing in Italy, see Sharon Wood, *Italian Women's Writing, 1860–1994* (London: Athlone Press, 1995) [*IWW*] and Sharon Wood, introduction to *Italian Women Writing*, ed. eadem (Manchester: Manchester University Press, 1993).

2. Julie Rivkin and Michael Ryan, 'Feminist Paradigms', *Literary Theory: An Anthology*, ed. iidem (Oxford: Blackwell, 1998), 527–32.

3. Elaine Hedges and Shelley Fisher Fishkin (eds.), *Listening to 'Silences': New Essays in Feminist Criticism* (New York: Oxford University Press, 1994).

4. Patricia Laurence, 'Women's Silence as a Ritual of Truth', ibid., 156–67 at 157–8, 166.

5. Bella Brodzki and Celeste M. Schenck (eds.), *Life/Lines: Theorizing Women's Autobiography* (Ithaca, NY: Cornell University Press, 1988), 10–11.

6. Ursula Fanning, 'Sibilla Aleramo's *Una donna*: A Case Study in Women's Autobiographical Fiction', *The Italianist* (Nov. 2000), 164–77, citing Paul de Man, 'Autobiography as De-Facement', *MLN* 94 (1979), 919–30 at 921.

7. Eakin, *Touching the World*, 80, 190.

8. See Bibliography for full references to writings on Sanvitale by Paola Blelloch, Ann Caesar, Fiammetta Filipelli, Sharon Wood, Simona Wright.

9. Bruno Bettelheim, *The Uses of Enchantment* (London: Penguin, 1976); Jack Zipes, *Breaking the Magic Spell: Radical Theories of Folk and Fairy Tales* (London: Heinemann, 1979).

10. Stith Thompson, *The Folktale* (New York: Dryden Press, 1946; repr. Berkeley: University of California Press, 1977).

11. S. Baring-Gould, *The Lives of the Saints*, new and rev. edn, 16 vols. (London: John C. Nimmo; New York: Longmans, Green, 1897–8; first pubd 1872–7), ix. 53, quoted in C. Grant Loomis, *White Magic: An Introduction to the Folklore of Christian Legend* (Cambridge, MA: Medieval Academy of America, 1948), 126.

12. Giambattista Basile, *Il pentamerone [...], overo Lo cunto de li cunte* (Naples: Salvatore Scarano, 1634–6). For the publishing history of Basile's text, see Michele Rak, *Napoli gentile: La letteratura in 'lingua napoletana' nella cultura barocca (1596–1632)* (Bologna: Il Mulino, 1994), 295–6.

13. For detailed analysis of this aspect with many examples, see the chapter 'The Silence of the Fathers', *BB* 335–52.

14. Warner devotes a chapter to this topic, 'The Silence of the Daughters: The Little Mermaid', *BB* 387–408.

15. For an enlightening discussion of the importance of the myth of Philomela, see Patricia Klindiest, 'The Voice of the Shuttle is Ours', *Literary Theory*, ed. Rivkin and Ryan, 612–29.

16. See *BB* 396–8 for more on this story.

17. Ruth B. Bottigheimer, *Grimms' Bad Girls and Bold Boys: The Moral and Social Vision of the Tales* (New Haven and London: Yale University Press, 1987), 177–87.

18. Ibid., 76–7.

19. Maurizio Bettini, *The Portrait of the Lover*, trans. Laura Gibbs (Berkeley: University of California Press, 1999), 148, in the chap. 'The Life of the Gaze'.

20. Michael Jay, 'In the Empire of the Gaze', *Foucault: A Critical Reader*, ed. David Couzens Hoy (Oxford: Blackwell, 1986), 175–204 at 175–7.

21. E. Ann Kaplan, 'Is the Gaze Male?', eadem, *Women and Film: Both Sides of the Camera* (London and New York: Methuen, 1983), 321–38.

22. Ibid., 326.

23. Ibid., 330.

24. Ibid., 334.

25. Ibid., 336; emphasis original.

26. See Bruce Merry, *Dacia Maraini and the Written Dream of Women in Italian Literature* (Townsville: Department of Modern Languages, James Cook University of Northern Queensland, 1997), and *IWW* 216–31, for bibliographies and detailed analyses of Maraini's work, in which the motif of silence is clearly significant.

27. Paola Capriolo, *La grande Eulalia* (Milan: Feltrinelli, 1988); Francesca Duranti, *La casa sul lago della luna* (Milan: Rizzoli, 1984).

28. Angela Carter, *Nights at the Circus* (London: Chatto & Windus, 1984).

29. Michel Foucault, *Surveiller et punir: Naissance de la prison* (Paris: Gallimard, 1975). All three writers, Capriolo, Carter and Foucault, are inspired by Bentham's *Panopticon*.

30. This point has been made and elaborated upon by many commentators on women's autobiography. See e.g. in Bibliography, Brodzski and Schenck, Gilbert and Gubar.

31. Lisa Ginzburg, preface to Natalia Ginzburg, *È difficile parlare di sé*, ed. Cesare Garboli and Lisa Ginzburg (Turin: Einaudi, 1999), pp. v, vii–viii.

32. Ann Jefferson, 'Autobiography as Intertext: Barthes, Sarraute, Robbe-Grillet', *Intertextuality: Theories and Practices*, ed. Michael Worton and Judith Still (Manchester: Manchester University Press, 1990), 108–29 at 109.

33. Francesca Sanvitale, *Camera ottica: Pagine di letteratura e realtà* (Turin: Einaudi, 1999).

34. Dorothea Brande's classic handbook for aspiring writers, *Becoming a Writer* (London: Macmillan, 1996; first pubd 1934), depends on this notion. See in particular chap. 5, 'Harnessing the Unconscious'.

35. Wood, *Italian Women Writing*, 19.

36. Eakin, *Touching the World*, 80; chap. 3, 'Self and Culture', gives an excellent summary of research in this area.

37. For a book-length study on women and the mirror, see Jenijoy La Belle, *Herself Beheld: The Literature of the Looking Glass* (Ithaca, NY: Cornell University Press, 1988). A fundamental point of departure is also, of course, Jacques Lacan, 'The Mirror Stage as Formative of the Function of the I as Revealed in Psychoanalytic Experience', *Écrits*, 1–8.

38. Ann Hallamore Caesar, 'Francesca Sanvitale, Investigating the Self and the World', *The New Italian Novel*, ed. Zygmunt G. Barański and Lino Pertile (Edinburgh: Edinburgh University Press, 1993), 184–99 at 188; *IWW* 244.

CHAPTER 6

The Einaudi Publishing House,
Public Attitudes and the
Perception of Truth

In this chapter I am concerned with the influence of the publishing house Einaudi and of individual editors within it, and how public attitudes and editorial decisions were intertwined, reflecting and strengthening one another. As an illustration of how awareness of public reception of a text can affect not only a writer's output, but can also distort 'memory', I examine the autobiography of Tina Pizzardo, 'la donna dalla voce rauca', a woman whom Pavese loved but also denigrated in his diaries.

All the writers I discuss in this book have at some stage been published by the Turin publishing house Einaudi, and some have had very close links with it. Cesare Pavese was one of the founding members of the company, since he and Leone Ginzburg were its first salaried workers, and Natalia Ginzburg was taken on by Giulio Einaudi as an employee after the war. Primo Levi's first book was eventually published by Einaudi, after the company famously refused it in the first instance, and in more recent times some of Francesca Sanvitale's works have been published by Einaudi, including *Madre e figlia*.

Einaudi has an almost fabled renown in Italy as a publishing house. Its history is closely linked with the country's political, literary and even social history. It has inspired affection, debate and entire publications, most recently Luisa Mangoni's *Pensare i libri*.[1] In the course of the long interview contained in Severino Cesari's *Colloquio con Giulio Einaudi*, Giulio Einaudi, the founder of the publishing house, talks of his view of the role of the publisher in society, distinguishing between 'editoria sí e no'. He identifies this role as

un impegno civile, che una parte dell'editoria ha preso con la società.

L'editoria 'sí' è quella che invece di 'andare incontro al gusto del pubblico', gusto che si pretende di conoscere ma che si confonde spesso col proprio, introduce nella cultura le nuove tendenze della ricerca in ogni campo, letterario artistico scientifico storico sociale, e lavora per fare emergere gli interessi profondi, anche se va contro la corrente. Invece di suscitare l'interesse epidermico, di assecondare le espressioni piú in superficie ed effimere del gusto, favorisce la formatura duratura. Di un gusto, appunto; e anche di un pubblico, di un mercato se vuoi.

Quel 'no' di 'editoria no' caratterizza invece gli editori che non si pongono in questa prospettiva, ma cercano di soddisfare i desideri piú ovvi del pubblico. [...]

Dico spesso: editoria è conoscenza degli uomini. E la bellezza, la chiave di questo lavoro è che deve essere premiata l'intelligenza.[2]

He goes on to say that he deliberately juxtaposed, employed as editors working together, writers who had conflicting ideas, such as Vittorini and Pavese, in order to stimulate creativity in the company:

La storia Einaudi è la storia di un gruppo, di un collettivo formato, in tempi diversi, da molte e diverse intelligenze 'conflittuali': questo vuol dire che c'era un legame profondo, fecondo e contraddittorio tra di noi e con la realtà [...].[3]

An earlier book, *Frammenti di memoria*, provoked Natalia Ginzburg to query the selection of 'fragments' he chose to recount.[4] As he points out in a postscript, 'avrebbe voluto che parlassi anche dei fatti recenti, da me solo accennati' (*Frammenti*, 195). These 'fatti' seem to be the practical and financial difficulties experienced by the company, which eventually resulted in its sale to the Berlusconi media empire. It remains to be seen what effect this will have on the imprint in the twenty-first century.

However, there is no doubt that during the Fascist years, the Einaudi publishing house had a significant political role, succeeding in providing a forum for anti-Fascist activists without being openly anti-Fascist, since this would have entailed closure. Giulio Einaudi speaks of his father Luigi's 'dissimulazione onesta' with regard to the Fascist authorities (*Frammenti*, 35), adding:

Bisogna avere vissuto quel periodo per riconscoscere che una 'dissimulazione onesta' era assolutamente produttiva e positiva. Altro è stata la lotta armata della Resistenza, altro è stata la lotta di quanti hanno patito negli anni del regime carcere e persecuzione, altro è stata l'attività di chi si è prodigato per mantenere certe idee di democrazia: le uniche oggi riconosciute valide.

In this distinction between active resistance and conspiracy, and a respectable but quiet pretence at abiding by Fascist rules whilst at the same time undermining them, he pinpoints an attitude that was understandable and probably far more commonplace and likely at the time than outright heroism. The circle of Giulio Einaudi's friends and colleagues included some well-known anti-Fascists, not only Leone Ginzburg and the Levi brothers but also Augusto Monti, Massimo Mila and Giaime Pintor. Vittorio Foa, in his article after the publication of *Frammenti di memoria*, emphasizes the importance of the political element in these early years and for the whole history of Einaudi:

La cultura come un livello della politica fu il terreno (e il senso) dell'incontro di Giulio con Leone. La casa editrice nacque quindi come una iniziativa 'politica', anche se non nel senso corrente della parola, e tale rimase anche nel suo straordinario percorso semisecolare.[5]

Giulio Einaudi was constantly under surveillance from the Fascist authorities, but the publishing house managed to preserve a delicate relationship with Fascism (*Frammenti*, 35). He says at the time many people thought Fascism would never be over, so they had to find a modus vivendi for the publishing house. The journal *Primato* offered a middle way (36):

rivista che faceva barriera contro le tendenze peggiori e più urlatrici del fascismo. C'era ad esempio chi, dalle colonne del 'Secolo d'Italia', chiedeva che la Einaudi, una casa editrice che pubblicava russi giudei e massoni, venisse soppressa. E ci fu una difesa su 'Primato', scritta da Pintor.
    Era un momento curioso. Bottai, il direttore di 'Primato', aveva apprezzamenti sinceri nei nostri confronti. Era molto gentile, non c'era volta che gli mandassimo un libro e lui non rispondesse apprezzando il gesto, entrando anche nel merito del libro. Mentre imperversavano in Italia intellettuali modello 'Difesa della razza', occorreva che tipi come Bottai potessero difenderci da questi cani rabbiosi. Quelli che ci bruciavano i libri. In certi momenti, persino a Torino, sfondarono le vetrine che avevano in mostra le edizioni Einaudi.

With this political history, it is particularly surprising to us now that Einaudi did not accept Levi's book in 1947, as we have discussed in an earlier chapter. Giulio Einaudi offers the by now familiar explanation that the public were not ready for it, but admits there is no record in the archives why the book was rejected, and this excuse does not tally with his description of what 'editoria sí' entailed, which should, according to his definition, have been capable of seeing beyond the public's immediate tastes. The most likely reason remains Natalia's general statement in *Lessico famigliare*, that in the immediate post-war years there was a widely-felt sense of indecency in speaking of certain traumas. As Einaudi was run on such a personal level, it is possible that even if this was simply her own reaction, it carried the day. The following comment by Giulio Einaudi's about Natalia Ginzburg is possibly a veiled reference to her decision on Levi and the reasons behind it (*Frammenti*, 162):

[Natalia] non tollera certi autori, certi problemi trattati in modo sciatto e approssimativo. Certe volte può anche sbagliare, può odiare libri e iniziative importanti solo perché non entrano nel suo schema, alla fine però le tollera. Ma non tollererebbe certo, immagino, libri della nuova storiografia che sminuisce l'Olocausto.

Whilst Giulio Einaudi is unlikely to be suggesting that Ginzburg thought *Se questo è un uomo* was 'sciatto e approssimativo', even in its first version, he could quite possibly be hinting that she did make a mistake regarding this book, a connection supported by the fact that he goes on to mention Holocaust literature in the same breath. On the refusal of the book specifically, he throws no new light on the matter, returning to Primo Levi's own suggestion in later years that the public was not ready at the time for such a book (*Frammenti*, 174):

non esiste invece traccia, nell'archivio Einaudi, delle motivazioni secondo cui nel 1946 'la proposta venne declinata con una formulazione generica' [...] Forse, come scrive l'autore, in quel tempo di aspro dopoguerra la gente non aveva molto desiderio di ritornare con la memoria agli anni dolorosi appena terminati.

The portrait of Cesare Pavese as a colleague that emerges from this *Colloquio*, with his 'infischiarsene' (*Frammenti*, 45), a catch-phrase already familiar to us from *Lessico famigliare*, is affectionate, but even Giulio Einaudi is disconcerted by the *Taccuino*. He attempts to justify some of it by claiming the writer was imagining the possible thoughts of characters in future novels, and in particular *La casa in collina*. He links the scene in *La casa in collina* of the protagonist's disgust at the sight of the body of a young Fascist with the more troubling remarks in the *Taccuino*. Nevertheless, he notes with some resignation the contents of a letter sent by Pavese, in which the author criticizes the company Einaudi's political stance (46):

Scorgo una frase revelatrice in una lettera del 25 agosto 1943 a Giaime Pintor: 'sono nauseato dall'indaffaramento politico della casa editrice, il quale da un mese ci blocca ogni lavoro', la stessa nausea che manifesta nel *Taccuino* segreto per le chiacchiere dei suoi amici antifascisti. E nel *Mestiere di vivere* cosa troviamo ai momenti cruciali della nostra storia? Nulla al 25 luglio, caduta del fascismo, nulla all'8 settembre, armistizio, nulla al 25 aprile 1945.

Giulio Einaudi goes on to admit that Leone Ginzburg and Massimo Mila 'vengono "nel taccuino implicitamente aggrediti"' (*Frammenti*, 47, quoting Dionisotti in the article that revealed the *Taccuino* to the public). Whilst accepting that there were differences in literary philosophy, political outlook and commitment between Pavese and his 'amici crociani del partito d'Azione', Giulio Einaudi finds parts of the *Taccuino* hard to swallow, not so much 'la sua ammirazione per il programma della Repubblica Sociale' but 'la giustificazione delle atrocità naziste, che lo portò a scrivere: "forse il vero difetto di noi italiani è che non sappiamo essere atroci"' (ibid.), phrases he, like most commentators, cannot fail to interpret as anything other than supportive of the worst excesses of Fascism, as we have already noted in an earlier chapter.

The Einaudi publishing house developed its image very deliberately in a coherent series of marketing exercises that in retrospect mark its modernity. Its heyday is perceived to be in the nineteen-fifties and sixties, when Italo Calvino and Natalia Ginzburg were important editorial figures. Calvino devised an information leaflet that would advertise books already on the company's list or about to be published. This was seen in terms of creating a market for the kind of books the company was producing, 'costruire un pubblico', as Giulio Einaudi calls it (*Frammenti*, 86), and went alongside special financial help in the immediate post-war years for students or young people wishing to buy books, with a scheme to pay by instalments. Commercial requirements, an appreciation of the market and a desire to educate went hand in hand.

However, the publishing house was not just a commercial enterprise, it was an artistic environment, affecting its writers and allowing itself to be influenced by them in a symbiotic relationship. Giulio Einaudi feels that times have changed: then, a young writer wrote and also selected and helped other writers. Pavese was Calvino's mentor, and in his turn Calvino nurtured new writers (*Frammenti*, 215–16):

Un giovane scrittore era una volta un intellettuale che in un certo senso sposava la casa editrice che lo pubblicava. La sposava e quindi si interessava anche ai 'libri degli altri', e non solo di letteratura. Non so se un Calvino che nasce oggi avrebbe la fortuna che ha avuto Italo Calvino. Che sí, ha influito con la sua vita e la sua intelligenza sulla casa editrice, ma forse ha anche influito su di lui l'ambiente in cui ha lavorato.

This image of a publishing house in which political, literary and intellectual diversity flourished as a result of the interaction among individual writers, and which influenced the reading and education of a generation, is a beguiling one. It is particularly interesting in the context of this book because it offers a microcosm of attitudes within a certain educated section of Italian society, both of the producers of literature and the consumers of literature. However, there is abundant evidence that that despite the policy of 'editoria sí', the publishing house largely reflected prevailing public attitudes in its output.

The 1950s are not years in which liberal views flourished. Despite the 'dolce vita' image of Italy during the economic boom, in Italy as elsewhere in Europe, public attitudes endorsed ways of life that seemed to offer security. This was clearly a reaction to the shattering insecurity of the war years throughout Europe, but it does seem to have brought with it an unfortunate 'backlash', particularly in matters related to sex and the role of women in society. It is well documented that women who had worked perfectly capably at 'men's' jobs during the war were quickly relegated to hearth and home, and that traditional 'family values' were held up as an ideal, heavily supported by America's film output. The underbelly of the apparently flawless and optimistic society depicted in the cheery advertisements of the time has only relatively recently been exposed, with the revelation in Britain, for instance, of the incarceration of single mothers in mental homes on the basis that their sexual behaviour suggested mental derangement, sexual abuse of children in orphanages, the shipping of children to Australia, often to effective servitude, and the active role of the Church, particularly the Roman Catholic Church, in all this. Public attitudes to sexuality in Italy were at least equally narrow, as Paul Ginsborg points out:

The Italy of the boom was still a society full of taboos about sexual behaviour. The restrictive codes of official morality were deeply intertwined in the South with codes of honour. Sexual mores were to change almost more slowly than anything else in Italy. However, in the early 1960s there were a few signs of a more open approach. [...] The first cracks in the official morality had appeared, but it was to be another decade at least before sexual mores underwent any major change. [6]

This veneer of propriety is reflected in some of the publishing decisions of the Einaudi company and of its writers in those years. Italo Calvino is an interesting example. It has already been pointed out that he altered his own earlier work, expunging detail that he felt was too sexually explicit in the moral climate of the 1950s and, presumably, according to his own maturer sensitivities. In his *Fiabe italiane* he took earlier versions of fairy-tales, collected often in dialect form as a literal transliteration of the oral accounts, and converted them into standard Italian. In the process, he made certain alterations, tending to standardize the tales and adjust them to contemporary taste by 'decreasing the narrator's visibility, reducing retributive justice, condensing, conflating variants, rationalizing, bowdlerizing, reducing religion, and increasing the unity of the tales'. [7] Folklorists and anthropologists were not best pleased by this treatment, because the result was, partly owing to Calvino's eventual reputation as a writer, partly owing to increased literacy nationally, that Calvino's collection was viewed by the reading public as definitive, and oral versions and elaboration of stories ceased. Calvino defended himself, somewhat disingenuously, by insisting, 'Anch'io ho il diritto di produrre delle varianti.' [8]

The 'bowdlerization' includes the deletion of scatological references (for example, the episode of the simpleton with his head on back to front watching himself defecate, noted by Marc Beckwith). However, it also entails the removal of the mildest sexual references. For instance, in one source story, 'El re del sol', taken from Imbriani's *Novellaja fiorentina*, after various misadventures the hero and heroine of the tale get married, in proper fairytale style, and the source text states boldly 'hin andàa in lett lo sposo e la sposa'. [9] Calvino renders this as 'i due sposi ebbero una stanza per loro nel palazzo', in a prim dilution of the image of the wedding night. Many readers sense in Calvino's writing an almost perverse rejection of the personal and the sensual. This is far too broad a subject to approach here in any detail (and there is, in any case, what amounts to a critical industry centring on Calvino's works) but even Giulio Einaudi implies as much when he comments (*Frammenti*, 81):

Nella scrittura di Calvino è come rimanesse sempre una traccia di dolore, sotto forma di una figura che appare e poi scompare, una figura del desiderio, che si insegue e non si raggiunge.

Whatever the reasons for Calvino's reluctance to touch upon the sexual in his own writing, his attitudes generally would certainly have influenced Einaudi's output. Giulio Einaudi stresses (ibid.):

Calvino è stato importantissimo, proprio dal punto di vista della casa editrice. È stato importantissimo. In un primo periodo è stato capo dell'ufficio stampa, poi direttore letterario. Ha curato per anni i rapporti con gli scrittori, non solo italiani.

After Pavese's death, as I have already mentioned in an earlier chapter, Natalia Ginzburg and Italo Calvino edited together the manuscript of *Il mestiere di vivere*. It would appear that the politically and personally incriminating *Taccuino* had been left by the author separate from the rest of the diary, and Calvino and Ginzburg chose not only not to publish it, but to conceal it indefinitely, and the location of the original of this section of the diary remains secret. The rest of the diary was purged of material 'dove il contenuto era di carattere troppo intimo e scottante, e dove si trattava di questioni private di persone viventi', as the editors note in their introduction to the original edition in 1952 (*MV* 9). It is understandable that they wished to protect the identity of people named in the text, particularly as many of the comments excised are so disparaging, but one does wonder how far the omissions were intended to protect Pavese's reputation rather than that of the people mentioned, whose names could simply have been deleted. In any case, the real reasons for the omissions were most likely to have been squeamishness on the part of the editors and a general understanding that the Italy of the 1950s was not receptive to material of this nature. Other important instances of reticence already discussed in this study, which are likely to be the result of this same combination of influences, include the reluctance to publish Primo Levi's book and, as late as 1973, Ginzburg's denial of the importance of feminism; and there is no doubt that Einaudi's output as a whole must have been nuanced by these factors.

'La donna dalla voce rauca' is Finally Heard: Tina Pizzardo and *Senza pensarci due volte*

Tina Pizzardo (1903–89), the inspiration for 'la donna dalla voce rauca' of Pavese's fiction and the butt of his misogynist comments in the unexpurgated version of *Il mestiere di vivere*, wrote an autobiography, completed in 1962 with the title *Memorie*, but not published until 1996, when it appeared under the title *Senza pensarci due volte*. The book is in part a response to Davide Lajolo's biography of Pavese, *Il vizio assurdo*, published in 1960, which Pizzardo felt verged on the 'fumettistica'. However, only a small proportion of the book describes the relationship with Pavese, and a great deal more space is dedicated to the account of one woman's active and independent life at a volatile time, so the text cannot be considered in any sense a homage to Pavese or merely an addition to the extensive material available about Pavese. Though it is unlikely to be prized as a great work of literature, it does have significant value, not only as a document of conditions for female anti-Fascists during the Fascist and war years, but also as an example of how external attitudes affect individuals' actions and their own view of themselves. Consideration of this autobiography brings together a number of questions that have been approached elsewhere in the present study, including how fiction and autobiography become blended, the particular nature of women's revelations about themselves, the subjective interpretation of events and 'truth', perception of sexual morality and how writers are influenced by awareness of the responses of their potential readership.

As we have noted in an earlier chapter, Fascist ideology was not favourable to women, undoing any earlier advances in their status and reinforcing the historical restrictions placed upon them by tradition, taboo and religion. Men's stance towards women and towards all forms of sexuality was confused and repressive. Fascism was associated with 'piccolo-borghese' ideals, and its approach to women chimed with those ideals. In theory, Communism should have rejected these attitudes to women along with its rejection of bourgeois ideals. Certainly, from the 1920s, work outside the home was seen by Communists as a means of achieving status for women, and the PCI adopted the Soviet model of the 'madre/operaia' as the ideal. Nevertheless, whatever the official line, there is ample evidence to suggest that women were still considered to be inferior to men, even by the Communists. Communist men were products of their upbringing in this area of their psychology as much as anyone else of any political adherence and subscribed to the same prejudices regarding what women 'should' look like and how they should act. Within clandestine organizations, the women's fate was to be *compagne* performing the familiar domestic duties at home and indeed for the *compagni*, and only auxiliary functions within the political organization. They were also expected to behave in a traditionally 'respectable' manner:

Nella clandestinità, alle donne si richiedeva di offrire in pubblico un *surplus* di rassicurante normalità; non importava soltanto 'comportarsi bene' secondo gli standard comunemente accettati, ma soprattutto bisognava 'essere giudicate bene', quasi che l'*apparenza* fosse uno dei doveri in più imposti alle donne dalle norme cospirative.[10]

Women did, however, enjoy the dubious equality of being arrested, interrogated and imprisoned by the authorities. Their jailers were normally nuns (whereas men were guarded by State employees), and the natural antagonism of the Church towards Communism meant these women were often regarded with a particular hatred by their captors:

Alla routine burocratica, ottusamente sempre uguale a se stessa, che ispirava i rapporti tra il regime carcerario e i detenuti maschi, nelle sezioni femminili subentrava un maggiore coinvolgimento, anche emotivo, da parte delle suore, animate da un esplicito intento missionario e da una interpretazione assolutamente gratificante del proprio ruolo.[11]

Contact between the sexes was also as fraught in Communist circles as in society at large, Communist men demanding similar proprieties from their girl-friends. Open sexual expression was seen as a moral and physical health risk. Again, Fascism, Catholicism and traditional taboos combined to limit sexual freedom, even between married couples, and certainly there existed 'una netta distinzione tra le donne con le quali ci si poteva "divertire" e le altre "da sposare"'.[12] These matters were discussed avidly and seriously as part of political philosophy amongst anti-Fascists, as Tina Pizzardo's autobiography recounts, but the result was that women in left-wing circles were perceived in exactly the same way as in Fascist-influenced society at large:

In quanto al mondo della cospirazione antifascista, e in particolare agli ambienti legati al partito comunista, i ricordi dei suoi militanti ci restituiscono non solo gli elementi salienti del moralismo sessuofobico di matrice cattolica e piccolo-borghese ma anche le identiche forme repressive di controllo comunitario contro ogni tendenza trasgressiva.[13]

This sociological background is invaluable if we are to begin to understand the undercurrents marking the accounts of Pavese, Pizzardo, the editorial and creative reticence of Calvino and Ginzburg and, to some extent, Primo Levi's unease when discussing sexual matters. All these writers were brought up in an atmosphere that decried all sexual activity outside marriage and sought to interfere with relationships even within marriage.[14] It would be inappropriate and deluding to expect the products of this society to have been completely unaffected by its sustained propaganda during their formative years.

In Tina Pizzardo's memoir we witness these effects on someone who was clearly an independent-minded, courageous woman, but who nevertheless felt constrained by the mores of the time to conceal her amorous activities. More surprisingly, many years later, when writing her memoirs, she still feels constrained to conceal the reality of her various liaisons, not only from the reader, but also, one suspects, from herself. *Senza pensarci due volte* is a disconcerting read, offering on the one hand an account of the hardships endured by its narrator at the hands of the Fascist regime, but at the same time a list of romantic encounters, all of which, except that with Altiero Spinelli, according to the narrator, stop short of full sexual consummation, and which end with her happy marriage to the best suitor. Far from following the model of a political memoir, the book is rather a picaresque tale of amorous adventures, and a traditional love-story dominates the text. It also seems to be untrue, or at least evasive, if set against other people's accounts of the same events.

There are three main relationships that interest us at this distance in time, one with Altiero Spinelli, one with Cesare Pavese and the last with Henek Rieser, the Polish-Jewish émigré whom Tina eventually married. Tina's perception of these relationships, the picture of them that emerges from between the lines of her own account and the picture that two of the men themselves present (Spinelli and Pavese: Rieser has maintained a discreet silence), are all different. In his introduction to *Senza pensarci due volte*, Ugo Berto Arnoaldi makes the point that 'la verità [...] qui come nel tormentato caso di Pavese, starà nell'incrociarsi di sguardi diversi sullo stesso oggetto, nell'irriducibilità stessa delle visioni differenti'.[15] Spinelli went rather further and noted in 1979 that Tina 'sta scrivendo le sue memorie, ma vedo che ricorda cose che non ci sono mai accadute'.[16] Many of the lacunae or distortions in Pizzardo's account seem to lie in the area of sexual involvement, and, since Pavese's comments about her in his diary are of a highly sexual nature and indicate an attitude to sex verging on the dysfunctional, it would seem that it is in this particular area that we can discern the most complex layers of concealment: Pizzardo alters the truth to herself and to her readers later on; Pavese blames Pizzardo for his own psychological problems (and possibly physical ones too) and so distorts a particular truth for himself whilst otherwise recording quite frankly what happened between him and Pizzardo; Calvino and Ginzburg conceal this material from readers of the future.

Altiero Spinelli had been a Communist since he was 17 years old, and at 18 had already been promoted to a senior position within the clandestine network, within a very short period running the Communist youth section for the whole of the north of Italy. Tina, though older than he (23 years old), was considered very much his inferior, in terms of political maturity and, of course, because she was female and therefore was automatically accorded a minor role in the organization. What might have been a brief, youthful flirtation of no consequence acquired enormous significance because, almost immediately, Altiero was arrested and condemned to a terrible sentence of 16 years and 11 months imprisonment, of which he served 11 years. The brief but passionate relationship was sustained through letters over almost the whole of Spinelli's incarceration.

It would have been understandable if Tina had discontinued this relationship, rather than going along with the delusion that the two would one day be reunited and marry; however, the mores of the time insisted that a betrothal had taken place. Tina was part of the family and exchanged letters with Altiero's mother, in a recognizable, even clichéd mother-in-law/daughter-in-law relationship characterized by De Luna as 'difficile e sofferto'.[17] The fact is that Tina and Altiero consummated their relationship and therefore were bonded by convention, confusingly so, since Altiero suffered from the 'moglie/amante' delusion, to the extent that his only physical sexual encounters up until this point had been with prostitutes. He is frank about all this in his own autobiography.[18] Pizzardo mentions it bitterly in hers (*SP* 39): 'La disgustosa lettera dove, col pretesto di assoluta sincerità, mi racconta di aver cercato una prostituta e di essersi con lei "saziato come un porco"'. The story of this couple, tormented by the confusion of their own sexual desires contrasted with the demands of contemporary 'morality', makes painful reading. Time together alone was infrequent and snatched. Both write of an episode in the hills near Turin, when Altiero attempted to have sexual intercourse with Tina and she rejected 'quel rozzo tentativo'. She adds (ibid.):

Certo, se non fossi stata vergine lo avrei egualmente respinto, per il modo, il luogo, ma non avrei detto la fatale parola che [...] lo ha di colpo inibito.

This hint at impotence is confirmed in Spinelli's own account (*Come ho tentato*, 106):

L'emozione fu così forte che uno strano timore prevalse sul desiderio e mi tolse ogni forza. Rimasi umiliato di questa improvvisa e inspiegabile impotenza. In incontri successivi mi ritrovai nella stessa vergognosa situazione.

The 'love' between the two is now conditioned entirely by a psychological trauma brought about by their attempt to have full sexual relations in the moral atmosphere of the time. Altiero is unable to reconcile the attitudes inspired by his upbringing with the prospect of physical relations before marriage with a woman he loves. This makes him both impotent and spiteful, as Pizzardo recounts (*SP* 39–40). Eventually, full sexual consummation takes place, an encounter that Pizzardo laconically notes as 'la nostra prima e deludente intimità' (*SP* 41) but Spinelli describes in euphoric terms: 'per tre notti e tre giorni non facemmo che prenderci e darci ebbri e felici' (*Come ho tentato*, 106). Clearly, while the event (sexual intimacy), its date (April 1927) and its location (Milan, a room in Corso Buenos Aires) can be assumed to be historical fact, the quality and exact nature of the encounter is open to such infinite interpretation within the boundaries of the two descriptions that it acquires an almost tragicomic flavour.

This confusion of response seems to be repeated on both sides in the relationship between Pizzardo and Pavese. At no point in her autobiography does Tina Pizzardo ever admit that she had full sexual relations with Pavese; however, in the unexpurgated version of *Il mestiere di vivere*, it is clear that a great deal of sexual activity was going on, however oblique the references. For example, the entry for 5 January 1938 actually states: 'Chi le ha chiesto di tornare? Chi le ha chiesto di tornare a letto?' (*MV* 76; see p. lxviii for a full list of the diary entries in which Pavese writes about sexual matters).

Once more, impotence becomes an issue. It seems that, at its simplest, Tina Pizzardo was a sexually active woman, yet at the same time was a teacher and a political activist and therefore did not fit into the 'loose-woman' mould that contemporary mores and propaganda expected. This was confusing for her and for the men involved with her, with the result that they suffered psychological and physical disturbance, and she is reluctant to admit that she was sexually active, maintaining the attitude of a 1950s teenager to 'going all the way', even at many years' distance. When she tired of her partners, for whatever reason, and moved onto the next, the rejected partner was even more confused and distressed and responded with anger and vitriol. In other words, a 'respectable' but sexually active woman like Tina Pizzardo did present a puzzle in sociological terms and, by turning the 'rules' of contemporary society on their head, both wielded power but also left herself open to opprobrium. As an interesting aside, it would seem that Pavese's impotence, however, was probably even more complicated than this and may have had a physical cause. Pizzardo offers the following information (*SP* 187):

C'è un episodio che nessuno, credo, conosce e io lo riferisco perché mi pare che getti un po' di luce sul suo segreto tormento. Ricordo il suo povero sorriso mentre diceva di essersi fatto fare da un medico confinato con lui un piccolo intervento ... 'qualcosa come la circoncisione'. 'Così ... per niente ... per prepararmi alle nozze ...'.

There are not many operations that could have been carried out under these rather primitive circumstances, but a likely possibility is the cutting of the fraenulum of the prepuce, a simple procedure which would alleviate difficulties with maintaining an erection in cases where the difficulties derived from this particular physical cause. Psychological difficulties are another matter and could still persist, even if they were initially exacerbated by the physical defect. Tina Pizzardo has been more discreet than I am here, but nevertheless she has given us enough information to indicate that there were problems of this kind with Pavese, something borne out by his own admissions in *Il mestiere di vivere* (e.g. *MV* 392, 9 March 1950). This physical/psychological problem seems to have been linked in Pavese's mind with his political failings (*MV* 396, 27 May 1950), a link in its turn leading back to his sexual dealings with Tina Pizzardo, the political and sexual activist, and reflected artistically in the conflation of commitment to a woman and commitment to a cause that we see in *La casa in collina*. In other words, what may seem a prurient and inappropriate investigation here on my part is pertinent to the psychological and political development of Pavese and many other young men of that time. De Luna makes this clear in his very sensitive study of the links between the personal and the public in *Donne in oggetto*.

Tina Pizzardo's attitude to Pavese was teasing; by her own admission, 'Io pensavo a una sorta di scanzonato flirt' (*SP* 154). At the time of her first encounter with Pavese she had already met Henek, and, though she describes him as 'il compagno Henek', nevertheless she cannot resist seeing him as possible lover, 'purché non s'innamori di me', she observes (*SP* 157). The rigid structure imposed on male–female relationships meant that the possibility of sexual involvement acquired an air of inevitability, a common phenomenon in all societies where sexual energy is perceived as dangerous. Carlo Levi describes this same effect in *Cristo si è fermato a Eboli*, set in the same years and in an extremely restrictive community. In present times, the enforced wearing of all-enveloping clothing by women in strict Muslim communities, or even the covering of the hair, all imply that the sexual urge is so strong and women so naturally provocative that sex will automatically ensue when men and women are together in any circumstance. In this sense, Tina Pizzardo's teasing and flirting and her assumption that men would 'fall in love' with her, described throughout her autobiography, paradoxically comes about because she is a product of a sexually repressive society. When it transpires that Henek is in love with someone else and feels sorry for her, her response makes her psychological confusion clear; having said she preferred him not to fall for her, now that he has indeed avoided this pitfall, she feels betrayed (*SP* 159):

Pietà per me! Non potevo sopportarla. Gli avrei fatto vedere se avevo bisogno di pietà. Sempre di fronte a una disillusione, un tradimento, il mio impulso è agire, punire, vendicarsi, far qualcosa e non star lì a piangerci su.

She therefore approaches Pavese again and, with obscure reasoning, blames him for her situation (*SP* 161): 'Se avessi avuto la sua amicizia non sarei andata a cercare altro e non mi sarei ridotta a ispirare pietà.' Soon her relationship with Pavese has progressed to a romantic stage, involving 'qualche leggero rapido bacio' (*SP* 163), but she insists that it is all 'per scherzo', even Pavese's halting declarations of love. At this point (February 1934), Tina is seeing both Pavese and Henek and still writing to Altiero in prison. She is thirty-one, Pavese twenty-six. In March, Tina tells Pavese she would like to be just friends with him, he bursts into tears (*SP* 165: 'Ricordo la delusione, il fastidio, l'imbarazzo per quei lacrimoni che venivano giù a pioggia e rotolavano sul bavero del paltò') but accepts her conditions. Nevertheless, by the end of April 1934, something has happened between them. She calls it 'niente' initially (*SP* 166), but goes on:

E poi un momento, solo un momento di lucida follia, d'abbandono. E mentre, rinsavita, mi rallegro che non sia successo niente, lui è già in ginocchio e dice che ora dobbiamo sposarci e saremo tanto felici.

There follows 'la bella estate', but also a disastrous winter, when Pavese disgraces himself by sulking on a skiing trip. Clearly the relationship was not going well, at least from Tina's point of view. She introduces the chapter concerning the arrest of Pavese and the others with an uncompromising picture of his behaviour on the mountain. This suggests that for her the separation was already taking place and was not the result of Pavese's exile. Pizzardo is adamant that Pavese's arrest was not caused by his possession of politically incriminating letters for her from Maffi and dismisses such claims as 'fantasiose sciocchezze' (*SP* 179). She explains that had Pavese been at all politically astute, he would have realized that the Italian secret police (OVRA) were likely to arrest and question randomly the friends and contacts of those they actually knew to be involved in the Giustizia e Libertà organization. As ex-editor of the journal *La Cultura* he was bound to be questioned, but, she argues, with a little 'avvedutezza', could have avoided the matter going further. She explains, scathingly (*SP* 179):

Perché si sentiva politicamente innocuo e de 'La Cultura' s'infischiava, perché aveva sempre vagheggiato di rovinarsi per una donna, Pavese ha preferito credere di esser finito al confino per i biglietti di Maffi e quindi per colpa mia. Questo lasciava capire nelle lettere e, tornato dal confino, è andato dicendo a tutti.

Come 'al confino per colpa di lei' si sia poi trasformato in: 'al confino per salvare lei', non riesco a capirlo. Da lui io no l'ho mai sentito.

Mentre scrivo mi viene d'un tratto in mente che, col passar del tempo, Pavese può averlo veramente creduto. Sì, più tardi, quando la sofferenza si è mutata in rancore può aver pensato: 'Io ho saputo tacere ciò che avrebbe potuto comprometterla: l'amicizia con Ginzburg, con la Barbara Allason, con quelli che frequentavano il salotto di Barbara e soprattutto tacere che mi ha sempre respinto perché non condividevo le sue idee. Così, a mio rischio, l'ho salvata.'

This passage offers a fascinating example of the 'incrociarsi di sguardi diversi sullo stesso oggetto' with its alternative (and believable) interpretation of events. It also offers an insight into how an autobiography can take shape, with an opinion apparently forming on the page as we read and transmuting to 'truth' before our eyes, the matter further complicated by the fact that this 'truth' is a self-deception assumed to have taken place in someone else's mind, which here becomes concrete, in the form of direct speech.

Pizzardo's next chapter is called 'Il tradimento', referring ironically to her supposed betrayal of Pavese by marrying while he was in exile. She makes this ironic intention clear when she debunks the myth perpetrated by Lajolo that Pavese learnt of her marriage as he descended from the train on his return, and promptly fainted (*SP* 184; italics original):

Noto, perché è un bell'esempio della sua impostazione fumettistica, che nel libro di Lajolo Pavese arriva a matrimonio avvenuto, gli danno la notizia appena scende dal treno e perciò: tre tonfi. Lui e le due valige, tutti e tre sbattuti a terra dal *tradimento*.

She points out that her wedding did not take place until 19 April 1936, but Pavese returned on 19 March. This is borne out by Pavese's letters and his diary entries. Nevertheless, Tina's clarity of vision regarding this matter blurs when questions of romantic involvement arise: her marriage to Henek Rieser could be viewed as a triple betrayal or *tradimento*: of Spinelli in prison, of Pavese in exile and of Rieser himself, since she describes the marriage as 'nient'altro che una mossa di strategia amorosa' (*SP* 181), undertaken with the knowledge that as it was a mixed Catholic/Jewish union it would be possible to divorce later, and also embarked upon, the writer claims, as a kind of challenge, since 'la legge polacca che vietava il matrimonio tra ebrei e cattolici era un ostacolo forse insormontabile' (*SP* 182).

This should have been the end of the story as far as Pavese and 'la donna dalla voce rauca' were concerned, but fifteen months after her marriage, in July 1937, Tina contacted Pavese again while her husband was away in Poland visiting his father. Pavese notes in capitals in his diary: 'IL 4 LUGLIO È RITORNATA TINA'; they see one another every day, Pavese wants Tina to divorce, but Henek is due back on 15 July, and on the 13th Tina 'breaks' with Pavese. In October, Pavese sends her a letter of hatred, a letter she destroys, though its contents can be imagined, as, of course, this period coincides with the most vitriolic and misogynist entries in the unexpurgated edition of *Il mestiere di vivere*. Tina and Pavese saw each other a few more times up until May–July 1938, when Pavese offered Tina his diary as a goodbye token. She refused it, 'per quella sciocca generosità di cui ho sempre di che pentirmi' (*SP* 196) and was horrified when it was published within a relatively short time.

Again, we are offered fascinating insights into how a 'true' document might have changed its nature: Pizzardo claims that Pavese states that he offered her the only and complete version of his diary.

However, she expresses doubts about this on two counts, firstly because she had seen published 'poesie, racconti di cui io avevo "l'unica copia"' and secondly because 'nel diario integrale ho trovato passi ingiuriosi che non ricordavo di aver letto' (*SP* 196). She paints a somewhat comical picture of bullying Italo Calvino into showing her the pre-publication typescript, which she again describes as possibly inauthentic (ibid.):

Quando prima della pubblicazione mi è stato concesso, per la timidezza di Italo Calvino che non ha osato rifiutare, di leggere la copia dattiloscritta integrale, ho avuto il sospetto che Pavese avesse ritoccato la parte che mi riguarda, o tolto, per rancore, alcuni passi illuminanti.

Tina ends her story at more or less this point, confirming the tone of the book as a personal romantic odyssey rather than a political memoir: she is pregnant with her husband's child and she lives happily ever after. The problems of the war, the racial laws, the horrors taking place over Europe and no doubt afflicting her husband's friends and family, are all merely hinted at and dismissed as not part of her story (*SP* 197):

Uscito Pavese dalla mia vita, nonostante le tempeste (campagna razziale, guerra, resistenza e sempre miseria e lavoro), ho trovato pace nell'amore per Henek e per nostro figlio.

These words are echoed almost exactly in the final sentence of the book, as if to reassure the writer and the reader of their authenticity (*SP* 201):

Uscito Pavese dalla mia vita non è più stato il caso a segnarmi la strada, ma solo l'amore per Henek e per nostro figlio.

There could be no more contradictory a pair of accounts than Pizzardo's and Pavese's representations of their relationship, both filtered through each writer's distorting glass: the glass of guilt and a false sense of propriety on one side, and of humiliation, hatred and resentment on the other. According to Pizzardo, her actions and intentions with regard to Pavese were always innocent and honorable; according to Pavese, Pizzardo was manipulative, conniving and dishonest. If we were to take a single lesson from this reading, it would be that all writing is fiction of a kind, even when it purports to be truth.

In the introduction to this study, I wrote that I intended to examine what authors left unsaid in their texts, in other words, alternative ways of saying. Often, as in this case, what we find ourselves examining and determining are alternative ways of seeing. Furthermore, a writer's interpretation and evaluation of his or her environment, whether refashioned as fiction or 'fact', will always be coloured by external influences. If we add to this psychological effect the demands of editors, publishers and public, we see that often the only route to the 'truth', metaphorical or actual, is by way not of what is said, but of what is not said.

Notes to Chapter 6

1. Luisa Mangoni, *Pensare i libri: La casa editrice Einaudi dagli anni Trenta agli anni Sessanta* (Turin: Bollati Boringhieri, 1999).
2. Severino Cesari, *Colloquio con Giulio Einaudi* (Rome and Naples: Theoria, 1991), 10–11.
3. Ibid., 11.
4. Giulio Einaudi, *Frammenti di memoria* (Milan: Rizzoli, 1988); cf. Natalia Ginzburg, 'Memoria contro memoria', *Paragone*, no. 462 (Aug. 1988), 3–9.
5. Vittorio Foa, 'Einaudi in frammenti', ibid., 10–15 at 12.
6. Ginsborg, *A History of Contemporary Italy*, 244.
7. Marc Beckwith, 'Italo Calvino and the Nature of Italian Folktales', *Italica* 64 (1987), 244–62 at 257.
8. Quoted ibid., 261, from a conversation with Alessandro Falassi in May 1980.
9. Vittorio Imbriani, *La novellaja fiorentina*, 2nd edn (Livorno: F. Vigo, 1877), 413.
10. De Luna, *Donne in oggetto*, 103.
11. Ibid., 163.
12. Ibid., 202.
13. Ibid., 205.
14. Ibid., 201.
15. Ugo Berto Arnoaldi, introduction to Pizzardo, *Senza pensarci due volte*, p. v.
16. Altiero Spinelli, *Diario europeo*, 3 vols. (Bologna: Il Mulino, 1989–92), iii. 261 (10 Feb. 1979).
17. De Luna, *Donne in oggetto*, 292.
18. Altiero Spinelli, *Come ho tentato di diventare saggio* (Bologna: Il Mulino, 1988), 46.

CONCLUSION

In the Introduction to this book I suggested that the writers I was about to discuss had selected themselves to some extent, because I found that it was only by examining elements of the unsaid in their work that certain 'puzzles' within their writing could be solved. I should like to return to the reasons for my selections and point out that there were other unifying factors, other reasons for writing this particular book.

Martin Amis speaks of a search for 'prose works which address the American century'.[1] In global terms it will probably seem to future generations that the twentieth century was indeed 'the American century'. Despite this probability, and perhaps because of it, I was looking for works and writers that address the European century, and particularly the second half of the twentieth century, after the Second World War. For Europeans, the twentieth century has been a white-hot crucible of change, not least owing to the effects of two devastating wars. America's influence has been of undeniable cultural, political and social importance in Europe as elsewhere, but the twentieth century was the last era when Europe was divided into discrete cultures and rivalries and before rapid communications smudged the differences between European countries. Whatever the future brings for Europe politically, it seems impossible that there will ever be this cultural separation again.

Historically, the turning-point of the twentieth century was the Second World War, with the great cruelties of the Third Reich marking a terrible hiatus in our perception of mankind's moral and cultural progress. Whilst there have been large-scale atrocities before and since, the breathtaking scandal of Nazi occupation and the concentration camps has made all thoughtful people aware that civilization is not a continuous upward graph. Atrocities since the war, in whichever part of the world and however appalling, are regarded with a sense of weary inevitability, since we all now realize that if barbarity could rage so recently in the heart of cultured and civilized Europe, it would be foolish and illogical to assume that 'progress' can offer any protection against mankind's primitive urges.

Alongside this sense of mistrust of human progress however, major positive social change has taken place, attempts by those in power genuinely to better existence for fellow human beings, unparalleled in other centuries. Divisions based on class and wealth have been broken down, sexual mores and the role of women in society have altered radically. Whatever 'backlash' responses pundits may predict, whatever the failures of our society, it is unlikely that these movements can ever be put into reverse, short of the total disintegration of the world as it is at present (a prospect that the threat of nuclear war has of course made a distinct possibility, though, after a brief period of public apprehension in the 1960s and 1970s, we all now live as if it still remains improbable).

As Europe in the twentieth century therefore, and particularly the second half, has been the cauldron for profound change, and as one of the purposes of great literature is to reflect something of human experience, I wanted to choose writers that reflected these changes. Italy is renowned for its centrality in the Renaissance; I felt that Italy had a significant role culturally, historically and artistically in the twentieth century too. In terms of history, it is not a role the Italians themselves always relish dwelling upon: Italian Fascism, the Second World War, alliance and then dissociation from Nazi Germany, these are sources of dissent and discomfort for Italians even today, not least because most of the ordinary Italian citizens who lived through those times experienced that era as a time of hardship and distress, whatever the political rhetoric under which they lived out their daily existences might have claimed. My choice of authors meant looking squarely at some of these difficult issues: as we have seen, Pavese's work centres on the crisis of conscience connected with Italy's wartime role; Levi and Ginzburg experienced at first hand the dire consequences of Italy's ill-judged alliance with Nazi Germany; Sanvitale was brought up in the insidious miasma of Fascist influence.

Primo Levi's importance as a literary and historical figure is now well established world-wide. The psychological complexity of his work and the insights it offers in the context of twentieth-century Europe, his specifically dual position as a scientist and author, Italian and Jew, liberal and product of his 1920s upbringing, made him an essential choice for any study of the unsaid or the unacknowledged.

Cesare Pavese's fortunes with the critics rise and fall periodically, a fact not unconnected with his undeniable misogyny, neurosis and political fallibility. Again, it was clear that a study of the repressed and unexpressed in such a writer was bound to be rewarding.

The canon in Italy has been highly resistant to female writers, and it is a sad paradox that many Italian women writers are better respected abroad than in Italy, at least in academic circles, and so it was important to me that my book should give equal weight to female writers as to male ones and redress the balance, at least within its pages. Natalia Ginzburg and Francesca Sanvitale, both excellent and accomplished writers aside from any considerations of gender, offered the opportunity to consider not only women's role as forgers of literary culture, but also their role within society. There are clear and undeniable links between feminist issues, class divisions and changes in public perception of morality, sexual and otherwise. These two writers explore these areas without being didactic or prescriptive, and bring humanity, insight and understanding to our perception of those fluctuating times; in short, we come to know what it was like to live then, and recent history emerges from a clutter of 'factual' detail as warm and actual.

By the 1950s, Freudianism and psychological realism, the great innovations of the early part of the century, were part of literary culture and indeed of everyday life. Post-war marketing and public-relations techniques took account of Freudianism as never before and began to shape our everyday experience. Our interpretation of the world around us became ever more self-aware, and postmodernism brought with it a kind of loss of innocence. My choice of authors therefore occupies a space when the fundamentally influential shock waves of the two wars had not yet died down, when psychological realism was an accepted norm in literature, but a neurotic self-awareness had not yet taken hold of writing. All four authors were shaped in pre-war or inter-war years and so are poised between two cultures, often uncomfortably so, giving rise to the gaps and ellipses upon which this book has focused. Francesca Sanvitale's work brings us close to the present day and shows us a way through and beyond the unsaid, revealing new expressive idioms.

The strong culturally-defining role of the publishing house Einaudi offered an irresistible opportunity to examine a microcosm of Italian society, the context within which all four important writers worked. The complicated network of relationships between these individuals and their public roles, the way in which they were all connected socially, culturally and professionally through this publisher all rewarded study. Again, Sanvitale represents a view outwards and forwards: her link with the publisher was only as one of its authors, but her role as a significant literary critic, editor of a literary journal and television scriptwriter all point towards a broader canvas, emphasizing by contrast the extent of Einaudi's power in the immediate twenty or so years after the war when the cultural field of operation was more circumscribed (and circumspect).

Tina Pizzardo is a figure who unconsciously brings together many of the elements discussed in this book: someone who was involved historically in the turmoil of the war, who appears in others' books and diaries, who has written autobiography, but in whose writing all the inconsistencies of narrative, all the pressures of society at different times are evident. She is a figure of many and contrasting identities, pressed into different moulds by the times she lived in, the people she met, the prevailing moral atmosphere about her, accorded a place in history only by chance, an 'ordinary' person made extraordinary by circumstance and by literature. As the recent biographies of Primo Levi have shown, she was even eventually at the centre of a kind of literary salon in 1950s Turin, a salon Levi himself frequented.[2]

Late-twentieth-century literary theory has tended to distance readers from stories, dehumanize them, break the links between the writing and the human beings behind it. Theories of the unsaid have been no exception; indeed, the abstraction of the concept of the unsaid has made it most attractive to those constructing complex and alienating analytical edifices around the human stories in the texts. In this book, my intention has been to take crucial texts, by significant individuals of historical and cultural importance, within a country central to Europe's destiny in the twentieth century, and by means of the notion of the unsaid to focus on the doubts, inconsistencies, regrets, in short, the humanity, of those writers and on the role the unsaid played in the creation of their texts.

Notes to Chapter 7

1. Martin Amis, *The War against Cliché* (London: Vintage, 2001), 379.
2. Angier, *The Double Bond*, 542; Thomson, *Primo Levi*, 277–8.

BIBLIOGRAPHY

Primary Sources

BASILE, GIAMBATTISTA, *Il pentamerone [...], overo Lo cunto de li cunte* (Naples: Salvatore Scarano, 1634–6).

CALVINO, ITALO, *Fiabe italiane* (Turin: Einaudi, 1956).

—— *Il sentiero dei nidi di ragno* (Milan: Mondadori, 1993).

—— *Lettere 1940–1985*, ed. Luca Baranelli (Milan: Mondadori, 2000).

CAPRIOLO, PAOLA, *La grande Eulalia* (Milan: Feltrinelli, 1988).

CARTER, ANGELA, *Nights at the Circus* (London: Chatto & Windus, 1984).

DURANTI, FRANCESCA, *La casa sul lago della luna* (Milan: Rizzoli, 1984).

EINAUDI, GIULIO, *Frammenti di memoria* (Milan: Rizzoli, 1988).

GINZBURG, NATALIA, *Lessico famigliare* (Milan: Mondadori, 1974; orig. pubd Turin: Einaudi, 1963). [*LF*]

—— *Cinque romanzi brevi* (Turin: Einaudi, 1964).

—— *Opere*, 2 vols. (Milan: Mondadori, 1986–7).

—— 'Memoria contro memoria', *Paragone*, no. 462 (Aug. 1988), 3–9.

—— *È difficile parlare di sé* [interviews with Mario Sinibaldi], ed. Cesare Garboli and Lisa Ginzburg (Turin: Einaudi, 1999).

IMBRIANI, VITTORIO, *La novellaja fiorentina*, 2nd edn. (Livorno: F. Vigo, 1877).

LEVI, PRIMO, *Opere*, ed. Marco Belpoliti, 2 vols. (Turin: Einaudi, 1997).

—— *Conversazioni e interviste, 1963–1987*, ed. Marco Belpoliti (Turin: Einaudi, 1997).

MARAINI, DACIA, *La lunga vita di Marianna Ucría* (Milan: Rizzoli, 1990).

PAVESE, CESARE, *La luna e i falò*, introd. Gian Luigi Beccaria (Turin: Einaudi, 2000; first pubd 1950). [*LEF*]

—— *Il mestiere di vivere*, ed. Marziano Guglielminetti and Laura Nay (Turin: Einaudi, 1990; first pubd 1952). [*MV*]

—— *Lettere 1945–50*, ed. Italo Calvino (Turin: Einaudi, 1966).

—— *La casa in collina*, idem, *Prima che il gallo canti* (Milan: Mondadori, 1967), 137–281. [*CC*]

—— *Il taccuino segreto*, La Stampa (8 Aug. 1990), 15–17.

—— *Racconti* (Turin: Einaudi, 1994).

PIZZARDO, TINA, *Senza pensarci due volte* (Bologna: Il Mulino, 1996). [*SP*]

PROUST, MARCEL, *A la recherche du temps perdu*, 4 vols., ed. Jean-Yves Tadié et al. (Paris: Gallimard, 1987–9).

SANVITALE, FRANCESCA, *Madre e figlia* (Turin: Einaudi, 1980; repr. 1994). [*MF*]

—— *Verso Paola* (Turin: Einaudi, 1991). [*VP*]

—— *Camera ottica: Pagine di letteratura e realtà* (Turin: Einaudi, 1999). [*CO*]

SPINELLI, ALTIERO, *Come ho tentato di diventare saggio* (Bologna: Il Mulino, 1988).

—— *Diario europeo*, 3 vols. (Bologna: Il Mulino, 1989–92).

STEINBERG, PAUL, *Speak You Also: A Survivor's Testimony* (London: Allen Lane, 2001).

VITTORINI, ELIO, *Le opere narrative*, ed. Maria Corti, 2 vols. (Milan: Mondadori, 1979).

WIESEL, ELIE, *La Nuit* (Paris: Minuit, 1958).

Secondary Sources

AMIS, MARTIN, *The War against Cliché* (London: Vintage, 2001).

ANGIER, CAROLE, *The Double Bond: Primo Levi, a Biography* (London: Viking, 2002).

BAKHTIN, MIKHAIL, *Esthétique et théorie du roman* (Paris: Gallimard, 1978).

—— *The Dialogic Imagination: Four Essays*, ed. Michael Holquist, trans. Caryl Emerson and Michael Holquist (Austin: University of Texas Press, 1981).

BARANI, VALERIA, 'Il fondo Natalia Ginzburg', *Autografo* 3/23 (June 1991), 71–7.

BARAŃSKI, ZYGMUNT, and VINALL, SHIRLEY (eds.), *Women and Italy: Essays on gender, Culture and History* (London: Macmillan, 1991).

BARTHES, ROLAND, *Le Degré zéro de l'écriture* (Paris: Éditions du Seuil, 1972).

—— *Essais critiques: Le Bruissement de la langue* (Paris: Éditions du Seuil, 1985).

BECKWITH, MARC, 'Italo Calvino and the Nature of Italian Folktales', *Italica* 64 (1987), 244–62.

BELPOLITI, MARCO, *Primo Levi* (Milan: Mondadori, 1998).

—— 'Levi: Il falso scandalo', *La rivista dei libri* (Jan. 2000), 25–7.

—— (ed.), *Primo Levi: Riga 13* (Milan: Marcos y Marcos, 1991).

BENSTOCK, SHARI (ed.), *The Private Self: Theory and Practice of Women's Autobiographical Writings* (London: Routledge, 1988).

BETTELHEIM, BRUNO, *The Informed Heart* (London: Penguin, 1986; first pubd 1960).

—— *The Uses of Enchantment* (London: Penguin, 1976).

BETTINI, MAURIZIO, *The Portrait of the Lover*, trans. Laura Gibbs (Berkeley: University of California Press, 1999).

BLANCHOT, MAURICE, *La Part du feu* (Paris: Gallimard, 1949).

—— *L'Espace littéraire* (Paris: Gallimard, 1955).

—— *The Writing of the Disaster / L'Écriture du désastre*, trans. Ann Smock (Lincoln: University of Nebraska Press, 1982).

BLELLOCH, PAOLA, 'Francesca Sanvitale's *Madre e figlia*: From Self-Reflection to Self-Invention', *Contemporary Women Writers in Italy: A Modern Renaissance*, ed. S. L. Aricò (Amherst: University of Massachusetts Press, 1990), 125–37.

BLOOM, HAROLD, *The Anxiety of Influence* (New York: Oxford University Press, 1973).

BONFANTINI, M., 'Il muto segreto di molte esistenze', *Corriere della sera* (14 Feb. 1965), 3.

BORRELLI, CLARA, 'Lirismo narrativo di Natalia Ginzburg', *Annali dell' Istituto Universitario Orientale di Napoli* 29 (1987), 289–310.

BOTTIGHEIMER, RUTH B., *Grimms' Bad Girls and Bold Boys: The Moral and Social Vision of the Tales* (New Haven and London: Yale University Press, 1987).

BRANDE, DOROTHEA, *Becoming a Writer* (London: Macmillan, 1996; first pubd 1934).

BRODZKI, BELLA, and SCHENCK, CELESTE M. (eds.), *Life/Lines: Theorizing Women's Autobiography* (Ithaca, NY: Cornell University Press, 1988).

BUDICK, SANDFORD, and ISER, WOLFGANG, *Languages of the Unsayable: The Play of Negativity in Literature and Literary Theory* (New York: Columbia University Press, 1989).

BULLOCK, ALAN, *Natalia Ginzburg* (New York and Oxford: Berg, 1991).

CAESAR, ANN HALLAMORE, 'Francesca Sanvitale, Investigating the Self and the World', *The New Italian Novel*, ed. Zygmunt G. Barański and Lino Pertile (Edinburgh: Edinburgh University Press, 1993), 184–99.

CALVINO, ITALO, *Una pietra sopra* (Turin: Einaudi, 1980).

CAREY, JOHN, *The Intellectuals and the Masses* (London: Faber and Faber, 1992).

—— *The Faber Book of Science* (London: Faber and Faber, 1996).

CAVAGLION, ALBERTO, *Primo Levi e 'Se questo è un uomo'* (Turin: Loescher, Il passo del cavallo, 1993).

CESARI, SEVERINO, *Colloquio con Giulio Einaudi* (Rome and Naples: Theoria, 1991).

CHEYETTE, BRYAN, 'The Ethical Uncertainty of Primo Levi', *Modernity, Culture and the Jew*, ed. Bryan Cheyette and Laura Marcus (Cambridge: Polity Press, 1998).

CICIONI, MIRNA, *Primo Levi: Bridges of Knowledge* (Oxford and Washington: Berg, 1995).

CIXOUS, HÉLÈNE, and CLÉMENT, CATHERINE, *La Jeune née* (Paris, 1975).

COLLINS, CHRISTOPHER, *The Poetics of the Mind's Eye: Literature and the Psychology of the Imagination* (Philadelphia: University of Pennsylvania Press, 1991), 268–81.

DAVIS, COLIN, *Elie Wiesel's Secretive Texts* (Gainesville: University Press of Florida, 1994).

DE GRAND, ALEXANDER, *Italian Fascism: Its Origins and Development*, 2nd edn (Lincoln: University of Nebraska Press, 1989).

DE LUNA, GIOVANNI, *Donne in oggetto: L'antifascismo nella società italiana, 1922–1939* (Turin: Bollati Boringhieri, 1995).

DERRIDA, JACQUES, *Writing and Difference*, trans. and with an introd. and additional notes by Alan Bass (Chicago: University of Chicago Press, 1978).

DIONISOTTI, CARLO, 'Per un taccuino di Pavese', *Belfagor* 46 (1991), 1–12.

DUCROT, OSWALD, *Dire et ne pas dire: Principes de sémantique linguistique* (Paris: Hermann, 1972).

EAKIN, PAUL JOHN, *Touching the World: Reference in Autobiography* (Princeton: Princeton University Press, 1992).

ECO, UMBERTO, with RORTY, RICHARD, CULLER, JONATHAN, and BROOKE-ROSE, CHRISTINE, *Interpretation and Overinterpretation*, ed. Stefan Collini (Cambridge: Cambridge University Press, 1992).

FANNING, URSULA, 'Sibilla Aleramo's *Una donna*: A Case Study in Women's Autobiographical Fiction', *The Italianist* (Nov. 2000), 164–77.

FILIPELLI, FIAMMETTA, 'Memoria e realtà nell'itinerario narrativo di Francesca Sanvitale', *Annali Istituto Universitario Orientale, Napoli: Sezione Romanza* 33 (1991), 217–29.

FOA, VITTORIO, 'Einaudi in frammenti', *Paragone*, no. 462 (Aug. 1988), 10–15.

FOUCAULT, MICHEL, *Madness and Civilisation*, trans. Richard Howard (New York: Pantheon, 1965).

—— *Surveiller et punir: Naissance de la prison* (Paris: Gallimard, 1975).

GARBOLI, CESARE, Introduction to NATALIA GINZBURG, *Lessico famigliare* (Milan: Mondadori, 1974), pp. x–xv.

—— 'Fortuna critica', *Natalia Ginzburg: Opere*, 2 vols. (Milan: Mondadori, 1986–7), ii. 1577–91.

GILBERT, SANDRA, and GUBAR, SUSAN, *The Madwoman in the Attic: The Woman Writer and the Nineteenth Century Literary Imagination* (New Haven: Yale University Press, 1979).

GILLIGAN, CAROL, *In a Different Voice: Psychological Theory and Women's Development* (Cambridge, MA: Harvard University Press, 1982).

GINSBORG, PAUL, *A History of Contemporary Italy: Society and Politics, 1943–1988* (London: Penguin, 1990).

GIOANOLA, ELIO, *Cesare Pavese: La poetica dell'essere*, 2nd edn (Milan: Marzorati, 1972).

GORDON, ROBERT, '"Per mia fortuna ...": Irony and Ethics in Primo Levi's Writing', *Modern Language Review* 92 (1997), 337–47.

—— 'Pasolini contro Calvino: Culture, the Canon and the Millennium', *Modern Italy* 3 (1998), 87–99.

—— *Primo Levi's Ordinary Virtues: From Testimony to Ethics* (Oxford: Oxford University Press, 2001).

GRIGNANI, MARIA ANTONIETTA, 'Un concerto di voci', *Natalia Ginzburg: La narratrice e i suoi testi*, ed. eadem (Rome: La Nuova Italia, 1986), 48–54.

GUSDORF, GEORGES, 'Conditions and Limits of Autobiography', *Autobiography*, ed. James Olney (Princeton: Princeton University Press, 1980), 28–48.

HEDGES, ELAINE, and FISHKIN, SHELLEY FISHER (eds.), *Listening to 'Silences': New Essays in Feminist Criticism* (New York: Oxford University Press, 1994).

HEILBRUN, CAROLYN, *Writing a Woman's Life* (New York: Norton, 1988).

HORROCKS, ROGER, *Male Myths and Icons: Masculinity in Popular Culture* (London: Macmillan, 1995).

HOWE, IRVING, 'How to Write About the Holocaust', *New York Review of Books* (28 Mar. 1985), 14–17.

JAY, MARTIN, 'In the Empire of the Gaze', *Foucault: A Critical Reader*, ed. David Couzens Hoy (Oxford: Blackwell, 1986), 175–204.

JEFFERSON, ANN, 'Bodymatters: Self and Other in Bakhtin, Sartre and Barthes', *Bakhtin and Cultural Theory*, ed. Ken Hirschkop and David Shepherd (Manchester: Manchester University Press, 1986), 152–77.

—— 'Autobiography as Intertext: Barthes, Sarraute, Robbe-Grillet', *Intertextuality: Theories and Practices*, ed. Michael Worton and Judith Still (Manchester: Manchester University Press, 1990), 108–29.

JELINEK, ESTELLE C. (ed.) *Women's Autobiography: Essays in Criticism* (Bloomington: Indiana University Press, 1980).

KAPLAN, E. ANN, 'Is the Gaze Male?', eadem, *Women and Film: Both Sides of the Camera* (London and New York: Methuen, 1983), 321–38.

KERMODE, FRANK, *The Sense of an Ending: Studies in the Theory of Fiction* (New York: Oxford University Press, 1968).

—— *The Genesis of Secrecy* (Cambridge, MA: Harvard University Press, 1979).

KLINDIEST, PATRICIA, 'The Voice of the Shuttle is Ours', *Literary Theory: An Anthology*, ed. Julie Rivkin and Michael Ryan (Oxford: Blackwell, 1998), 612–29.

LA BELLE, JENIJOY, *Herself Beheld: The Literature of the Looking Glass* (Ithaca, NY: Cornell University Press, 1988).

LACAN, JACQUES, *Écrits: A Selection*, trans. Alan Sheridan (New York: Norton, 1977).

LAJOLO, DAVIDE, *Il vizio assurdo* (Milan: Il Saggiatore, 1960).

LAURENCE, PATRICIA, 'Women's Silence as a Ritual of Truth', *Listening to 'Silences': New Essays in Feminist Criticism*, ed. Elaine Hedges and Shelley Fisher Fishkin (New York: Oxford University Press, 1994), 156–67.

LEJEUNE, PHILIPPE, *L'Autobiographie en France* (Paris: Armand Colin, 1971).

—— *Le Pacte autobiographique* (Paris: Éditions du Seuil, 1975).

LOOMIS, C. GRANT, *White Magic: An Introduction to the Folklore of Christian Legend* (Cambridge, MA: Mediaeval Academy of America, 1948).

LYOTARD, JEAN-FRANÇOIS, *Le Différend* (Paris: Minuit, 1983).

MCLAUGHLIN, MARTIN, *Italo Calvino* (Edinburgh: Edinburgh University Press, 1998).

MAGRINI, CLAUDIO, 'Lessico famigliare di Natalia Ginzburg', *Letteratura italiana*, dir. Alberto Asor Rosa, viii: *Le opere*, iv/2: *Novecento: Ricerca letteraria* (Turin: Einaudi, 1996), 771–810.

MANGONI, LUISA, *Pensare i libri: La casa editrice Einaudi dagli anni Trenta agli anni Sessanta* (Turin: Bollati Boringhieri, 1999).

MERRY, BRUCE, *Dacia Maraini and the Written Dream of Women in Italian Literature* (Townsville: Department of Modern Languages, James Cook University of Northern Queensland, 1997).

MINGHELLI, GIULIANA, 'Ricordando il quotidiano: *Lessico famigliare* o l'arte del cantastorie', *Italica* 72 (1995) 155–73.

MUSUMECI, ANTONINO, *L'impossibile ritorno* (Ravenna: Longo, 1980).

NEHER, ANDRÉ, *L'Exil de la parole: Du silence biblique au silence d'Auschwitz* (Paris: Éditions du Seuil, 1970).

O'HEALY, AÍNE, *Cesare Pavese* (Boston: Twayne, 1988).

OLNEY, JAMES, *Metaphors of Self: The Meaning of Autobiography* (Princeton: Princeton University Press, 1960).

—— (ed.), *Autobiography: Essays Theoretical and Critical* (Princeton: Princeton University Press, 1980).

OLSEN, TILLIE, *Silences* (New York: Delacorte Press/Seymour Lawrence, 1978).

PIETTE, ADAM, *Remembering and the Sounds of Words* (Oxford: Clarendon Press, 1996).

RAK, MICHELE, *Napoli gentile: La letteratura in 'lingua napoletana' nella cultura barocca (1596–1632)* (Bologna: Il Mulino, 1994).

RIVKIN, JULIE, and RYAN, MICHAEL, 'Feminist Paradigms', *Literary Theory: An Anthology*, ed. iidem (Oxford: Blackwell, 1998), 527–32.

SCHWENGER, PETER, *Fantasm and Fiction: On Textual Envisioning* (Stanford: Stanford University Press, 1999).

SIBELMAN, SIMON P., *Silence in the Novels of Elie Wiesel* (New York: St Martin's Press, 1995).

SOAVE BOWE, CLOTILDE, 'The narrative strategy of Natalia Ginzburg', *Modern Language Review* 68 (1973), 788–95.

SODI, RISA, 'An interview with Primo Levi', *Partisan Review* 14 (1987), 355–66.

SONTAG, SUSAN, *Against Interpretation* (London: Eyre and Spottiswoode, 1967).

STEINER, GEORGE, *Language and Silence* (London: Faber and Faber, 1967).

STERN, SHEILA, *Swann's Way* (Cambridge: Cambridge University Press, 1989).

SUMELI WEINBERG, M. G., 'La forza della negatività: La dialettica del soggetto parlante nella *Lunga vita di M.U.* di Dacia Maraini', *Otto/Novecento* 19 (1995), 177–86.

THOMPSON, STITH, *The Folktale* (New York: Dryden Press, 1946; repr. Berkeley: University of California Press, 1977).

THOMSON, IAN, *Primo Levi* (London: Hutchinson, 2002).

TODOROV, TSVETAN, *Poétique de la prose* (Paris: Éditions du Seuil, 1971).

—— *The Fantastic: A Structural Approach to a Literary Genre*, trans. Richard Howard (Cleveland: Press of Case Western Reserve University, 1973).

WARNER, MARINA, *Monuments and Maidens* (London: Weidenfeld & Nicholson, 1985).

—— *From the Beast to the Blonde: On Fairytales and their Tellers* (London: Chatto & Windus, 1994). [BB]

WLASSICS, TIBOR, *Pavese falso e vero* (Turin: Centro Studi Piemontesi, 1985).

WOOD, SHARON, *Italian Women's Writing, 1860–1994* (London: Athlone Press, 1995). [IWW]

—— (ed.), *Italian Women Writing* (Manchester: Manchester University Press, 1993)

WOOLF, JUDITH, *The Memory of the Offence: Primo Levi's 'If This is a Man'* (Hull Italian Texts; Market Harborough: University Texts, 1995).

WORTON, MICHAEL, and STILL, JUDITH (eds.), *Intertextuality: Theories and Practices* (Manchester: Manchester University Press, 1990).

WRIGHT, SIMONA, 'Intervista a Francesca Sanvitale, Roma 17 luglio 1995', *Italian Quarterly* 127–8 (1996), 87–110. [SW]

—— 'Francesca Sanvitale: A Poetic and Narrative Exploration', *Rivista di studi italiani* 16 (1998), 255–77.

YOUNG, LAURENCE, *Writing and Rewriting the Holocaust: Narrative and the Consequences of Interpretation* (Bloomington: Indiana University Press, 1988).

ZIPES, JACK, *Breaking the Magic Spell: Radical Theories of Folk and Fairy Tales* (London: Heinemann, 1979).

INDEX

Page numbers in bold type indicate the principal discussion of the subject in question